The Great European Stage Directors

Volume 3

The Great European Stage Directors
Series Editor: Simon Shepherd

Volume 1
Antoine, Stanislavski, Saint-Denis
Edited by Peta Tait

Volume 2
Meyerhold, Piscator, Brecht
Edited by David Barnett

Volume 3
Copeau, Komisarjevsky, Guthrie
Edited by Jonathan Pitches

Volume 4
Reinhardt, Jessner, Barker
Edited by Michael Patterson

Volume 5
Grotowski, Brook, Barba
Edited by Paul Allain

Volume 6
Littlewood, Strehler, Planchon
Edited by Clare Finburgh Delijani and Peter M. Boenisch

Volume 7
Barrault, Mnouchkine, Stein
Edited by Felicia Hardison Londré

Volume 8
Bausch, Castellucci, Fabre
Edited by Luk Van den Dries and Timmy De Laet

The Great European Stage Directors

Volume 3

Copeau, Komisarjevsky, Guthrie

Edited by Jonathan Pitches
Series Editor: Simon Shepherd

methuen | drama
LONDON · NEW YORK · OXFORD · NEW DELHI · SYDNEY

METHUEN DRAMA
Bloomsbury Publishing Plc
50 Bedford Square, London, WC1B 3DP, UK
1385 Broadway, New York, NY 10018, USA
29 Earlsfort Terrace, Dublin 2, Ireland

BLOOMSBURY, METHUEN DRAMA and the Methuen Drama logo are trademarks of
Bloomsbury Publishing Plc

First published in hardback in Great Britain 2019
Reprinted 2019
This paperback edition 2024

Copyright © Jonathan Pitches and contributors, 2019

Jonathan Pitches and contributors have asserted their right under the Copyright, Designs
and Patents Act, 1988, to be identified as authors of this work.

For legal purposes the Acknowledgements on pp. xi–xii constitute an extension of this
copyright page.

Cover design by Adriana Brioso
Cover image: The Shakespeare Memorial Theatre, circa 1890.
(© London Stereoscopic Company/Hulton Archive/Getty Images)

All rights reserved. No part of this publication may be reproduced or transmitted
in any form or by any means, electronic or mechanical, including photocopying,
recording, or any information storage or retrieval system, without prior
permission in writing from the publishers.

Bloomsbury Publishing Plc does not have any control over, or responsibility for,
any third-party websites referred to or in this book. All internet addresses
given in this book were correct at the time of going to press. The author and
publisher regret any inconvenience caused if addresses have changed or sites
have ceased to exist, but can accept no responsibility for any such changes.

A catalogue record for this book is available from the British Library.

A catalog record for this book is available from the Library of Congress.

ISBN: HB: 978-1-4742-5396-3
        HB Set: 978-1-4742-5411-3
        PB: 978-1-3504-4579-6
        PB Set: 978-1-3504-4598-7
        ePDF: 978-1-4742-5990-3
        eBook: 978-1-3504-6190-1

Series: Great Stage Directors

Typeset by Integra Software Services Pvt. Ltd.
Printed and bound in Great Britain

To find out more about our authors and books visit www.bloomsbury.com
and sign up for our newsletters.

CONTENTS

LIST OF FIGURES

NOTES ON
CONTRIBUTORS

Roberta Barker is Associate Professor of Theatre in the Fountain School of Performing Arts, Dalhousie University, Halifax, Nova Scotia. A practising director of theatre and opera, she is the author of *Early Modern Tragedy, Gender and Performance, 1984–2000* (2007), co-editor of *New Canadian Realisms* (2012) and General Editor of the series *New Essays in Canadian Theatre*. Her articles on early modern and modern drama in performance have appeared in such journals as *Shakespeare Survey*, *Shakespeare Quarterly*, *Modern Drama*, *Early Theatre*, *Shakespeare Bulletin* and *Nineteenth-Century French Studies*, as well as in a number of edited collections. Her current book project, *Symptoms of the Self: Tuberculosis and the Making of the Modern Stage*, is under contract with the series 'Studies in Theatre History and Culture'. She is an elected member of the inaugural cohort of the College of New Scholars, Artists, and Scientists of the Royal Society of Canada.

Tom Six is Lecturer in Theatre and Performance at The Royal Central School of Speech and Drama, University of London, and also works as a director and dramaturg. He is the author of articles about the histories and practices of acting and directing for journals including *New Theatre Quarterly*, *Shakespeare Bulletin*, *Shakespeare Studies* and *Theatre, Dance and Performance Training*, as well as contributions to edited collections. Forthcoming projects include a special issue of the journal *Contemporary Theatre Review*, co-edited with Caridad Svich, on the director Katie Mitchell, and two book projects, a monograph: *Theatre Studios: Historicizing Ensemble Theatre-Making* (2018) and an edited collection: *Michael Chekhov in the Twenty-First Century: New Pathways*, with Cass Fleming (Bloomsbury, 2018). He was the winner, in 2017, of the David Bradby Award for Early Career Research in European Theatre and serves on the editorial board of the journal *Studies in Theatre and Performance*.

Mark Evans is currently Associate Dean (Student Experience and Quality and Accreditation) in the Faculty of Arts and Humanities at Coventry University, and since 2012 he has also held a personal chair as Professor of Theatre Training and Education. He trained originally at the École Jacques Lecoq, and with Philippe Gaulier and Monika Pagneux, in Paris. His research interests are in the movement training of actors and performers and the history of physical theatre training and performance. As well as teaching and researching theatre practice he has over fifteen years' experience of directing and performing in new plays, site-specific performances and community projects. He is an Associate Editor of the *Theatre Dance and Performance Training* journal and has published widely on performer training and the history and development of physical theatre, including *Jacques Copeau* (2006), *Movement Training for the Modern Actor* (2009) and co-editing the *Routledge Companion to Jacques Lecoq* (2016).

Cass Fleming is Senior Lecturer in Theatre and Performance at Goldsmiths, University of London. She is a theatre director and teacher of acting, directing and devising. She trained at WAC, Goldsmiths, Royal Central School of Speech and Drama and obtained a PhD on the use of play in actor training addressing the work of Chekhov and Bing under the supervision of Professor Ramsay Burt and Mike Huxley. Over the past twenty-five years she has undertaken training in a range of physical practices, including acting, dance, mime, mask, yoga and also Chekhov Technique with Graham Dixon and David Zinder. She has taught Chekhov Technique to undergraduate and postgraduate students at Goldsmiths, Central School and to directors at the Royal National Theatre Studio and those involved with the Genesis project at the Young Vic Theatre. Her production experience as a director has included dance-theatre, radical adaptations of texts and devised embodied theatre. Much of her current work is based on Michael Chekhov Technique and she is a Core Associate of MCUK (www.michaelchekhov.org.uk).

Jonathan Pitches is Professor of Theatre and Performance at the University of Leeds in the School of Performance and Cultural Industries. He specializes in the critical study of performer training, intercultural performance, environmental performance and blended learning. He is founding co-editor of the journal of *Theatre, Dance and Performance Training* and has published several books in this area: *Vsevolod Meyerhold* (2003), *Science and the Stanislavsky Tradition of Acting* (2006/9) *Russians in Britain* (2012) and *Stanislavsky in the World* (with Dr Stefan Aquilina, 2017). He is currently working on an AHRC-funded fellowship *Performing Landscapes: Mountains* (2018), which will culminate in a monograph of the same name for Palgrave Macmillan.

Claire Warden is Senior Lecturer in English and Drama at Loughborough University. Earlier she was Reader in Drama at the School of Visual and Performing Arts at De Montfort University. She joined the School in September 2015, having previously been a postdoctoral fellow at the Institute for Advanced Studies in the Humanities and the University of Edinburgh, and Senior Lecturer at the University of Lincoln. Her research focuses on cross-disciplinary modernism, British and Continental European theatre, performance theory and contemporary performance aesthetics, particularly in relation to sport and entertainment. She is the author of *British Avant-Garde Theatre* (2012), *Modernist and Avant-Garde Performance: An Introduction* (2015) and *Migrating Modernist Performance: British Theatrical Travels through Russia* (2016), as well as multiple journals articles and book chapters. She is associate editor of Wiley-Blackwell's *Encyclopaedia of Modernist Literature* (2018) and, proving she is nothing if not diverse, is also co-editor of *Performance and Professional Wrestling* (2017).

DEDICATIONS AND ACKNOWLEDGEMENTS

Dedications

Roberta Barker would like to dedicate her contribution to this collection in loving memory of her father and stepmother Stephen and Susan Barker, two great lovers of the performing arts, who first introduced her to Guthrie and Moiseiwitsch's stage at Stratford, Ontario.

Tom Cornford would like to dedicate his contribution to this collection to the memory of Ken Washington (1946–2014), Director of Company Development at the Guthrie Theater.

Mark Evans would like to dedicate his contribution to Vanessa Oakes, in recognition of her love and support.

Cass Fleming would like to dedicate her contribution to the memory of Suzanne Bing (1885–1967) and to Lorelei and Johanna, in recognition of their playful inspiration, support and love.

Jonathan Pitches would like to dedicate his contribution to Ceri, Harri and George and to the memory of Edward Braun, whose influence on Russian theatre is inestimable.

Claire Warden would like to dedicate her contribution to Rebecca, Emma and Morgan, the next generation of artists and world-changers.

Acknowledgements

Mark Evans and Cass Fleming would like to acknowledge the support, advice and help of Catherine Dasté, Professor Thomas Donahue (Saint Joseph's University), Professor Judith Miller (New York University), Suzy Willson (Clod Ensemble), the Bibliothèque nationale de France (Fonds Copeau) and the Archives de Beaune.

Jonathan Pitches and Claire Warden would like to acknowledge the help and support of Simon Shepherd; Richard Thompson; the Houghton Archive,

Harvard; the Cadbury Research Library, University of Birmingham; Georgia de Chamberet at Bookblast.

Roberta Barker and Tom Cornford would like sincerely to thank the archivists of the Victoria and Albert Museum, London; the Stratford Festival, Stratford, Ontario; and the Guthrie Theater, Minneapolis, for their help with research for this project.

Every effort has been made to trace copyright holders and to obtain their permission for the use of copyright material. The publisher apologizes for any errors or omissions in the above list and would be grateful if notified of any corrections that should be incorporated in future reprints or editions of this book.

Introduction to the Series

Simon Shepherd

The beginnings of directing

Directors have become some of the celebrities of contemporary theatre. Yet for most of its life, and across a range of practices, theatre has managed perfectly well without directors, celebrated or otherwise.

This is not to say that it has lacked direction, so to speak. Some form of directing, by actors, prompters, stage managers, designers, has always featured as an activity within theatre's processes. What was new was the concept that directing should be done by a role specifically dedicated to that purpose. Emerging around the 1890s after many centuries of theatre, it was both a historical novelty and geographically limited, to Europe and North America.

What these cultures had in common, at the start of the twentieth century, were the ideas and practices which we now call Modernism. In the arts it is associated with particular sorts of innovation made by short-lived movements such as Constructivism, Dada, Expressionism and Surrealism. But modernist thinking also influenced industrial innovation. This is seen in the creation of what F.W. Taylor called 'scientific' management, the systematization and hence separation of the role of a manager who bears responsibility for planning and oversight of the production process. As I have argued before,[1] the concept of director comes to be formulated at the same time as a managerial class is becoming defined. The value put upon the activity of management might be said to create the conditions for, and justify, the creation of a separable role of director.

This was apparent to Barker in 1911 when he observed that in Germany it was precisely the proliferation of management duties that made it impossible to combine the role of manager with that of actor. But German practice was perhaps in advance of the rest of Europe. Many of those now regarded as the founders of directing appeared to work in very similar ways to those who are not categorized as directors. Antoine ran his own company, selected the repertoire, took acting roles and directed plays, as did Stanislavski and Copeau. In this respect their practice differed little from, say, Henry Irving or Herbert Beerbohm Tree, both regarded as actor-managers.

Where the practice of the early directors seems consistently distinct throughout Europe is in its cultural, and sometimes political, positioning. Antoine, Copeau, Barker, Piscator, among others, positioned themselves against a dominant theatrical culture which they aimed to challenge and change. This positioning was an ideological project and hence brought with it an assumption of, or claim to, enlightened vision, artistic mission, the spirit of innovation. Adopting this rhetoric Antoine declared that directors had never existed before – that he was the first of a kind. When P.P. Howe wrote his 1910 book on that new organizational phenomenon the repertory theatre he distinguished the new director from the old stage manager on the grounds that, while the stage manager was adept at controlling the 'mechanical' aspects of the stage, the director was the guardian of the 'vision'.[2] This aesthetic formulation is, though, wholly cognate with management as industrially understood, as Alexander Dean makes clear. In 1926 he recommended that each company should have one person in the role of overall director because the director is not only responsible for each production but also, crucially, is 'the great connecting link between all parts of the organization'. Furthermore: 'Every organization needs a leader who has a vision; who sees a great achievement ahead.'[3] The non-mechanical visionary is also the Taylorist planner.

But some, it seems, were more visionary than others. You will have noted that none of the directors so far mentioned is North American. Yet while Antoine, Copeau and others were founding their theatres outside the mainstream, the same was happening in the United States. The Little Theatres of Chicago and New York started in 1912, the Neighbourhood Playhouse (New York), Portmanteau Theatre and Washington Square Players followed in 1915–16. Contemporary commentators such as Constance D'Arcy Mackay (1917) saw both the European and the American experiments as part of the same 'little theatre' movement.[4] Their practices look similar: founding theatres, against the dominant; culturally selecting audiences, possibly by a membership scheme; working with amateurs; performing explicitly naturalist dramatists, such as Ibsen. But while Antoine and Copeau have entered the canon of great directors, Winthrop Ames and Alice and Irene Lewisohn have not.

Reflecting on the contrast between North American and European practices, William Lyon Phelps suggested in 1920 that the United States lacked a public discourse that would take theatre as seriously as cars. His argument built on Moderwell (1914) and was taken up by Dean (1926).[5] Both saw little theatres as the mechanism for developing a larger theatre-going public, and hence were primarily interested in their success as organizational and economic entities, being much less interested in directors as artists. In Britain similar arguments proposed repertory theatre and the amateur movement as the mechanisms for building both democracy and a dramatic renaissance. Theatre, Barker argued in 1910, is a 'sociable' art. Thus North American and British discussions proposed that theatre could develop the cultural accomplishments of civil society. European discourses, meanwhile, were more interested in, and driven by, avant-gardist movements and experiment. For instance, Antoine positioned himself within an already existing public discourse about art, allying himself with the naturalist, and anti-racist, Zola; staging censored playwrights; distributing Strindberg's polemical preface to *Fröken Julie* (*Miss Julie*) – and making sure to invite reviewers to his theatre. For Piscator and Brecht the energizing link was to activists and ideas within both the political and the artistic avant-garde. The European director thus acquired the status of artistic activist, linked to and recognizable by existing networks of activists and makers, with their own mechanisms for dissemination and publicity. The European avant-garde, long celebrated as the supposed origins of performance art, was perhaps more clearly the originating moment of the theatre director.

The discursive position of European directors was consolidated by their own pronouncements and publications. Each of the early directors was adept in an established theatre craft, as were actor-managers. But when Barker, Meyerhold or Saint-Denis lectured on and wrote about the crafts of theatre, and even more when directors established regimes of training, they were showing themselves to be not just practitioners but theorists of a craft, not so much mechanics as visionaries. The early directors, and indeed directors since, claimed to understand how theatre works as an art form, and to have proposals for its future developments. In this sense they show themselves to be not only guardians of the vision of the play but also guardians of a vision of how theatre itself can and should work. The success of the claim to be visionary is evidence that what the director manages is not just the company or production but also the discourse about them.

Taken together new ideas about management, avant-garde practices and theories of theatre enabled the formulation of, and justified, a separated role of director. The role could then be seen as providing a specialism, missing hitherto, which is necessary to ensure the artistic seriousness and importance of theatre.

While the mechanism that formulated the role of director may have been discursive, its consequences were much more than that. Properly to carry out the guardianship of the vision meant taking responsibility for ensuring the aims and coherence of the processes of theatre-making. The artistic visionary slides into place as Dean's industrial manager. The discursive formulation results in actual power over other theatre workers. The director's control can determine not just that which is staged but also the hiring, if not firing, of those who stage it.

With the invention of directors a new power structure emerges. Yet it had been, and is, perfectly possible to make theatre without that role and its power structure. So there is a potential tension between the effectiveness and productivity of the crafts necessary for theatre and the new, but not demonstrably necessary, power structure that came to claim organizational authority over those crafts. This tension has made the role of director important and yet unstable, treated as celebrity and yet, after only a century, subject to questions as to whether it is actually necessary.

Those questions have been asked not least by directors themselves. Tangled up with the other issues summarized above they run through the volumes of this series. For the directors here have been selected not only because they are generally taken to be important, indeed 'great', but also because they reflect in interesting ways on the role of directing itself. Of course there are other important names, and interesting reflections, which have not made it into the selection list. Decisions such as these are usually difficult and almost always never satisfactory to everybody. But more stories are told than those of big names. The featured directors are not important because they possess some solitary essence of greatness but because they offer ways into, and are symptomatic of, a range of different practices and ideas. The discussion of each featured director frequently involves other directors, as well as designers, writers and actors with whom they worked and by whom they were influenced. For example, the authors of Volume 3 insist that we move our focus outwards from the featured male directors to attend to the women with whom they collaborated and on whom they depended.

The series begins with some of the earliest examples of the practice, but the only other chronological principle governing the distribution of directors is the decision to create two groups of volumes falling roughly either side of the midpoint of the twentieth century. What this arrangement highlights is the extent to which the practice of directing generates a system of self-reference as it rapidly developed an extensive discourse of its own very new art. Thus, for example, Volume 6 features directors who engage with, and perpetuate, the practices and legacy of Brecht.

Rather than suggesting a chronologically seamless evolution of practices the distribution of the directors across the series seeks to call attention to debate. Volume 1 deals with Naturalism, Volume 2 with critiques of Naturalism. The aim is to provoke thinking not so much about the director as an individual as about the art of directing in its different approaches and concerns. The vision of which the director is guardian and the assumptions as to what constitutes the art of directing are revealed as diverse and provisional. For some directors their creative work mainly involves the staging of their ideas about the world, for others creativity comes in the design of processes and the management of people, for yet others creativity has to do with the design and management of theatres. While Brook's philosophy of life may have constructed powerful and influential stagings, Guthrie's philosophy of life more or less invented the equally powerful, and perhaps more influential, concept of the role of artistic director.

If Volumes 1 and 2 display contrasted aesthetic approaches, Volume 3 has us focus on directors as founders and managers of companies and theatres. That topic of company formation and management returns again, in the context of the latter part of the twentieth century, in Volume 7. In a similar way Volume 4 brings together directors who may be seen as auteurs working within a modernist climate while Volume 5 gives us auteurs emerging from a post–Second World War Europe. In Volume 8, the directors are also auteurs, perhaps most powerfully so in that there is often no dramatist's text. But at the same time here the role of director begins to wobble, blurring into that of choreographer or visual artist.

In exploring the various directors, it becomes clear that, as noted above, some directors are major contributors to the discourses about directing, both reflecting on practices in general and foregrounding their own work in particular. This has an effect on their apparent status within the field. The existence of texts authored by directors often facilitates the study of those directors by others, which in turn generates more texts and elevates their apparent status, as a sort of greatness-construction machine. But there are other directors who are less textually established, perhaps because the director actively refuses to document their work, as did Planchon, or perhaps because there are cultural or geographical boundaries that English-speaking academics tend not to cross, as is the case of Strehler. Or it may be that directors have simply fallen out of theatrical or academic fashion, as, say, for Saint-Denis. That they are no longer, or ever were, serviced by the contemporary greatness-construction machine does not make these directors any less significant. Celebrity is not in itself necessarily relevant to being important.

Introduction to Volume 3

Jonathan Pitches

The novelty and complexity of theatre directing

If clarity of nomenclature or stability of definition was the aim of this book, then the three chapters which follow, outlining the work of stage directors Jacques Copeau, Theodore Komisarjevsky and Tyrone Guthrie, will have fallen at the first hurdle. Agreement as to what constitutes the job of directing within their own practices is seldom to be found, let alone consensus between them. In the collective eyes of these three twentieth-century practitioners, the director is: a producer, a metteur-en-scène, a régisseur (or rezhisseur) a conductor, a creator-interpreter, an editor, a critic, a chairman, a stage manager and an actor-manager. In more colourful terms, ones typical of Tyrone Guthrie's dissertations on the subject, the director

> is partly an artist presiding over a group of other artists, excitable, unruly, childlike and intermittently 'inspired'. He [*sic*] is also foreman of a factory, the abbot of a monastery tree, and the superintendent of an analytical laboratory. It will do no harm if, in addition to other weapons, he arms himself with the patience of a good nurse, together with the voice and vocabulary of an old-time sergeant-major.[1]

Such expansive understandings of the role of the director are partly cultural. Komisarjevsky was an émigré from Russia; Copeau was a pivotal figure in French theatre and Guthrie was from a hybrid Anglo-Scots-Irish heritage, working extensively in the United States and Canada later in his career. As a triumvirate of directors, they represent three great traditions of Western theatre directing with very different, if at times interconnected, histories. The **Life** sections of the three chapters which follow sketch in detail the specifics of these varied cultural backgrounds and help explain how they impact on the particular **Art** each director practised. But the eclectic range of directorial definitions used by Komisarjevsky, Copeau and Guthrie is also a symptom of two other things: the newness of the role of director itself and the complexity of theatre direction as a craft.

In terms of novelty, all three directors were instrumental in affirming directing as the key responsibility in the theatre, before it was a fully recognized role. Komisarjevsky was a contemporary of the better-known Russian directors, Stanislavsky and Meyerhold, witnessing first-hand how the latter challenged the model of actor-manager represented by Komisarjevsky's entrepreneurial sister, Vera Komissarzhevskaya. 'Only a little more than a century old'[2] as a term, the first two decades of the twentieth century marked the birth of directing and Komisarjevsky was in the midst of its genesis in Russia, before he moved to Britain in 1919. Copeau, too, launched his directorial career just as the role was gaining purchase, in his case in France, following in the footsteps of the pioneers of French-directed theatre, André Antoine and Aurélien Lugné Poë and debuting with a little-known classical text in 1913. Younger than his Russian and French counterparts, Tyrone Guthrie was born in 1900, a fitting date, as Samuel Leiter notes, at the 'start of the century during which the art of directing came into its own'.[3] Though twenty years 'behind' in years, Guthrie in fact worked in a parallel theatre world to Komisarjevsky in England in the early 1930s – both freelanced for the Shakespeare Memorial Theatre in the same year (1933) directing *Richard II* and *Macbeth*, respectively. Though his period of influence begins later, Guthrie may nevertheless be seen at the vanguard of directing in Britain, a role which only seriously began to shake off the traditions of the actor-manager in the interwar period, following the lead of Harley Granville Barker before the First World War.[4] As an emergent role with a patchwork of precursors it is unsurprising the art of direction was understood and described in different ways by each of our featured stage directors.

As far as directorial complexity goes, Copeau, Komisarjevsky and Guthrie offer a persuasive case study, a paradigm of the numerous functions associated with direction. Indeed, even the range of definitions above does not capture the breadth of capacities each of them conceived to be part of the job of directing. Though critical of Wagner, Komisarjevsky fashioned himself as provider of a total theatre and his actors as 'universally' practised. His long list of personal competencies comprised scene designer, lighting and costume designer, architect, composer of the stage picture, scene analyst and actor-trainer. Guthrie as an altogether more proficient administrator than his Russian counterpart preferred to eschew the artistry of direction in favour of its organizational demands: 'he [*sic*] arranges the agenda of each day's work, sets the pace and determines the amount of time devoted to this or that'.[5] But this bureaucratic reading of the role did not impede his desire to make significant embellishments and amendments to the play texts he interpreted, nor to occupy what Samuel Leiter called the directorial school of 'total freedom', when he wanted.[6] In his writings on theatre directing, Copeau appears humbler than either Komisarjevsky or Guthrie, claiming that the key to success in working on any text is a kind of dramaturgical empathy: 'I try to enter into it without any preconceived notions or ready-made ideas. I do all I can to espouse it as it is and live with it.'[7] But he too conceived directing as multifaceted, drawing on his own journalistic background to define the director as a critic 'better able [...] than the playwright himself [sic] to discern errors in playwriting'[8] while considering the wholesale retraining of the actor an imperative.

The novelty and complexity of directing, then, underline much of what follows in the three chapters dedicated to each director. But too tight a focus on the singular director as trailblazer and polymath conceals one of the most important connecting points between these three: the director as collaborator. While the names of these renowned men grace the face of this book as *Great Stage Directors*, their success and impact as artists, identified in the **Importance** sections of each chapter, owe much to a cast of lesser-known players. Many of these unseen contributions are from women and no matter how many times one uses a square bracketed '*sic*' to signal the archaism of the masculine-gendered director, a more sustainable strategy has to be to extend, where possible and appropriate, the web of influences which surround each of the directors in this volume. Reading against the grain, therefore, to expose the concealed circles of creative collaboration for these directors, is a significant aim of this book. For Mark Evans and Cass Fleming writing on Copeau, that means a renewed focus on the figure of Suzanne Bing as well as a section on female contemporary makers of Copeau-inspired theatre. For Jonathan Pitches and Claire Warden, Komisarjevsky's debt to actress Phyllada Sewell, teacher Ernestine Stodelle and writer and designer Lesley Blanch are foregrounded, relationships which went way beyond the Russian director's oft-quoted predilection for short-lived romantic liaisons. Critical revision is similarly part of Tom Cornford and Roberta Barker's examination of Tyrone Guthrie as they challenge what they call the 'fairy godfather' narrative of Guthrie's impact on North America and debunk some of the wilder claims for his influence on twentieth-century theatre architecture. Although he spent much of his time in a closed-shop of male collaborators, the designer Tanya Moisewitch's significance as Guthrie's creative mainstay is elaborated upon in this chapter, another example of the collaborative networks which feature so clearly in this book.

Though there is a clear drive to revise some of the histories around these influential theatre practitioners and to elaborate on their creative partnerships, readers new to Copeau, Komisarjevsky and Guthrie will be able to garner key information about them without difficulty. Each chapter has a summary of their lives, outlining their key productions and explaining how their theoretical ideas were (or were not) achieved in practice. New archival materials on each director have been carefully integrated with established primary and secondary sources so that the result, we hope, is of a fresh but accessible examination of the craft of directing as it emerged in the hands of three prolific artists working in the first three quarters of the last century. We have taken the approach of co-writing each chapter, rather than dividing them up into smaller single-authored sections. This has meant considerable to-ing and fro-ing of drafts and multiple conversations within pairings. It has demanded a collaborative *writing* process in keeping with the subject matter and, while stimulating for the team, we hope it is also reflected in the range of perspectives brought to bear on the directors and in the positioning of their histories as contingent, based not always on agreement or narrative linearity.

Some connecting tissues

Collections like these often throw up strange or unforeseen juxtapositions; there are no other books dedicated to the art of theatre direction which consider Copeau, Komisarjevsky and Guthrie together, for instance. But although each director operated within their own artistic circles and cultural milieu, there are some significant meeting points between them which are worth highlighting in this introduction and which only manifest themselves by virtue of their unique combination here. These can be summarized under the themes of (i) migration, (ii) the architecture of the stage, (iii) approach to the classics and (iv) the ensemble.

A 'pull to the West' is a feature of each of the director's career paths, one which resonates with other director-practitioners in this period of the twentieth century, such as Brecht, Piscator and Michael Chekhov. For Komisarjevsky, the move was permanent after his apprenticeship in Russia and his twenty years in England (1919–39) and he died on the East coast of the United States in 1954. Guthrie spent considerable time in Canada (specifically Ontario) and the United States (chiefly in New York and Minneapolis) after developing his reputation in London and Stratford (England). His legacy is substantially built on the two new theatres he founded in the two North American cities but unlike Komisarjevsky – whose mobility was stymied by the Second World War – Guthrie continued to flit between the British Isles and North America and he ended his days back in the bosom of his family home in County Monaghan in Ireland. For Copeau, the draw of America, and specifically New York, was brief (just two seasons in 1917–19). But it still led to powerful influences on his, and Bing's, theatre practice and, conversely, a palpable reaction from the US theatre cognoscenti and the embryonic Group Theatre (née the Theatre Guild).

These migrations, whether final or fleeting, are an essential part of the story of theatre directing in this period of theatre history and mapping them, as we do in each of the following chapters, helps explain the extent to which the new role of director was already part of a geopolitical complex of influences and practices. Whether it is the rebalancing of the German influence in New York with the invitation of the Frenchman, Copeau; the playing out of old colonial hierarchies in Guthrie's 'enlightenment' project; or the continuing sense of cultural alienation felt by Komisarjevsky, once he settled in the United States, this book is defined by stories of travel, (im)mobility and intercultural exchange across Europe and North America.

Both Komisarjevsky and Guthrie are lauded for their contribution to twentieth-century building design, even if it was only the Russian who was formally trained in the profession. Komisarjevsky's most visible legacy in this area was in cinema, not theatre design, with interior designs across London to his name.[9] But, as Pitches and Warden set out in their chapter, he brought the sensibility of an architect – the belief that space should be constructed to assist its inhabitants – to his creative process. 'The real producer', he says in *Myself and the Theatre*, 'devises the sets, lighting and costumes to *serve the purposes* required by the acting'.[10] Guthrie's intervention in the development of theatre architecture was altogether more bombastic, with no less an aim than 'recasting the theatre experience', as Barker and Cornford debate in their chapter. But although others have suggested that 'Guthrie's most lasting contribution to modern theatre practice was his participation in the revival of the open, or thrust stage',[11] Barker and Cornford seek to put this claim in context with Guthrie's other innovations and successes. It is not so much an architectural impact which we should be celebrating, they argue, but an administrative one. Copeau, too, was a stage innovator, if on a smaller scale than his European compatriots. Like Guthrie he looked back to go forward, taking his model not from Shakespeare but from the *commedia dell'arte*. As Evans and Fleming discuss, Copeau sought to remodel the performance space of his acting school, the Vieux-Colombier, along the lines of the simple, raised and naked stage used by the commedia troupes in Italy from the sixteenth to the eighteenth centuries. In doing so he sought to attain a more 'sincere' (a key word for him) and direct audience–actor relationship.

This turning back to a bygone stage in order to envision a contemporary theatre for the mid-twentieth century is of course fraught with contradictions and these are drawn out with dexterity in the coming pages: Guthrie as a conflicted radical-conservative; Komisarjevsky as establishment-experimenter; Copeau as an autocratic-democrat. They played out these contradictions working on several genres of plays but each director developed a defining approach to the Western theatre canon – as it was constructed then – and most prominently to Shakespeare. In Komisarjevsky's case he was tasked with dragging the Shakespeare Memorial Theatre's approach to the Bard into the modernist era of 1930s England. He did this with the help of his some-time designer, Lesley Blanch and working within the limitations of unbelievably short rehearsal periods. Guthrie, even more than Komisarjevsky, built his export capital on the reputation he had as a bold (if not brazen) interpreter of Shakespeare, one built at the Shakespeare Memorial Theatre, too, as well as at the Old Vic. Plying what Barker and Cornford reveal as his trademark combination of a virtuoso lead actor, control of rhythm and cleverly arranged ensemble scenes, Guthrie set about transferring this modus operandi to two developing theatre contexts in North America. Copeau, working with Bing, was as prepared as Guthrie to modify Shakespearean text and they built their approach to adaptation around the simple platform staging mentioned above. Molière was even more important to the development of Copeau's directorial approach, with the landmark production of *Les Fourberies de Scapin* (The Tricks of Scapin) featuring in the New York tour and in revival in Paris a few years later. Again, the contradictions are in evidence as his 'new' approach to the Classics was not, Copeau stressed, revolutionary but a policy of back to basics. It nevertheless led to critics claiming the production was 'Molière reborn'.[12]

As a concluding connection, the three directors' attitude to the theatre ensemble is noteworthy and once again signals the tensions and contradictions associated with the function of the director. With varied theatre roots and cultural backgrounds, each director had a different paradigm of the theatre ensemble on which to draw. Copeau drew inspiration from the French tradition and, as noted, from the simplicity and physicality of the *commedia dell'arte*. Komisarjevsky had Stanislavsky's Moscow Art Theatre as a reference point, as well as his own sister's approach at the Vera Komissarzhevskaya Theatre. Guthrie's model was inspired by the British repertory system and by his love of Shakespeare's stage, both of which he sought to reinstall in the theatre buildings he founded in Ontario and Minneapolis. This was in the belief that the principles of a theatre organization feed the ethos of performing or, as Leiter puts it, 'from the ensemble situation of collective activity in repertory came ensemble playing'.[13]

The ensembles that Komisarjevsky, Copeau and Guthrie fashioned were not bastions of democracy, however. Each considered the ensemble to be an organism dependent on its leader, not on its peers. 'Every such theatre must be a community following a "master",' declared Komisarjevsky, citing a host of European examples.[14] Copeau agreed, calling himself the 'patron' of the Vieux-Colombier and in Mark Evans's terms, creating 'an ensemble shaped in the image of its director'.[15] Guthrie, for his part, moulded the ensemble with a very sure hand – through the brilliance of his staging and the seemingly innate talent he had for organizing crowd scenes.[16] He was, as Barker and Cornford point out, very happy to give his star actors the liberty and space to shine and be noticed – Alec Guinness and Laurence Oliver, for example. But the ensemble were subject to the terms of theatre direction as he saw it, and that meant 'the imposition of a musical and choreographic pattern on the acting and above all the pulling together into a unity of what would otherwise be a series of isolated, even contradictory, impulses and impressions'.[17]

In this book we have veered away from such unifying intentions, preferring to focus where necessary on the contradictions inherent in the craft of directing and embodied in the careers of Copeau, Komisarjevsky and Guthrie. I have in this introduction offered some aspects where their ideas and approaches may be pulled together and the common pattern adopted in the chapters in terms of their **Life, Art** and **Importance** will ensure that further comparisons can be made and threads drawn out. These three stage directors are important (if not 'Great') not just because of their individual contributions to the world of theatre directing but because they speak to the development of the role itself, in all its instability and contentiousness. Theatre directing, viewed through the lives and practices of these men is a tough battle ground of pragmatism and creativity, commercialism and artistry, single-mindedness and partnership, played out on a field which had not yet had the lines chalked out – a landscape of potential weathered by challenge.

1

Jacques Copeau

Mark Evans and Cass Fleming

Introduction

Much that we take for granted in modern contemporary theatre can be traced back to the innovations and experiments of Jacques Copeau and his collaborators during the early decades of the twentieth century. Copeau's close collaborators over this period included Suzanne Bing,[1] Michel Saint-Denis,[2] Louis Jouvet,[3] Charles Dullin,[4] Jean[5] and Marie-Hélène Dasté (née Copeau)[6] and Jessmin Howarth.[7] A brief list of these innovations would include mime and physical theatre; mask theatre; the twentieth-century renaissance of the *commedia dell'arte* and the theatrical clown; physical actor training; ensemble acting; the use of play and improvisation; devised theatre, and the integration of song, dance, movement and text; the writer as collaborator; the modern school for actor training; and the bare stage and simple 'unit' set.

Despite his success and influence, and the impact of his collaborators, Copeau is still little known outside of France. This is in part because he did not, despite his experience as a theatre critic, write down anything that might be construed as a manifesto or an instruction manual, in the manner of Konstantin Stanislavsky or Bertolt Brecht. Instead it is the work and the teaching that have done the talking, the result being, many actors around the world will have been trained or rehearsed in regimes that owe a significant debt to Copeau, Bing and Saint-Denis. Many audiences will

FIGURE 1.1 *Jacques Copeau in 1927. Photo courtesy of Catherine Dasté/BnF.*

marvel at devised theatre, ensemble performance and collaborative physical theatre, without realizing the multiple connections such work has with the experiments in Paris and Burgundy by a small community of French actors in the early twentieth century.

Copeau was affectionately known as *Le Patron* (The boss) by his collaborators and the members of his companies. The term is a complex one – meaning not only the chief or head person, but also a father-figure or owner. It is a term that reflects something of the complexity of his relationship with his colleagues. They all owed a great debt to Copeau, who inspired them and transformed their careers. But they all felt the need to escape from his influence in order to move on and to flourish in their own right. The notion of a 'Great Director' is in some respects problematic when discussing Copeau's work. He was certainly a visionary and highly creative director, but because his remarkable achievements came through his collaborations with other artists and students, as with many of the other directors featured in this volume, the archetype of the solitary genius suggested by the title of 'Great Director' is not necessarily appropriate from a twenty-first-century perspective. Copeau was also more than just a 'Director' and his significance needs to be viewed not just in terms of his important theatre productions but also in relation to how he integrated many different roles during the course of his career. In addition to being a talented and daring director he was also an excellent analyst of theatre practice, the founder and director of two trail-blazing theatre companies and of one of the most innovative and influential actor training schools in Europe, a mentor of new theatre writers, a playwright and skilled adapter of extant plays, a successful actor and a forerunner in the practices of both devised and community theatre.

Because of these important collaborations and complexities, our narrative in the three sections: **Life**, **Art** and **Importance**, will, at times, extend outwards in a more genealogical formation, to provide space to discuss the often overlooked contributions by his collaborators. A fuller feminist analysis of Copeau's practice is beyond the remit of this chapter and has been done elsewhere,[8] but by making these detours at various points we hope to give an account of Copeau that is less dominated by a patriarchal and linear historiography that would obscure his creative collaborations, his multiple roles and the richness of his Life, Art and Importance. We have sought to bring into equal focus the work of Copeau's female collaborators (Bing, Howarth and Marie-Helene Dasté) with that of his male collaborators (whose contribution is already well documented). The sections on Life and Art consequently overlap and occasionally revisit key periods and events in order to draw out multiple significances, although the broad chronological narrative of Copeau's life remains in place as a useful frame within which to view the changes and transformations in Copeau's work.

Copeau's Life

Early years

Jacques Copeau was born in Paris on 4 February 1879. His parents, Victor and Hélène Copeau, were reasonably prosperous and firmly middle class.

They owned a small iron factory in Raucourt in the Ardennes, and this family business secured them a comfortable life in the tenth *arrondissement*[9] of the capital city, Paris. During his youth, he became increasingly interested in the theatre, attending performances at leading theatres of the time: 'I used to sneak out of the house to go and spend a few sous.[10] I had carefully saved from my pocket money to attend the theatre.'[11] Among the work that inspired the young Copeau was that of a leading figure in the development of theatrical naturalism, André Antoine (1858–1943): 'Everything he did fascinated me.'[12] Antoine offered the young Copeau support and encouragement and Antoine's leadership of his own theatre was clearly an inspiration for Copeau's later work at the Vieux-Colombier. In his last year at the lycée there was a clear indication of where Copeau's interests and ambitions lay when he directed his classmates in a production of his own play *Brouillard du Matin* (The Morning Fog).

In 1901 his father died, and faced with this moment of personal loss and upheaval he decided to curtail his studies at the Sorbonne and to see the world. In Scandinavia, he met up with a young Danish woman, Agnès Thomsen, whom he had encountered some six years earlier. They were married in 1902, and their first child, Marie-Hélène, arrived within a year. Although money was tight for the young family Copeau managed to continue to write articles for various Parisian periodicals, catching the eye of some influential authors, such as André Gide (1869–1951), who encouraged Copeau in his efforts. Copeau returned to Paris, but was soon forced to leave again in order to look after the family business in the Ardennes – a task he dutifully, but one senses somewhat reluctantly, fulfilled until 1905 when the business went bankrupt.

In order to support his family, he worked at an art gallery for four years, during which time he tried to continue with his own writing. He was a passionate champion for change and theatrical reform, and in 1907 he was offered the opportunity to share this passion with a wider readership when he was made drama critic for the *Grande Revue*. This was a major turning point for him, enabling him to find a place among the leading radical thinkers of his time. Within another two years, together with Gide, Jean Schlumberger, André Ruyters and Henri Ghéon, he had founded the *Nouvelle Revue Française* (New French Review), which was to become a leading French journal. Copeau was a compelling writer and critic – he was well read, knowledgeable and incisive. He was not afraid to take on the mediocrity and superficiality of the boulevard theatres, which he did in a wide range of contemporary journals and newspapers. He had a lifelong abhorrence of anything that smacked of what he called *cabotinage*, 'the malady of insincerity, or rather of falseness. He who suffers from it ceases to be authentic, to be human'.[13]

A new stage in his career was to open up for him when he was offered the opportunity to write a play for the 1910–11 season of the Théâtre des Arts. He chose to adapt and stage Fyodor Dostoyevsky's novel *Les Frères*

Karamazov (The Brothers Karamazov). His bold decision worked, and after the production opened on 6 April 1911 it was widely acclaimed by the Parisian critics. This moment of success was to be an important stepping stone towards his next and much more significant project – the creation of his own theatre.

Théâtre du Vieux-Colombier

Such an undertaking required a theatre space and a company of actors that would be suited to his vision. He found the space he was looking for in the Théâtre de l'Athénée Saint-Germain on the rue du Vieux-Colombier, a small and intimate venue on the Left Bank. He had the old space stripped of the conventionally ornate decoration and demanded that it be replaced with a pared back design that allowed more direct contact with the audience. In line with the functional stage design and the fresh new innovative approach, he named his new theatre after the road on which it stood. In response to the responsibility he felt to his prospective audience of students, artists and intellectuals, the seats were modestly priced – among the cheapest in Paris.[14]

The beginnings of the new company of actors was in place already. Copeau knew that he wanted to continue to work with Charles Dullin (1885–1949), who had performed in his adaptation of *The Brothers Karamazov*. Dullin shared Copeau's passion for the *commedia dell'arte*. He had performed the role of Pierrot at the Théâtre des Arts in 1910 (connecting with a long tradition of French Pierrots) and had frequently worked as a street performer.[15] In Spring 1913, Copeau held auditions in Dullin's studio in Montmartre. According to his memoirs, he chose not to focus on the auditionees' conventional talent and experience, but rather 'sought to discern each one's natural, inner self'.[16] He quickly gathered together a small company of actors, also initially enlisting Louis Jouvet (1887–1951) as *régisseur* (or stage manager). Kurtz suggests that Dullin probably voiced what many of the young company were feeling when he said, 'At a time when I needed to believe in what I was doing [...] Copeau brought me what I was looking for.'[17] Kurtz also tells how the young Suzanne Bing (1885–1967) drove a deal with Copeau that she would not have to provide her own wardrobe for the characters she played.[18] This seemingly simple agreement swept away a theatrical convention that had financially burdened actors for centuries. Bing, as we shall see, was to go on to become one of Copeau's most important collaborators.

Copeau's plan was to launch the company with a repertory season, including new plays and classic revivals. Copeau realized that in order to generate the kind of ensemble of which he dreamed he would need to find ways in which he could bond them together and give them some shared understanding of the challenges they would face. In order to achieve this, he decided to take the actors 'outside the theatre into contact with nature and with life'.[19] He took them to Le Limon, a village east of Paris. There, for a period of ten weeks, he instigated a strict regime of rehearsals, sight readings, analysis of plays, open air exercise and improvisations. Living and working together in this manner quickly created a camaraderie that would support them over the years and the challenges to come. It is easy, looking back from the twenty-first century, to forget how innovative such an approach to rehearsals was. The use of improvisation and the notion

FIGURE 1.2 *The Vieux-Colombier company rehearse at Le Limon. Photo courtesy of Catherine Dasté/BnF.*

of company exercises were practically unheard of outside the work of Stanislavsky.[20]

The company finally emerged into public view in October 1913. On 15 October, Paris woke to find posters for the opening of the theatre plastered on the walls around the Left Bank. The posters proclaimed a call:

> To youth: to react against all the cowardice of commercial theatre and to defend the freest, most sincere manifestations of a new drama.
>
> To the literary public: to maintain the recognition of the classic masterpieces, French and foreign, which will form the basis of the repertoire.
>
> To everyone: to support a company which will sustain itself by the affordability of its shows, by their variety, the quality of their interpretation and their staging.[21]

The opening production was Thomas Heywood's *A Woman Killed with Kindness*. By picking a relatively obscure classical text, Copeau made clear his intention that the company would be known for its artistic vitality and integrity rather than for any superficial sensationalism or attempt to pander to current fads. The company ethic of hard work, discipline, experimentation and physical expressivity was already distinguishing them from the normal commercial theatre fare.

The first major obstacle was the outbreak of the First World War. Many of the original company members were conscripted to serve on the Front – Dullin joined the dragoons, Jouvet the Medical Corps. Copeau himself was called up, but in 1915 he was discharged because of ill health. He used the subsequent period of recuperation to correspond constantly with Dullin and Jouvet in letters, and Bing in person, sharing ideas for the future of the company after the War. Copeau made contact with many of the leading figures in European theatre in order to inform and enrich his own ideas. He visited Edward Gordon Craig in Rome for a month and then made contact with Emile Jaques-Dalcroze, an innovative teacher who had created Eurhythmics, a practice that teaches rhythm and musical expression through movement. Dalcroze also introduced him to Adolphe Appia, an innovative stage designer whose designs sought to emphasize the three dimensional and symbolic in a theatre industry where designs had become two dimensional and representational. All three reinforced Copeau's belief in theatre as a plastic art, in which the finely tuned expressive skills of the actor could best operate within a three-dimensional and vibrant theatre space.

Copeau, excited by these new ideas, saw the break enforced upon him by the War as an opportunity to set up his own school, through which he could begin to train the actors of the future. Returning to Paris, he enlisted Bing as a key collaborator in the founding of the first iteration of the Vieux-Colombier School in 1915. The initial intake was only twelve students attending on their day off from lycée. The training at the school started with the development of the students' physical expressivity – Copeau considered this a central element to the art of the actor. They learnt gymnastics, eurhythmics, ball games, dance, voice and improvisation through games and play, object work and the representation of animals and fables. However, these skills were not developed as a bag of tricks, but as a route to simplicity and clarity of acting.

The success of an extended lecture tour that Copeau undertook to the United States in order to promote French culture led to an invitation for the company to tour to New York for an extended period. The tour meant that those of his company on active service would now be released by the French War Ministry, and re-united with Copeau and Bing. After a long ship journey, the company together with various family members including Copeau's wife and children, arrived in New York on 11 November 1917 and opened their first performance, *Les Fourberies de Scapin* (The Tricks of Scapin) by Molière, two weeks later. After an uncertain initial critical reception, interest in the work of the company grew and responses became increasingly positive. They presented six plays in repertoire in the first season – with critics remarking on the authenticity, integrity and simplicity of the work.

FIGURE 1.3 *Copeau performing as Scapin. Photo courtesy of Catherine Dasté/ BnF.*

Experiments and collaborations in New York: Suzanne Bing, Margaret Naumburg, Jessmin Howarth and Marie-Hélène Dasté

During the company's two seasons in New York, Bing worked extensively as an actor, playing a large number of new roles in addition to her older parts in their revived productions at the Garrick Theatre, often to critical acclaim. Overall, the company produced what must have been an exhausting forty-four productions during the tour to America. Impressively, Bing somehow found the time also to develop a number of other strands of practice that were to become crucial to the Vieux-Colombier's larger project. While Bing's contribution has sometimes been downplayed or misunderstood, her work was of central significance to the project with Copeau and to what is seen as his theatrical legacy.[22]

In 1913 Bing and Copeau had started a long-term relationship and in 1917 Bing gave birth to their son, Bernard. Throughout this period, and for rest of their period of professional collaboration, Copeau seems to have created a situation for himself where he could draw on the creative, emotional and sexual relationship with Bing while also maintaining the domestic relationship that he had with his wife, Agnès, and their children.[23] Consequently, there was a complex merging of the personal and professional on many levels in this group of collaborators, which was challenging for both women. Copeau's manner of discussing Bing's contribution to this project varies and is often contradictory and inconsistent, but on occasion he is very clear about the centrality of her work as the 'doyenne' of the company.[24] Bing was a quiet but deeply significant pioneer of her generation of female theatre-makers in France, navigating pregnancy, childcare, financial hardship and life as a single unmarried mother, while contributing to the vision and project she shared with Copeau and their other long-term collaborators. While this may seem commonplace now, it was positively radical for a bourgeois woman in the early years of the twentieth century. Despite the many difficulties that the company faced in America, this was a very fertile period of experimentation for Bing and this fed into their shared project. However, her son reported that Bing in fact had ambiguous feelings about Copeau and that this reflected the complexity of their relationship during this period.[25] Equally it is also important to acknowledge that Agnès Copeau experienced the other side of this situation, for much of her marriage having to deal with Copeau's continuing infidelity, despite her protestations and complaints.

During his trip to America in 1917, Copeau had met Waldo Frank, the writer and editor. He also met Margaret Naumburg,[26] Frank's wife, who in 1914 had established a progressive educational school initially called the Children's School, later called the Walden School. In April 1918, Copeau and Bing visited Naumburg's school together and were greatly inspired by what they saw. Between 1918 and 1919 Bing was to spend as much time as she could at Naumburg's school leading creative classes for the children. She was able to observe the use of creative games and play as part of Naumburg's approach and learn about the way in which she blended aspects of the Montessori Method with other radical pedagogies and ideas about psychoanalysis. The influence of both Naumburg and Montessori is clearly evident in Bing's subsequent work with the Vieux-Colombier School and it undoubtedly enabled her and Copeau to develop their pedagogic approach and techniques more effectively for their own project.[27] Copeau maintained a level of actor training for the company during the time in America and Bing continued to experiment with the development of their approach. Bing also further experimented with these approaches during the summer rest period, where she 'trained the children of the actors of the Vieux-Colombier to observe birds and to imitate their behaviour'.[28]

Following on from their previous experiments with Eurhythmics Copeau had also invited Jessmin Howarth, who had trained with Dalcroze, to work with the company in New York as a movement teacher.[29] Another important experiment that took place during this period was to feed into both Copeau's later theatre work and the development of Bing's teaching. Marie-Hélène (Copeau's eldest daughter) undertook with Bing the company's first attempts to make masks for use in performance.[30] Although we know little about their early experiments, this was a highly significant moment for the company as they were to use both character masks and what was known as the Noble (or Neutral) mask[31] to facilitate creative play in training and in performance in the school and later projects.

Bing's collaborations with these three other women, and the resultant work she produced, was to cross-fertilize with Copeau's long-term interest in *commedia dell'arte* and the company's work on *The Tricks of Scapin* while in New York. The notebook L'École du Vieux-Colombier, from June 1918, notes the 'observation of a robin on the lawn of Cedar Court', presumably Bing's experiments, and goes on to suggest that in the new commedia (later to become what Copeau refers to as New Comedy[32]) they could seek 'comparison of the characters of certain types with the appearance of certain animals'.[33] This was a fundamental breakthrough for Copeau, Bing, Jouvet and their fellow collaborators.

Despite the overall success of the tour, the period certainly also presented challenges to Copeau, on a number of levels. Bing occupied a curious position as both a close collaborator and co-parent of their son, but also as an outsider; she was not Copeau's wife and so in social terms existed in an unconventional space. She was also differentiated from the rest of the company by her personal relationship with Copeau and by her seniority in relation to the evolving approach to actor training. This must have been difficult to navigate as dissention and bad feelings aimed towards Copeau grew among the actors during the summer the company spent preparing for the second season,[34] particularly as a result of a perception that Copeau was becoming more focused on the training than the productions. Nonetheless, when Copeau, Bing, Jouvet and the company returned to France they had the basis on which to re-start the company in Paris and subsequently re-open the school.

The return to Paris

The tour to the United States had exhausted the company, and Copeau in particular. The company retreated to the countryside to regroup and to begin rehearsals for a new season. Copeau returned to Paris to launch a passionate appeal to his supporters, which bore fruit in the foundation of Les Amis du Vieux-Colombier. Their financial support enabled him to re-open his theatre without the need for public subsidy or the pressures of commercial income generation. The Company once again flourished. Productions of new and classic plays won the approval of the Paris critics, including productions of Shakespeare's *The Winter's Tale*[35] adapted by Copeau and Bing, and Charles Vidrac's *Le Pacquebot Tenacity* (The Boat Called Tenacity). The Vieux-Colombier stage had been remodelled to provide a simple open stage space, brightly lit, that opened out easily into the auditorium. Sometimes the *tréteau nu* (naked stage[36]) was used on the Vieux-Colombier stage and sometimes not, but the principles were always present in the approach to staging. Indeed, in 1922 the company staged an open-air production of *The Tricks of Scapin* in the square outside the Saint-Sulpice church in the Latin Quarter on the Left Bank in Paris, using a raised platform stage. Through all

FIGURE 1.4 *Open-air performance of* Scapin *outside the Saint-Sulpice church in Paris. Photo courtesy of Catherine Dasté/BnF.*

of this he was inspired by the correspondence he had had for several years with the Russian theatre director and teacher Konstantin Stanislavsky, so he was delighted to be able to host Stanislavsky for a meal on the stage of the Vieux-Colombier when the Moscow Arts Theatre toured to Paris in 1921.

The Vieux-Colombier School (1920–4)

Copeau and Bing worked closely together to plan for the new iteration of the Vieux-Colombier School, which launched one week after the theatre re-opened. They continued to search for a training that would enable actors to achieve the sincerity and playful creativity they believed in, with the discipline and commitment this required. Copeau sought a rediscovery of fundamental principles and remained sure that the most productive approach would be to work with young performers, who would be more open and less formed than older actors. The School's first year (1920–1) ran with a programme taught by Bing, who went on to be the central pedagogue, devoting most of her time to teaching, although she was never given the title of Director of the School.[37] Despite Copeau's passionate belief in the importance of the School, he actually spent very little time teaching in Paris due to his work at the theatre and elsewhere. However, Kusler argues that when he did teach his work with the students in dramatic theory and dramatic education it was a 'vital unifying element'.[38]

Copeau was reportedly pleased with the outcome of Bing's work and decided to expand the School in 1921–2. The use of play, games, improvisation, animal study, elements and nature, rhythmic and musical play, and the inner sensation/feeling of movement/gesture that Bing had developed further in New York, underpinned the work of the older Apprentice Group in the School. Various people now contributed to the further development of some key initiatives within the School. Physical education classes were directed by Georges Hébert (1875–1957)[39] (although they were actually taught by his assistant M. Moyne) and drew on his system of natural gymnastics. This was to become a core component of their work and in later years Jean Dorcy took on the teaching of this area of the curriculum along with circus skills. In 1921, they introduced the use of masks as a training device drawing on Copeau's work with mask in *commedia dell'arte* and Bing's experiments in mask making (carried out with Marie-Hélène Dasté). Albert Marque (a technical adviser on the Workshop design course) later developed the Noble (or Neutral) mask and taught the young students more advanced mask-making skills. The use of both Noble and character masks was to become central to much of their later work and to the work of those following after them (Saint-Denis, Jacques Lecoq, Philippe Gaulier, Mnouchkine).

In 1923–4 the School budget was cut. Bing and Marie-Hélène worked hard to re-configure the curriculum and the programme for the Apprentice Group was now placed at the heart of the School. Bing mentored the students in the development of two mime pieces: *Marin* (Seafarer) and *La Guerre* (The War), which were what we would now understand as very early examples of devised mime performance. Jean Dasté felt that these performances best reflected their overall work at the School.[40] However, Copeau felt that the most successful end of year production was a Nō Theatre production of *Kantan* performed by the students and directed by Bing before the closure of the School in 1924.

Regardless of the challenges Copeau had faced at the Vieux-Colombier Theatre, by 1924 he and Bing had consolidated their different experiments into an original and coherent approach to actor training and had also developed a way of enabling the student actors to become 'creators' of new performance material in line with their vision. In effect, they had established a form of early devised theatre in the School's studio. In addition to this they had built a strong community of apprentice artists who were to become of central significance to their next project.

The Vieux-Colombier and the principle of liberty

In the end, the Vieux-Colombier Theatre's success and strength became its own weakness. Copeau resolutely refused to weaken his stance on the commercial exploitation of the successful productions or on refusing any subsidy or sponsorship that was not in his control. Jouvet, increasingly frustrated, felt that he had no option but to leave. Although Copeau begged Jouvet not to go, Jouvet clearly felt that he could not subsume his own artistic needs to that of his friend and director. Kurtz records Jouvet's response to Copeau: 'I am not leaving the Vieux-Colombier. The Vieux-Colombier has left me.'[41] Kurtz also indicates that Jouvet's departure must have been a terrible blow to Copeau – deserted by one of his oldest collaborators, someone whom he had come rely upon for his commitment, hard work and many skills and talents. Only Bing remained by his side, the co-author of many of their more innovative projects. A younger generation, who had come through the School, now stepped in to take the place of some of those who had left. Copeau's nephew, Michel Saint-Denis, became his trusted assistant within the company – a partial replacement for Jouvet, and complementing the role of Bing within the School.

He also refused either to move to a larger theatre or to increase the capacity of the Vieux-Colombier. This left the Theatre artistically rich but financially poor. The pressures of a continuously refreshed repertoire meant that costs never reduced and the struggle to market productions and fill the auditorium never diminished for a moment. Copeau was resolute, even stubborn, in his commitment to his principles – 'I do not wish to assure my future at the price of my liberty.'[42] The purity of his early vision would not be allowed to be sullied.

What I call living is for a man to assert himself according to his nature, to follow his spiritual destiny. Away from this course, I find death. It is to real death that you send us if you call us to an artificial life, if you do not respect our thoughts above all, if you can see only a material power in that which the spirit has alone created, if you wish *to exploit the idea of the Vieux-Colombier* before it has reached maturity, before the *fact* of the Vieux-Colombier has been achieved.[43]

Copeau's passionate defense of his position reads well, but it did not ultimately prevent further defections and a decline in interest and commitment from his supporters. Kurtz records how, for the 1922–3 season, only 25 per cent of Les Amis du Vieux-Colombier renewed their subscription.

What was to be the final season at the Vieux-Colombier also marked the tenth anniversary of its founding. The company was now skilfully adept at a range of theatrical genres. Over the preceding decade they had, despite, or perhaps because of, the difficulties they had faced, developed a strong company rapport, a light and poetic physical energy, and flexible physicality that lent itself particularly well to comedy. Copeau himself had now become deeply experienced as a director, actor, teacher and dramaturg. The 1923–4 season also included a play written by Copeau, *La Maison Natale* (The Birthplace). Based on an early idea he had been nurturing since 1901, this play was a daring new enterprise for him. For Copeau, Molière was the model of a theatre artist – an actor, writer and company manager – and producing a play of his own marked a special moment in his own artistic development. This idea of the complete theatre artist was now to start driving him towards the next project.

The critics did not however respond with universal approval to Copeau's play, and the theatre continued to struggle with its (undeserved) reputation for avant-gardism and a repertoire that catered for the Left Bank intelligentsia. Despite its struggles at this time, it is nonetheless necessary to recognize the significant impact that Copeau and the Vieux-Colombier had on Paris theatre. A generation of actors and playwrights benefitted enormously from the rigour and vision of Copeau's approach. Still, the pressures that he was under were immense and ultimately unbearable, he had become dangerously fatigued and the continuing departure of former colleagues only strengthened his belief that determined adherence to his ideals was the best way forward. However, he and Bing had also seen exciting developments in the School, which offered some hopeful possibilities for the future. Sensing that the only way to continue his project was to close the Vieux-Colombier project and to start again, Copeau bided his time in order to find the most opportune moment to make the break.

On 23 May 1924, Copeau formally announced the temporary closure of the theatre, necessitated, he stated, by his own state of health and by 'the launching of new projects'.[44] He handed over the right to use Vieux-Colombier actors and plays to Jouvet, effectively acknowledging that

Jouvet and Dullin would now carry the company flame in the capital city. In October 1924, he departed for Morteuil in Burgundy full of anticipation for the new project.

The move to Burgundy and Les Copiaus

As early as 1916 Copeau had expressed the desire to create a New Improvised Comedy that would involve the invention of characters and lead to the development of new and vibrant theatre. In a letter to Jouvet in 1916 he discusses this plan to 'invent … about ten modern synthetic characters of great breadth, representing characteristics, foibles, passions, the moral, social and individual absurdities of today'.[45] Copeau leased a property in Morteuil in Burgundy to house a re-configured company with Bing made up from a number of actors from the Vieux-Colombier and students from the Apprentice Group in order to make this desire manifest. This decision was also underpinned by his belief that his company should live and work in a more communal way, as they had in Le Limon and in America. Firmly believing that it would lead to a more authentic, sincere and accessible theatre a rural location was chosen, away from the cities, working closer to nature and to the communities that the company would live among. This project was a forerunner for practices of community and applied theatre, and contemporary ensemble theatre companies such as Footsbarn[46] and Kneehigh can be seen as a continuation of this type of approach in the twentieth and twenty-first centuries.

While the idea of the new project was exciting, the harsh reality of their financial and living circumstances required real commitment from Copeau, and the artists and students who moved with him. The building he leased turned out to be 'a large, imposing farm-house, situated in a damp hollow. It was filthy, had no electricity and the stoves did not work'.[47] This project was not for the faint-hearted and over the following years the collaborators made considerable personal sacrifices in order to bring their project to fruition. The committed artists and their family members included Copeau, his wife, Agnès Thomsen, their three daughters, including Marie-Hélène, Bing with Bernard, her son by Copeau, and her older daughter Claude Varese, who was to become an Apprentice. They were joined by a number of students and four actors from the Vieux-Colombier also committed to the reconfigured company, including Jean Dasté, Jean Dorcy and Etienne Decroux (1898–1991). On arrival, Copeau introduced the project, and his vision of the way in which they would live and work together. He had recently converted to Roman Catholicism (as Bing had done shortly before him) and his growing spiritual beliefs influenced the way in which he wanted this theatre community to live and work. In addition to stressing the importance of morality and discipline[48] he required the artists 'to accept poverty as a condition of discipleship'.[49]

Copeau felt passionately that this should be a training-company that would undertake research and experimentation in order to develop this new form of theatre, and they continued to draw on, and develop, the pedagogy from the Paris school. Copeau taught when he was present, but Bing was once again responsible for the training and was helped by Marie-Hélène and Jean Dasté (who married in 1928) and later by Saint-Denis and Villard. The combination of Copeau's vision of the New Improvised Comedy, his extensive experiments with *commedia dell'arte*, and Bing's development of the methods of extended play, rhythmic work, mime, mask and devised theatre-making techniques started to converge in exciting new ways and were to be used as the basis for a professional repertoire. Significantly they also continued to invent and to celebrate rituals in their everyday lives just as the Apprentice Group had done previously with Bing in the School. This started to feed directly into their work for public performance.

The first two performances were presented in January 1925 in Lille: *L'Impôt* (The Tax) and *L'Objet* (The Object). The latter piece allowed the group to generate their own performance material as they had done at the Paris school. It was based on a very loose plot concerning the search for an object,[50] which Rudlin notes 'turned out to be a jazz tune'.[51] Copeau had the actors 'improvise', he observed the outcomes and would then 're-stage and shape the action and write down the dialogue'.[52] In effect, Copeau and his collaborators became the 'poets', or authors, of their own work. They were becoming the 'complete' theatre-makers that Copeau had long dreamed of. This approach is now very common in devised theatre, but the use of these methods to make performance in the 1920s was revolutionary and far removed from the Vieux-Colombier's staging of theatre texts.

The audience in Lille did not respond well to the work and the company desperately needed sources of funding. In the light of these circumstances, Copeau brought the first phase of their project to an end. Eleven of the students who were not able to support themselves during this period left but all the others remained. As he was going to be frequently away, Copeau decided that during his absences his nephew, Michel Saint-Denis, would direct the troupe. In Paris Saint-Denis had been general secretary for the Vieux-Colombier for a period of time. He had not attended the School in any capacity,[53] was not an actor in the Vieux-Colombier company and only became a full member of the School-company following the move to Burgundy in 1924. Nonetheless, Saint-Denis had been closely connected to his uncle's work prior to the move, observed, and on occasion participated in classes at the School, and was to quickly learn, and use, the techniques and making processes Copeau, Bing and their collaborators had developed.

This reconfigured troupe was to become known as Les Copiaus (an affectionate name bestowed by the local community) and they were to go on to create another fifteen productions between March 1925 and April 1927.[54] They produced a number of other original pieces of devised theatre, various adaptations of work by playwrights such as Corneille, Goldoni,

Moliere and Lopé de Rueda, and full productions of pre-existing plays. The company's new creations included invented characters such as Jean Bourgignon (a local wine marker from Burgundy, who was to become central to the Copiaus project), recreations of *commedia* characters (such as Pierrot), and performance pieces that combined songs, music and movement. Marie-Hélène and Jean Dasté, along with Saint-Denis and Jean Villard also acted as fairground barkers drawing and entertaining the crowds for their shows and this gave them the opportunity to more openly engage with their audiences as a travelling troupe of actors before and after the formally framed performance.

Bing, Marie-Hélène and Jean Dasté, Saint-Denis, Villard and the rest of the company were subsequently to create a number of the original devised pieces drawing on their existing methods, without Copeau as director. In 1925 they performed a short piece based on *Las Olivas* (The Olives) by Lopé de Rueda that dealt with 'the growing and harvesting of blackcurrants [...] expressed in mime, song and dance'.[55] The troupe subsequently performed to a large audience as part of a wine harvest festival where they presented a mime and movement-based piece *La Celebration du vin et de la vigne* (The Celebration of Wine and the Vineyard), which explored the work of the local people in the vineyards.

In December 1925, the company moved to a small village, Pernard-Vergelesses, to escape the damp Chateau where they had first lodged. After a period of protracted absences, and despite the increasingly problematic relationship between Copeau and the rest of the company, he wrote *L'Illusion*

FIGURE 1.5 *Masked improvisation with Michel Saint-Denis, Suzanne Bing and Jean Dasté. Photo courtesy of Catherine Dasté/BnF.*

(The Illusion) (1926) for them which drew more explicitly on their masked-play research and their own lives as a theatre troupe. Copeau explains: '[t]his is not, properly speaking, either a drama or comedy. It is a theatre game'.[56] Les Copiaus went on to develop four other pieces independently of Copeau and devised these pieces using mime and mask. The following year they developed this work into *La Danse de la Ville et des Champs* (The Dance of the Town and of the Fields) which contrasted ideas about rural and urban culture. Rudlin notes that '[f]or many of the company the performance was the apotheosis of the ideas it had been working on since the opening of the Vieux-Colombier School in 1920'.[57] Significantly, Copeau had not been involved in the making of the piece and had in fact been asked not to attend rehearsals by the company indicating how strained relations were by that point.[58] His feedback on the work was vehemently negative as Villard explains: '[w]e were waiting for constructive criticism. Alas, it was a demolition job, total and complete. Copeau was ferocious. All our efforts, all our passions, all our joy – there was nothing left. Nothing found favour in his eyes. His last word, full of a bitter derision worthy of Ecclesiastes was: dust'.[59] Rudlin argues that the 'new *commedia* project … had evolved empirically into a product that was, somehow, contrary to Copeau's vision'.[60] The troupe was bitterly disappointed with Copeau's criticism but they went on to create another piece without Copeau and were still rehearsing in May 1929 when Copeau decided to dissolve the company. Rudlin argues that Copeau's move away from his belief in the supremacy of the text towards a theory of action in these later years resulted in the written material they used having 'little value except as action'.[61] The actors had indeed become their own 'authors' or 'poets' but consequently this also changed the type, purpose and status of the text. This strand of practice had really become something that was more meaningfully owned by Bing and the younger company members, and had become more radical than perhaps Copeau had ever anticipated.

La Compagnie des Quinze: Suzanne Bing, Jean and Marie-Hélène Dasté, Michel Saint-Denis

When Copeau disbanded Les Copiaus in 1929 he was in declining health, which put him under great strain. Undoubtedly, as Baldwin[62] suggests, he was also being pulled in new directions – towards the possibility of prestigious posts in Paris and towards a stronger religious conviction that must have been at odds with elements of his personal life. The multi-generational nature of the company had initially been its strength – Copeau had built much of the new work on the willingness and enthusiasm of the young actors who had followed him through the School and into Les Copiaus. Now, the young actors, with the older and more experienced Bing, wanted to take on more of the direction of the work. Copeau seems to have felt this in part as a betrayal.

A year after Copeau disbanded Les Copiaus Saint-Denis reunited the artists to form the Compagnie des Quinze.[63] It was a company of fifteen made up of ten former company members including Bing and five students, led by Saint-Denis [see **Volume 1**]. Saint-Denis was ambitious, had a vision and believed in their new company. They produced six independent productions (1930–4), which, like their work in Les Copiaus, ranged in styles and periods, and staged four other works in three seasons. Bing was now the only person in the company member who had been a founder member of the Vieux-Colombier; the new company continued directly using her pedagogic and theatre-making practices.[64] The relationship between the new company and Copeau continued to be complex, but in terms of historical narrative it is Saint-Denis's accounts that tend to dominate our understanding of this last phase of the collaborators' work. Sadly, Saint-Denis does not acknowledge his application of Bing's pedagogy and theatre-making techniques in his two published books. Consequently, Bing's work and that of the other women, became further effaced in French theatre history.

Saint-Denis, taking advantage of the favourable reception of the Compagnie des Quinze in England, grasped the opportunity of support offered by several influential English theatre people, and moved to London to establish a career as a director and teacher. The company's early work, drawing on the outcomes of the Vieux-Colombier School and Les Copiaus, was highly innovative, but ultimately Saint-Denis returned to the more conservative notion that the text, and director's vision, should be the dominant aspect of theatre-making and the play, mime and mask work was now placed back within that more traditional hierarchy. Saint-Denis directed a number of important productions that involved leading actors of the time, quickly building a reputation for realism mixed with a sense of style and physicality. His success enabled him to make contact with like-minded theatre artists and those interested in challenging the actor training orthodoxy of the time. Although Bing participated in the Compagnie des Quinze and continued to adapt works for the Dastés after the company was disbanded, Saint-Denis's narrative pays little attention to her role or to the contribution of her early teaching and direction within the Vieux-Colombier School to the Compagnie des Quinze's and indeed Saint-Denis's later international success.

Copeau alone: Religious spectacle

After the disbanding of Les Copiaus, Copeau was to tread a very different path to his nephew for the remainder of his life. After a two-year period reflecting on his conversion to Catholicism and how he could connect this spiritual conviction and quest with his work in the theatre, Copeau was invited to direct a medieval Mystery play, *Santa Ulvina*, at Florence in 1933. This was followed by a second adaptation of a Mystery play in 1943, which was to be his last theatre production.

In addition to these religious mass performances, Copeau was to make two other significant contributions to French theatre at this time. In 1940, in the early years of the Second World War, Copeau was made director of the Comédie-Française. Copeau had long wanted to introduce significant changes to theatre and no doubt felt confident that he could bring about the renewal. However, he resigned several months into the post after coming into conflict with the Vichy Government and the Nazi regime over their insistence that he persuade his son to leave the resistance movement.[65] In 1941, he wrote an important essay that argued for a decentralized theatre culture and system in France. This decentralized structure would make theatre available in the regions outside Paris and, he felt, would also reflect the diversity of French culture. This essay was to have a considerable influence on the development of cultural programming and management in France; indeed, Evans argues that this 'was to be one of [Copeau's] most important and lasting legacies'.[66] By the 1940s Copeau had moved away from his desire to make work and to bring about renovation in French theatre. His health was not good but he continued to write both plays and articles until his death in Beaune on 20 October 1949.

Copeau's Art

Although there is a chronological coherence to the development of Copeau's artistic vision and to his theatrical achievements, this chapter proposes they can be best understood thematically. The 'Art' section is therefore structured around key themes that inform Copeau's work: his early vision for theatrical renewal; his interest in movement and play in the creation of new theatre; his commitment to collaboration, community and family; and, the development and use of innovative approaches to scenic design and lighting.

Copeau's vision and the Théâtre du Vieux-Colombier

Copeau's experience as a critic and his close friendship with many leading cultural figures in Paris meant that he would have been under no illusions about the scale of the task he was setting himself. He was effectively setting out to rebuild the art of theatre. To do so he looked for inspiration not to the modern experiments of the avant-garde, but to historical examples. Molière was the model that inspired Copeau – an actor and writer who drew on the rich heritage of the *commedia dell'arte* but also made it his own. He also moved focus away from the individual star actor and towards the ensemble of players and the rhythmic interplay of movement, voice and *mise en scène*. We can see the first attempts at this in his revival of his 1910 adaptation of *The Brothers Karamazov* in 1913. Kurtz describes how with the exit of old Feodor, 'Copeau made him start building up his exit in the middle of his scene so that when he finally left the stage, it was the result of a long-prepared sequence and a contribution to the dramatic impact of the scene, rather than a character simply walking off on a line or action cue'.[67]

There's no doubt that Copeau's vision was an inspiring one, announced by an inspiring man. The success of his experiments with *The Brothers Karamazov* spurred him on to plan for a theatre and a permanent company of his own. On the one hand, Copeau promised something quite substantial to the actors whom he sought to draw together for the Théâtre du Vieux-Colombier; 'an attempt at dramatic renovation'.[68] On the other hand, he offered little; he could afford to pay only modest wages and the theatre was run on the most economical basis possible. The idea of a rotating repertoire of plays was in part an aesthetic decision and in part a financial necessity. The theatre needed to be replenished with new audiences on a regular basis in order to keep the box office takings strong.

The Théâtre du Vieux-Colombier's first season in 1913 consisted of a range of works, including a revival of *The Brothers Karamazov*. But the momentum that was established was disrupted by the outbreak of war in 1914. The opportunity, when it came, to tour to New York was a crucial chance not only to re-unite the company, but also to integrate into the work many of the ideas that Copeau had been able to research during the period when he was invalided out of war service. It might seem odd that the production Copeau chose to open the company's season in New York was not a new play or even a revered classic European drama, instead it was Molière's comedy *The Tricks of Scapin*. *Scapin* was for Copeau however the perfect play with which to commence this next phase of the company's work.

In the midst of the violent currents of Modernism, Copeau could not ignore what he saw as the vital energies and scenic poetry of the great dramatists of the past. This play is a light comedy very much in the tradition of the *commedia dell'arte*, but it requires a strong sense of rhythm and energy from the actors and an ability to engage with the light comedy of the story in an appropriate manner. The play opened in New York on 27 November 1917, and remained in the company's repertoire until 13 May 1922, making it one of the longest running plays for the company. The play is a three-act farce, first performed by Molière's company in 1671. It tells a story very much in the mould of the traditional *commedia dell'arte* spectacles. Set in Naples, the play is based around the escapades of Scapin, a servant figure in the tradition of the Arlecchino figure in Commedia. The story is simple and can be seen as characteristic of the kinds of plots used for many traditional *commedia* plays. It revolves around the need for Scapin to play a series of tricks on two old fathers to ensure that their young sons can end up happy, prosperous and married to the women they love, and that he can exact some revenge upon his master, Geronte.

The New York production included an introduction (*L'Impromptu du Vieux-Colombier* [The Impromptu of the Vieux-Colombier]) and an epilogue (*Le Couronnement de Molière* [The Coronation of Molière]) both composed by Copeau and the company. The purpose of this framing device was partly to introduce the company members to a foreign audience and to celebrate French culture, but also to introduce the style of the performance and the ethos of the company. Both additional sections blurred the distinction between the actors as actors, and as representational figures, the theatricality of the whole event was in this way subtly emphasized. The introduction finished with the traditional signal of three loud knocks, announcing the start of the play.

The style of the performance was '*dans un mouvement rapide*' (in a fast movement).[69] This implies a brisk, light and yet urgent approach that was intended no doubt to capture the audience's attention and keep them engaged. The performance was played without interval and on a raised bare platform. The simplicity of the staging aided the rapid and rhythmical style of performance. The beat of the actors' feet on the bare boards of the platform added another level of musicality to the experience. Copeau himself played the role of Scapin, the trickster – perhaps a playful reference to his role as a master manipulator, able to turn all things round to the needs of the happy ending and to unite a disparate group through the power of his own charm and wiliness? He would also have been aware that Molière had played Scapin, an association that Copeau would have been proud of and that partly motivated his epilogue for the play. As a director, he managed to draw out from his actors performances that embodied the energy and playfulness associated with the theatrical traditions informing the original play. He sought to encourage the actors to build the performances from the body and from an intelligent but playful physicality and used this as the starting point to explore the play, rather than an intellectual understanding or analysis of the text.[70] Copeau's own performance as Scapin was hailed by critics who saw it as a triumph of physical acting: 'He was movement incarnate, cascading motility, leaping here and there, with long and lithe strides, stopping but for seconds – just enough time to think up new tricks, new deceits, acrobatic stunts, and rogueries.'[71] The language picks up on the dynamics of the movement; the phrase 'cascading motility' – though awkward to the ear now, creates an interesting image of a tumbling effervescence of movement in performance and indicates perhaps something of the difficulty facing a critic seeking the right phrase to capture that quality.

Copeau's qualities of lightness of touch, acrobatic movement and complete physicality – 'He talks with his face, feet and hands, as well as with his voice'[72] – were supported within an equally adept and skilled ensemble, creating a coherent experience that blended acting and direction in a manner wholly consistent with what Copeau understood and wanted to present as the nature of the text. Louis Jouvet, for instance, playing the part of Geronte, expressively captured the character's rapid emotional journey through greed, fear, anger and shame. Interestingly, two of the best insights into Copeau's vision for *The Tricks of Scapin* come from remarks made by Copeau and Roger Martin du Gard in their diaries after seeing what they considered a particularly conventional and uninspiring production at the Comédie-Française on their return from New York. Copeau remarked that the production had 'no movement and no shape'.[73] Martin du Gard was more detailed:

> Everything that makes for a sense of theatre was missing: rhythm and movement on the stage, composition of the characters positioned so as to make sense and express themselves with greater precision [...] Each actor has worked out a characterisation with meticulous care and often much understanding. But without any direction, without reference to the ensemble. From which comes a constant false note.[74]

These remarks give us some sense of what Copeau's production sought to achieve: rhythmic movement; coherent, purposeful and meaningful stage composition; and rich ensemble playing.

Whereas before the war, only a small proportion of new work had been included in the repertoire, on the return to Paris Copeau became more committed to a search for the future poets of the theatre with whom he could work and collaborate. The ethos and reputation of the company meant that many writers approached the company – however Copeau was clear that he was looking for those who could best fulfil the opportunities that the company offered. One important example was Charles Vidrac's play *Le Paquebot Tenacity* (The Boat Called Tenacity) (1920) – a simple and sensitive play that became a significant success for the company. Vidrac was initially a poet, but had been drawn towards the theatre through his association with other writers who were also part of the circle of artists aligned to the Vieux-Colombier. For this play, Jouvet created another simple stage set, using only minimal additions to create a sense of place. The collaborative nature of the Vieux-Colombier is evident in Vidrac's account of how he assisted Jouvet in painting parts of the set.[75] The use of lighting from above and from the side of the stage, and the abolition of footlights, were also important innovations for the time, drawing on Copeau's memories of his conversations with Edward Gordon Craig.[76] The subtle use of the new lighting configurations became another part of the stage poetry, supporting the stage composition and the rhythm and movement of the actors. What stood out for the reviewers and critics was the 'sympathetic precision'[77] of the acting. By avoiding the kinds of overt comic theatricality previously employed in *The Tricks of Scapin*, and instead placing subtle emphasis on telling details of characterization, presented without interpretation or affect, the actors, under Copeau's direction, achieved something delightful, alive and more than the sum of its parts. Its success demonstrated that the company was not limited to one theatrical and presentational style.

Play, mime, mask and devised theatre

Physical expressivity, playful creativity and his notion of 'sincerity'[78] were always part of Copeau's vision for his actors and the related training and making methods that came from this quest were developed in close collaboration with Suzanne Bing. The techniques and devised theatre-making methods developed at the School underpinned the later work created by Les Copiaus. Indeed this strand of their practice arguably went much further than Copeau could ever have anticipated. At the start of their project, Copeau sought to develop psycho-physical training and skills for his actors in that they were based on a model of an integrated body and mind. This approach explored the constant imaginative interplay between an actor's movement and the way in which it triggers internal sensations, feelings and what we might understand as a character's psychology. Copeau had been inspired by Stanislavsky's insistence that the actor find a truth, and imaginative justification, in their characterization,[79] and he wanted his actors to achieve this in their physicalized performances of characters in non-Naturalistic theatre.

> Copeau felt that the natural movement of craftsmen at work or children at play could be developed in actors by exercises linking the external action with an internal state of mind. Although he tended to work from the outside, or the physical action first, he wanted to develop an accompanying 'state of intimate consciousness, particular to the movement accomplished'. Thus Copeau seems to have shifted his focus from a psychological study of the character's inner state of mind to a focus on the inner feeling of the action itself. For Copeau, lack of sincerity in movement often stemmed from lack of internal preparation and follow through – a self-consciousness rather than an action-consciousness.[80]

In order to achieve this vision, Copeau required a broader range of movement and highly developed imaginative, physical, kinesthetic, rhythmic and ensemble skills, from his actors and a pedagogic system that could train them in these areas.

To understand this development, we need to explore further Copeau's close collaboration with Bing. When Bing and Copeau taught weekly classes for children in Paris during the First World War, in addition to developing a number of seminal techniques, she also started to reflect on the style and manner of her teaching. Although Copeau attended fortnightly (and this established the pattern that was to continue during all the years of their collaboration), it was Bing who acted as the central and consistent pedagogue. There was already a distinct difference between their pedagogic styles and abilities at this time, nonetheless they shared the same vision and Copeau could clearly see that Bing had the capacity to build the innovative pedagogic approach they would need for their project. Bing's stay in America (see Life section for details) then enabled her to act on three key encounters with Margaret Naumburg, Jessmin Howarth and Marie-Hélène Dasté.

Bing's time spent at Margaret Naumburg's progressive school in New York was pivotal to the further development of their work with play, mime and pedagogy.[81] Naumburg had studied with John Dewey, Maria Montessori and Marietta Johnson, three radical reformers of education who all advocated student-centred and experiential learning in self-determined environments, which challenged the models of autocratic and top-down education that had dominated in the nineteenth century. Naumburg had also studied Eurhythmics and was influenced by Alexander Technique, and aspects of these embodied techniques were filtered through her additional interest in Freudian Psychoanalysis. Naumburg's rebellious and avant-garde blend of training, skills and interests was used at her school when Bing joined to lead creative sessions and observe the teachers. Bing learnt to use careful observation of movement and behaviour (from Montessori and Naumburg's approaches), to reflect on her teaching style, and to learn key skills. Crucially, Naumburg placed creative play, with its innate connection to mimicry and storytelling, at the very heart of her school and she took it seriously as the 'groundwork for education'.[82] As Copeau had noted, this type of play demonstrated what they thought would be desirable to their theatre project: '[C]hildren who play well, who *know how* to play, are models of verve, naturalness and invention. They are masters of improvisation'.[83] Consequently Bing's time at Naumburg's school provided her with skills to use creative play as the basis for actor training and theatre-making. Indeed, Felner argues that this experience with Naumburg inspired Bing to develop 'what we call theater games today [...] designed to free the "child-like instincts for play," break down blocks, and release spontaneous movement'.[84]

The second encounter was with Jessmin Howarth, who had trained with Jacques Dalcroze and joined the company as the movement teacher. Howarth trained the company in rhythmic gymnastics, improvisation in dance and mime, and she also attended rehearsals. She used play, games and improvisation to teach rhythm and musicality, and movement in more general terms. Eventually Copeau and Bing felt that an application of Eurhythmics in a 'pure' sense was problematic because it contained a level of stylization in the movement practice that did not seem capable of responding flexibly to their ideas about the actor's sense of internal rhythm and had not been fully integrated by their actors. The stylization also did not suit the demands of their repertoire. In contradistinction to Eurhythmics, Bing argued that rhythmic exercises are 'always unsatisfactory if they are not used exclusively to exercise the outer manifestation of the inner sense that one wants to develop'.[85] She came to recognize that it had not been possible to make a link between Eurhythmics and 'the free improvisation created, suggested, by a child's play (le jeu d'enfant), the interior music of this play'[86] that she and Copeau were searching for. Although this overall method was not retained in a 'pure' form, Evans argues that Bing and Copeau took aspects of Eurhythmics and incorporated it into their evolving approach to training.[87] This included a centralizing of inner/outer rhythm and a notion of musicality in their practice along with the use of musical concepts in their making and dramaturgical processes. There was a third point of cross-fertilization that also took place during this period which involved Bing and Marie-Hélène, Copeau's teenage daughter who had grown up in her father's theatre company and had accompanied them on the tour to America. During the summer break, Marie-Hélène and Bing, both of whom had a strong visual imagination and keen interest in image and form, started to carry out the Vieux-Colombier's first experiments in mask making. This was a significant step for the company in relation to Copeau's work with the masked characters in *commedia dell'arte* and because Bing was subsequently to use mask training in the curriculum of their School and for mime productions.

Consequently, the establishment of the Paris school gave Bing and Copeau the opportunity to synthesize this rich combination of collaborations and experiments they had undertaken, and move into a realm of radical invention. In the first programme for the School, taught solely by Bing, her classes were structured around a use of play, games and improvisation, extended into small performances through the use of fairy tales, simple scenarios and songs. This included the exploration of musical concepts, rhythmic patterns and ideas about dynamics, duration and space. Significantly, the final year performance was described as a *charade* on the saltimbanque (travelling/street performer), which was a short piece of original mime performance, with the narrative and atmosphere expressed solely through physicality and sound. Fleming[88] argues that at the School Bing also introduced a set of innovative pedagogic tools many of which are now common features of actor training, but which were groundbreaking in the 1920s and have fed into the development of devised theatre. Among other things, this included student-led working, mentoring the students in the devising of their own performances, and self and peer feedback. Central to this was the system of Student-Monitors and Group-Leaders, and Marie-Hélène was crucial to the success of the School in this capacity. Bing also supported them in the establishment of celebrations with masked dancing and games for birthdays and special events in their everyday lives. Copeau felt these activities were crucial to the development of the School, and a communal way of life, that he believed was the basis for their new form of theatre. They were to become important elements in the work of Les Copiaus.

Two new elements introduced to the syllabus in its second year were to be powerful catalysts for the final stage of development of this practice: the use of the Hébert system of natural gymnastics and the use of masks. 'For Copeau Hébert's system facilitated the goal of "the natural development of the instinct for play," through the building of physical prowess and the regaining of instinctive behaviour – two vital tools for the Copeau actor.'[89] This method of gymnastics 'works with fundamental groups, named families: pulling, pushing, climbing, walking, running, jumping, lifting, carrying, attacking, defending, swimming'.[90] They used this system to improve corporeal flexibility, control and balance of movements, and breath control. However, they were not interested in the aesthetic dimension of gymnastics, rather they sought to combine this practice with the inner feeling and rhythm, *le jeu d'enfant*, of the core gestures.[91] Copeau and Bing introduced the use of Noble (what we now call Neutral) and character masks for the training of their students. Bing developed masked chorus work known as the 'The Little Demons' with her students for use in the Vieux-Colombier production of Saul in 1922, directed by Copeau and written by Andre Obey. This represented the first transfer of the use of this type of extended mime and masked play into their professional repertoire. The two sides of the Vieux-Colombier project were finally brought together. Bing and the students then took this material further, drawing on their work with Hébert gymnastics, to create the students' end-of-year production *Play of Little Demons* (1922).

When the School was restructured the following year solely for the nine students in the Apprentice Group, it was decided that they would mount performances for the public. By this point they were achieving Copeau's vision of actors working as their own creators of performance: '[u]ltimately, free play gives way to small-scale productions for which people are entirely left to their own devices, as creators and workers'.[92] Bing had thus successfully mentored the students to develop their own mask and mime performance. As discussed earlier, the two mime pieces performed, Marin and La Guerre were what we would now classify as devised mime performance. Bing researched Japanese Nō Theatre and subsequently trained and directed the students in Kantan, a highly expressive and precise end-of-year school production in this genre. Although the piece was never to be performed to a full audience, the open rehearsal was to be an important point in the School's development and Copeau was delighted with the work.

By the time that Copeau closed the Théâtre du Vieux-Colombier and the associated school in 1924 he and Bing had developed a pedagogic process centred on play that developed a high level of mime and mask skill in their students along with the capacity to work as the 'creators', or devisers, of theatre. This area of their 'Art' practice was to become the central focus when Copeau moved the re-configured company to Burgundy. The subsequent work of Les Copiaus and the Compagnie des Quinze drew directly on this practice, and often re-visited material made at the School. Although Copeau was not directly involved with the work of the Compagnie des Quinze, their work was inextricably bound to the project that he had undertaken with Bing and she was to become a founding member of the new company, performing in a number of their key productions as the most experienced actor. Neglecting this connection skews the history of devised theatre-making and modern mime, and risks hiding Bing's work and Copeau's more radical practice under Saint-Denis's achievements as the next 'Great Director' in this French lineage.[93] This was a crucial aspect of Copeau and Bing's 'Art' which was to be of central importance to the development of this strand of theatre in the twentieth century.

Company, family and community – productions made in collaboration

Theatre companies often strongly resemble other forms of community or family grouping. They have their own dynamics and politics, but when they work well they generate relationships that, within the theatrical context, are more than just professional or utilitarian. Copeau was strongly drawn, throughout his life, to generating companies that were based on more than just commercial bonds. The Vieux-Colombier and later Les Copiaus were not surrogate families for Copeau; they *were* his family. This complex relationship between the professional and the personal is reflected in the involvement of his own children in the early experiments in theatre training and education, in his recruitment of his nephew Michel Saint-Denis as his assistant, in the relationship between him and Suzanne Bing (and their son, Bernard), and in the later construction of Les Copiaus around these close family and emotional ties.

Copeau's first experiment in the generation of this kind of artistic community came with the retreat to Le Limon with the core of the Vieux-Colombier company. For ten weeks, they trained intensively together; studying, improvising, living together as a group of theatre artists. Of course, the results were limited in this short timeframe; but the experience clearly fired a vision of what might be possible, and for Copeau and Bing at least, a determination to pursue the challenge further and an understanding that this would take time.

In October 1924, following the closure of the Vieux-Colombier, Copeau, Bing and the new company arrived in Burgundy. The new company, although communal in nature, was still under the guiding direction of Copeau, who maintained his role as *le patron*. The fact that many of the new company were students who had studied at the School and not professional actors with the baggage of past experience and theatrical habit was a particular bonus. Here, finally, was the opportunity for a genuine blank sheet of paper. Copeau took several key features of the theatre of the past as starting points for this new project: the chorus from classical drama, masked improvisation from *commedia dell'arte*, and full-face mask work from the Nō Theatre and Greek tragedy. To these he added the use of play, mime and movement that had been developed within the School by Bing. The chorus was a dramatic representation of the cohesion of the company as a whole – a group of people, moving, thinking and acting in unison and with a shared intention. The chorus generates and requires a common aesthetic within the group – how do they move and speak, what is their role within the drama? These are the building blocks of ensemble acting and represent a redefinition of the notion of ensemble as a space within which actors are not just acting together on a permanent basis, but also sharing and developing practices, processes and the aesthetic and dramatic principles that underpin them. Copeau's desire to explore a New Improvised Comedy grew out of the work that he had seen the students achieve under Bing's instruction within the School. The mask work that Copeau and Bing had explored in the School suggested the genuine value in masked improvisation – creating characters that were not just psychological constructs but that were realized in a profoundly physical sense as well. Tapping in to the creativity within physical improvisation that releases the actor's sense of playfulness and joy; emphasizing the plastic and dynamic aspects of theatre as well as the verbal and textual.

The whole experiment almost failed as the financial situation deteriorated and the expected backers failed to produce the necessary funds. Copeau was forced to return to Paris to seek support for the project. He instructed Saint-Denis to prepare for the disbanding of the new company after less than a year of activity. Despite Bing's seniority and experience, Saint-Denis assumed the mantle of leadership offered by Copeau, and the company moved from a training company, focused on experiment, to become a producing company. It seems that Bing's achievements were more strongly associated by Copeau with teaching, directing in a studio context, and performing than with direction and leadership of a new company. Copeau's decision reflects the

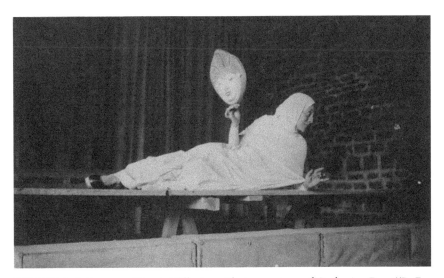

FIGURE 1.6 *Suzanne Bing in* L'Illusion. *Photo courtesy of Catherine Dasté/BnF.*

ideologies about gender that dominated in Europe during the early years of the twentieth century and the fact that there were very few female theatre directors at that time. In effect this decision passed control from one man to another, in a patrilineal manner, but nonetheless the work of the new company was to draw heavily on Bing's work in all areas, and her expertise as an actor.

The young company threw themselves at this new challenge, and in Copeau's absence became more democratic in their organization. This new democracy was to create some tensions during the periods that Copeau was able to return to Burgundy. Despite his plans for Les Copiaus as a group with(in) which to experiment and to research, Copeau seems to have found it difficult not to keep drawing the company back towards productions of his own naturalistic dramas and of classic texts. He may have found it hard to let go of his own aspirations as a playwright and he was also going through a profound period of personal and spiritual reflection which turned his attention inwards. The way forward arrived with the wine harvest in 1925. The company produced a performance, *The Celebration of Wine and the Vineyard* that was a direct response to the environment in which they were now located and drew on the types of ritual the Apprentice Group students had invented under Bing's supervision at the Paris school. Kusler explains that this included the creation of a school song; the making of a specific uniform; the invention of the new student initiation ceremony; and the establishment of celebrations with masked dancing and games for birthdays and special events in their everyday lives. Copeau had felt that this dimension of the school, the shared rituals and forms of play, were critical to the development of a communal way of life that he believed was the basis for their new form of theatre.[94] Bing will also have encountered the birthday ritual carried out in Montessori education and Naumburg's school during their time in New York and there are clear parallels here. In Burgundy they continued this practice in their training and everyday lives and sought to learn and use the rituals of the local community. To make the show, the company observed the working actions of the local people, talked to the local farmhands and practised the songs and dances of the people of the region. Building on this research they created character archetypes based on the kinds of people that they lived and worked among. The result was something quite new – something we would now understand as devised popular theatre. The combination of dances, song, mask-work, improvisation, physical comedy, mime and chorus work as a celebration of the life of the local people re-positioned theatre as something inextricably linked to the community within which it is situated.

Spurred on by the success of this show and the success of their ongoing research, they further developed their improvisations to create a more robust set of stereotypical characters. They toured the productions created through this work around the local villages and towns – establishing a strong rapport with the audiences: 'Because there was never a barrier between players and audiences, the spectators sensed how much they influenced the actors, how they could affect their performances, indeed, how at times they could lift the actors to a rare degree of exhilaration.'[95] However, something was needed to bridge the gap between the new collaborative devising and performing skills that the company was developing and their founder and director's vision. Copeau found a way to bring everyone together by writing an adaptation of Corneille's *The Illusion*. This blended the entertainments that Les Copiaus were so good at with some more complex themes and provided a framework within which their explorations of a new *commedia*, a New Improvised Comedy, could make sense. Blending the reality of the company's everyday lives with a particular theatrical reality, the integration of the mask work seemed natural, playful and part of the wider meta-theatrical conceit of the original play. The play revolved around the story of a young lover who joins a troupe of actors in order to escape his father's ire. The players set up in Pernand-Vergelesses, layering fiction over reality, and the actors and the young lover perform to the audience – the young man's father. The drama moves in and out of the fictional world and the 'real' world – so that the audience at points are watching actors pretending to be characters who are pretending to be actors who are pretending to be characters! The levels of illusion contribute to the overarching concept of reality itself as an illusion. Copeau prepared a prologue that he delivered as himself, 'The Old Actor', in which he considers the role of the actor in inhabiting the character he must play and then subverts that image with the 'bad dream' of the actor caught unprepared and having to improvise or to reveal his own vulnerability. 'I'm not acting anymore,' announces Copeau in his prologue. At a deeper level, we also sense a premonition of Copeau's eventual disengagement from his young company. Mask characters were central to this production and by this time they worked with four types: a Noble (Neutral) mask; a mask of terror, animality and the grotesque; a fairy-tale mask of dream/poetry worn by the Magician (Copeau); and a mask of an old woman, a sorceress (worn by Bing).[96] We can see in this layering of theatrical elements how the personas of, and relationship between, Copeau and Bing are dynamically represented within the piece in ways that also work to enhance the dramatic effect.

The Illusion was very well received, and a subsequent tour helped to raise the profile of the work and boost the company's coffers. The peace between him and the young company was short-lived however and Copeau too soon started to reassert his control over what he still perceived as his own project. Relationships became fractious, resulting in Copeau removing himself for longer spells from the daily work of the group. Rudlin suggests that at least in part this was because Copeau required recognition as an important international theatre practitioner and could not sustain such a profile without maintaining his own theatrical activities outside the company.[97] His financial contribution to the project was also important, of course. But at the heart of the growing tensions was in all likelihood the fact that Copeau had known most of the company members as students and young actors

FIGURE 1.7 *Copeau as the magician in* L'Illusion. *Photo courtesy of Catherine Dasté/BnF.*

and still saw the project as his opportunity to lead them towards further experiments and research. For many of these young actors, as had been the case for Dullin and Jouvet before them, they were starting to sense what they could do for and by themselves.

Les Copiaus went on to develop four other pieces independently of Copeau. *La Guerre* (The War), performed in 1927, was a direct development of the work that Bing and the students had undertaken in the Paris School. They also developed a short piece titled *Le Printemps* (Spring) the same year allowing them to continue their previous work on nature and the elements. Jean Villard explained that '[u]sing a chorus and masks, this piece was a "living fresco" of the renewal of spring – the sap mounting in plants and trees, flowers opening, the wind blowing, animals playing in the forest in the midst of people, their work and their loves'.[98] In his next absence, the group developed this work further into *The Dance of the Town and of the Fields*, which was presented as a complete ensemble piece; the programme listing only the actors and a list of scenes. The prologue was spoken by all the company and included an announcement that 'there were *no stars* among them'.[99] The performance involved a physical recreation of the cycles of the year and life in Burgundy and the story of one young character who is drawn away to the town. Their choral work contrasts the natural countryside with the mechanical dynamics of the town and they created atmospheric soundscapes, using only used minimal dialogue. As a counter-point to this story, another character (Oscar Knie, a masked character devised by Saint-Denis) makes a journey from the town into the countryside. The performance was a successful realization of the company's potential, and could be seen as the final stage of a journey begun in the various experiments Bing and Copeau had undertaken in the War years as they strove to establish their School. The work had moments of simplicity and serenity, drawn from the work with the Japanese Nō Theatre. It made use of the company's experiments in mime, rhythmic and expressive movement and gymnastics to genuine dramatic purpose. It celebrated the ensemble playing and showed what could be achieved through chorus work, especially with a group who had worked and trained together for such a sustained period. Finally, it suggested that a New Improvised Comedy, new and revitalized *commedia dell'arte*, was possible – that improvised characters could be developed that were meaningful beyond the realms of historical reconstruction. It was, essentially, a precursor to much of the devised and collaborative physical theatre of the end of the twentieth and the start of the twenty-first centuries.

As noted earlier, Copeau's response to the work was devastating and demoralizing for Les Copiaus. Did he see something genuinely worthless in the vibrant physical performance by his young ensemble who had become their own 'authors'? As 'authors' were they more sensitive to any criticism? Had they learned both too much and too little? From this distance, it is impossible to tell. However, this strand of practice had become more radically challenging to the status of the text than perhaps Copeau had anticipated or intended. The company continued to develop new work and to tour Europe. But by 1929 it was clear that this journey also, like the Vieux-Colombier journey before it, was drawing to a close. Copeau noted in his diary that autumn: 'My leaves are falling, like the season. Thus reduced, thus disengaged, will I ever re-engage myself? Is it not preferable that I show what I can achieve alone, and perhaps, can I only achieve alone?.'[100] Les Copiaus dispersed, but the core members, including Suzanne Bing, reformed under the direction of Michel Saint-Denis, as the Compagnie des Quinze. The new company continued to use Copeau and Bing's work on play, mime, mask and devised theatre and often drew on performance material and research that had been developed at the Paris school and under Les Copiaus.[101] Consequently, they continued to work much in the same vein as Les Copiaus, but Saint-Denis's vision was for a closer collaboration with the playwright as the central creative force. Bringing their considerable physical and theatrical skills to bear, they had notable successes with several pieces, including *Noe* by Andre Obey. Bing and Copeau, once such a powerful and creative pair of collaborators, seem to have drifted apart. Saint-Denis, as we have seen in the Life section above, took advantage of the success of the Compagnie des Quinze tour to London, turned exile, and built a very successful career in the UK as a theatre director and a teacher.[102]

Copeau, in the years after the closure of the Burgundy project, started to retreat from the creation of new performance work. He continued to give readings and to lecture abroad; lacking a troupe of his own, he relied upon invitations from others to direct. In 1933, he was invited to Florence to mount *Santa Ulvina*. The site for the performance, in the medieval cloisters of Santa Croce, allowed him to experiment with the location of the audience and the flow and movement of actors across the broad spaces. Rudlin argues that at this period he was most interested in finding a way to make theatre an act of 'communion'.[103] He had always believed in the social value of the great theatre traditions of the past, such as the *commedia dell'arte* and the ancient Greek Tragedy. His late exploration of the medieval Mystery plays is thus not so much of a surprise. This performance enabled his spectators to become a temporary community, through their involvement in this large-scale performance in a very specific location. He clearly believed that theatre had a unifying role within society. Something that he increasingly believed also had a spiritual and religious dimension, but that also fitted with the earlier theatrical journeys he had made. Mass performances and pageants became very popular during the 1930s – expressions of a need for communion and togetherness – but also as more complex and disquieting expressions of nationalism and cultural identity.

Scenic design, architecture and lighting

The designs for Copeau's first major theatre production, his adaptation of *The Brothers Karamazov* for the 1910–11 season at the Théâtre des Arts in Paris, were not particularly innovative. At that early stage in his career he was clearly drawing on the kinds of staging that were not untypical of the naturalistic styles of the time. The production was an important one for him however and he revived it several times during his career: it was part of the opening season of the Vieux-Colombier company as well as part of both of the New York seasons.

Photographic images of Copeau's early productions can sometimes give the impression that they were realist or naturalistic in style. While Copeau certainly wanted his actors to perform with sincerity, conviction and a certain degree of playful ease, in design terms he was actually aiming for something different and both more radical and ambitious. His focus on the rhythmic dynamics of the stage in fact places him closer in some respects to symbolism than naturalism. His direction and Jouvet's designs were intended to be suggestive as much as naturalistic. Kurtz describes how the steps that led from the mainstage to the forestage and on to the auditorium of the Vieux-Colombier theatre were a key example of the way in which the design of the space contributed to this effect.[104] Copeau's vision was of a presentational theatre, deliberately revisiting the historical ways that theatre had opened itself up to the audience rather than ignoring their role in the theatre event. He cleared out what he saw as mechanical trickery – 'for the new drama, let us have a bare stage'.[105]

In 1913, Copeau had substantially redesigned the old theatre building that was to become the Théâtre du Vieux-Colombier. However, his experiences on tour in New York several years later and his discussions during the First World War with leading figures in theatre design, such as Adolphe Appia and Edward Gordon Craig, meant that he was ready for further innovation when the Vieux-Colombier company returned from New York. His work with Jouvet to redesign the stage space at the Garrick Theatre in New York, opening up the stage to the back and sides and presenting the new innovation of the bare platform stage or *tréteau nu*, had shown him what might be possible with less structure and design but better used. Previously, after he was invalided out of the French army in 1915, Copeau had visited Craig's School in Florence. As well as confirming for him the value and importance of a School for the creation of the actors capable of reinvigorating the theatre, the visit also confirmed the value of a stage stripped of unnecessary decoration and ornament and the significance of the mask as a tool for the actor. If the stage was to be a place for scenic movement and expressive *mise en scène*, then heavy-handed naturalism would need to be removed. Craig showed Copeau what could be done with one simple staging idea augmented by the use of screens, lighting and movement. Copeau wrote enthusiastically to Jouvet, who was still at the Front: 'it is exactly what we need for our stage'.[106]

Copeau had already decided that simple staging was not an end in itself. Its purpose was to enable the dramatic work that was being produced to find its natural stage configuration. In his notes on his 1916 meeting with Adolphe Appia, Copeau records:

> The idea of stage settings emerging from the text, form the inner spirit of the dramatic work. It is a truism which he discovered before we did. To

tell the truth I do not think I learned it either from him or from Craig; I discovered it by myself. How much more important it is in relation to the movement and actions of an actual production.[107]

Copeau, in 1917, already realized the dangers of theatrical fashion. He noted the turn away from realistic design, as its aesthetic force diminished, but warned at the same time that 'the *new* idea, the idea of simplicity, which the modern chaps are making so much noise about' could pass and fade away just as quickly.[108] His realization that approaches to scenic design are not about the space itself, but about creating the most effective space in which the play can realize its dramatic potential, was a realization that was to shape the work of directors such as Peter Brook and Joan Littlewood in the years to come.

Copeau saw the value of recognizing the three-dimensionality of the theatre space. At the heart of the theatre event was the actor, and the other elements of the stage design needed, in his view, to be constituted in alignment with the physical presence of the actor: 'The stage is the instrument of the dramatic creator [...] It belongs to the actors, not the technicians or the scene-painters. It should always be ready for the actor and for action.'[109] Stage direction, for Copeau, was not simply a matter of moving blocks of actors around the stage to keep them out of the way of the lead actor. He recognized, as did many other leading directors of this time, the role of the director in designing a *mise en scène*. This was about the 'design of a dramatic action',[110] and represented the meeting place between the motivated gesture and action of the individual actor, the scenic vision of the stage designer and the rhythmical and dynamic design of the theatre director. None of these terms existed in the rich sense that we would now understand them – Copeau's achievement can in part be measured through his contribution to the development of this creative triangle of forces and their realization through his work with his collaborators at the Vieux-Colombier.

Appia, whom Copeau had met in 1916, claimed: 'Scenic art must be based on the one reality worthy of the theater [*sic*], the human body.'[111] Copeau takes this dictum thoroughly to heart; his theatre never forgets or misplaces the actor, the human figure. It never dwarfs the actor with scenic design or naturalistic backdrops. Copeau had chosen well in making Jouvet his stage manager. The two of them shared a vision for theatre design that was simple and eloquent, and that allowed the actors space to move. Furthermore, for both Copeau and Jouvet the spatial design was part of an overall concept for the stage space that included the lighting, costumes and props. The Vieux-Colombier had a wardrobe department of its own that created the costumes for their shows – an innovation that enabled a coherence of design that integrated the actor, their movement and the space within which they moved. The extensive wardrobe department was presumably also a direct consequence of Suzanne Bing's bold negotiation with Copeau when he hired her that she should not have to provide her own outfits.

The initial design of the Vieux-Colombier stage in 1913 had left a form of proscenium arch over the front of the stage. After the return from New York and the Company's experiences at the Garrick Theatre, Copeau and Jouvet arranged to have the proscenium removed. They also removed what remained of the wing space, leaving only simple entry/ exit points and opening out the stage to provide a more dynamic and shared space. Their rejection of naturalism, of the picture-box design and of stage machinery places Copeau and Jouvet alongside the other theatre pioneers of the time.

The empty stage space, first fully trialled in New York and then refined in Paris, created a kind of theatrical nakedness for the actor that made their every movement and gesture more expressive and of greater significance. It must also have been a creative provocation to the writers Copeau invited to collaborate with the Vieux-Colombier. Not only does the open stage emphasize the physical expressivity of the actor, but it also invites in the attention of the audience and encourages them to pay attention to the movement and composition of the actors in space, the language and rhythms of the text, even to moments of stillness and silence. Even small alterations to such a simple and open space became eloquent and expressive and can play a role in the dramaturgy of the work. Truth, for Copeau, lay not in stage conventions but 'in the feelings and actions of our characters'.[112] He believed that 'The greatest drama possesses its own eloquence'[113] and technical trickery was not needed to compel the audience into an emotional response.

It was not just any action, however, that Copeau saw enhanced by the bare Vieux-Colombier stage. He believed that the action that suited it best was the action of people at work:

> *Real action* is beautiful on our stage. The work being done by the artisans with their habitual movements, seems to be in its place on it. That is because they are really making something from what they are doing, and doing it well and consciously, absorbed in it. Their movements are sincere, in keeping with real time periods, and correspond to a useful purpose for which they are perfectly fitted.[114]

Such 'real action' (with all its complexities and problematics) needed a suitable stage, a stage which revealed the work of the actor as useful, purposeful, artisanal, creative and authentic. This idea of the value and importance of everyday actions and gestures is significant at several levels. It explains Copeau's commitment during the years of the Vieux-Colombier and Les Copiaus to a particular scale of theatrical space. It connects with his desire to 'untrain' actors of their theatrical habits and return them to a sense of sincere and authentic actions. It points forwards to the work in Burgundy, where the company trained, rehearsed and often performed in spaces that were open but intimate – the *cuveries* at Pernand-Vergelesses, and that were intimately connected with the working lives of the communities within which they were based.

From the start, Copeau's commitment to such scenic simplicity was complete and unwavering. In 1916, he writes in his notes to a French translation of plays by Cervantes, 'is it possible to go back, to ape such early naivety and penury? I say it is necessary. Let nothing remain. *We must*. Burn everything. Let nothing remain. Do not modify, improve, elaborate. *But abolish*'.[115] Throughout his life, he saw this purity as necessary, as important for the health of the theatre: 'It is not simply a question of building the most perfect theatre in the world, but the simplest and healthiest.'[116]

This section has examined the development of Copeau's central aesthetic principles and sought to outline how the work of a number of collaborators has been key to putting those principles into practice. In particular, the contribution of his female collaborators has been brought more consistently to the fore. The significance of these factors for the wider impact and influence of Copeau's work is what will now be addressed in the following section.

Copeau's Importance

Like Copeau's **Art**, his importance to theatre in France, Europe, America and beyond, was also multifaceted. His groundbreaking work with the Vieux-Colombier and Les Copiaus was of great importance to French and international theatre as well as to the emergence of mime and mask performance, of devised performance, of new playwrights working collaboratively with companies, and of a new generation of directors and theatre-makers. The impact of Copeau's work can still be felt today, although the lineage is not always fully understood. As he had originally hoped, his work did indeed present a challenge to the dominance of the boulevard theatres and the Comédie-Française and led to major changes in repertoire, production and acting standards and to ideas about what theatre could be. Although Copeau was not involved with the devised work of the later Compagnie des Quinze as a director, the company was inextricably bound to the wider project that he had begun with Bing. Moreover, Bing, Saint-Denis and Villard[117] were, within this company, directly drawing on the pedagogic and theatre-making processes that Bing and Copeau had developed since 1913. After the break-up of the Compagnie des Quinze, the key members each went their own way; by 1931, therefore, this strand of practice had completed a move from the classroom and the experimentation of Les Copiaus and the Compagnie des Quinze into early forms of devised mime, and often masked, performance. The work that emerged from this theatrical evolution was physically and rhythmically expressive and highly imaginative; it emerged from both a training and a making system

underpinned by play and improvisation, and was inspired by Copeau and
Bing's teaching. As the discussion in the rest of this section indicates, this
strand of theatre production, modern mime, mask work and devised theatre
was to be continued, developed and blended with other approaches by other
artists and pedagogues.

After the dissolution of the Compagnie des Quinze, Jean and Marie-
Hélène Dasté formed Les Comédiens de Grenoble (which later became
the Comédie de Saint-Étienne). They both were to become seminal in the
development of physically expressive theatre and of mime and mask work in
the French theatre. They also directed two Japanese Nō-inspired productions
Sumida (1947) and *Kakegiyo the Furious* (1951) both of which were liberally
adapted by Bing. Jean Dorcy claimed that this work enabled French theatre
to take 'a giant step forward'[118] and he argued that it was thanks to their
training by Bing that the Dastés knew this mode of performance, and the
various solo and chorus parts, well enough to mount these productions.[119]
Sumida forms another crucial node within the wider genealogical web of
this work, as shortly after the Dastés had invited the young Jacques Lecoq
(1921–99) to join their company the newcomer was asked to oversee the
movement of the boat in this production which was his first experience of
choreographing movement for performance.[120]

After his success with the Compagnie des Quinze, Saint-Denis was
approached by leading figures in the British theatre to direct and work
in London. Alongside his directorial successes, including a production of
Oedipus Rex (1945) and an English version of Obey's *Noah* (1935), Saint-
Denis was also interested in establishing his own training regimes. He
founded one drama conservatoire before the Second World War (London
Theatre Studio, 1936–9), and another one after (Old Vic Theatre School,
1947–52), both of which drew extensively on Copeau and Bing's pedagogical
innovations while also adapting them to the needs of a more conventional
repertoire. Echoes of the radical beginnings of his work emerge much later
in his involvement in the founding of an experimental studio within the
Royal Shakespeare Company in the 1961 and in Keith Johnstone's mask
work, inspired by the work of Les Copiaus.

The work of Copeau, Bing, Marie-Hélène Dasté and Etienne Decroux was
also central to Jean-Louis Barrault's theatre practice. As Felner explains,[121]
Barrault worked closely with Decroux on the development of Corporeal
Mime and both men acknowledge that they owed much to Bing and her
'masque playing'.[122] Kurkinen also notes that Barrault was in close contact
with Marie-Helene, as a mentor and collaborator, while making *L'Autour
d'une mère* (About a Mother)[123] and this show was to subsequently become
a cornerstone in French devised theatre. Barrault and Decroux both worked
as actors in the film *Les Enfants du Paradis* (Children of Paradise, 1945).
Barrault played the famous French mime, Jean-Gaspard Deburau,[124] and
Decroux played his father. This film linked the historical tradition of mime
to the practices developed by Copeau and Bing in the twentieth century,

which later become known as Modern or New Mime.[125] Barrault's company visited Edinburgh in 1947, and the success of this tour together with the achievements of Saint-Denis as a teacher and director both contributed to the recognition in the UK of the potential value of Copeau's work.

Jacques Lecoq opened his own school in Paris in 1956. He drew on his initial training with the Dastés and with Claude Martin, who had been a pupil of Dullin,[126] alongside his research into the techniques of *commedia dell'arte* and Greek Tragedy and his own background in sports and gymnastics. His school was to become a fundamental bridge between the mime and collaborative theatre skills developed by Copeau and Bing in the first part of the twentieth century and the practices that continued and evolved in the second half of the century in France, Europe, United States and beyond.

Different voices: Dialogue, collaboration and new lineages

Despite the contribution of several key female collaborators, Copeau's legacy can easily be misunderstood as a lineage between men, many of whom became 'Great Directors' in turn and whose contribution has been culturally privileged. The work of Dullin and Jouvet (both of whom became members of the influential Cartel des Quatres[127]), Jean Dasté, Dorcy, Decroux, Barrault, Villard and Saint-Denis can of course be seen as crucial in terms of the longer-term importance of Copeau's work and the ways in which it has been developed. However, as has also been argued earlier in this chapter, this well-rehearsed narrative denies and conceals the important role of the female artists and collaborators who were always central to Copeau's development of actor training, mime and devised theatre. Throughout this chapter on Copeau, we have sought to recognize and celebrate the contribution to Copeau's remarkable achievements and legacies by all his collaborators, but in particular by Bing, Marie-Hélène and Catherine Dasté, Naumburg and Howarth in order to offer some rebalance of the narrative.

In preparation for this section, we have talked with a number of established experts in order to draw together additional perspectives on the legacy of the work of Copeau and his collaborators. We spoke with Professor Thomas Donahue (Saint Joseph's University, Philadelphia), the author of several important books about Copeau and in particular his tour to America; about the impact of Copeau's work in America during the early part of the last century, and also about Bing's role with Professor Judith Miller (New York University, Abu Dhabi), an expert on the work of the French theatre director Ariane Mnouchkine, on the inspiring links from Copeau, Bing and Marie-Hélène Dasté, to contemporary French theatre practice, through the work of Mnouchkine; and with English theatre director and founder of the Clod

Ensemble, Suzy Willson, who reflects on how the strands of practice that have developed from Copeau have been important in her work in the UK. Willson also talks eloquently about the ways in which this practice relates to her desire to create community practice. Making use of these dialogues in this way is intended to re-emphasize the collaborative nature of knowledge and to represent the importance of taking multiple perspectives on Copeau's successes and achievements.

Copeau's influence in the United States

The main grounds for arguing for Copeau's influence on practitioners in the United States is through his initial lecture series in January 1917 and then the subsequent Théâtre du Vieux-Colombier tour to New York and residency at the Garrick Theatre (1917–19). Donahue suggests that

> Copeau's major influence was in New York and not elsewhere. [...] He came in as a 'saviour' of modern theatre; I think it was even announced in the New York Times, and that suited him just fine. People in the United States were terribly interested in listening to what he had to say; I'm not sure that his lecture series had a great impact, but there were reactions. They were not quite sure how his ideas were going to take shape, how they were going to be incorporated within the theatre at the time, which was terribly commercial. They were stuck very much within the Realist framework and it has always been very difficult for American Theatre to push beyond these parameters. [...] In Greenwich Village [the Théâtre du Vieux-Colombier] most definitely had influence with the people who were in the Art Theatre. The Art Theatres at that time, the small theatres, were very much a live movement in the United States, in the American context they were *avant-garde* definitely, and they were far removed from the commercialisation that you found in the rest of New York theatre.[128]

For Copeau, the lecture series and the tour were important opportunities to make money to support the company and to raise his own profile as an international theatre figure. However, Copeau's impact in America was also politically inflected; at the time the tour was proposed, America was still not in the First World War.

> There was a German language theatre in New York at this time too. The German Theatre in New York was quite vibrant, as was the Yiddish Theatre. One of the reasons that the 'tiger' Clemenceau[129] asked Copeau to come to New York was to balance that German influence in the theatre here. And I think Clemenceau made that very clear in his request and I think that touched Copeau in many, many ways.[130]

Copeau's commitment, despite his need to make money for the company's survival, to resist the demands of commercialization caused several problems for him throughout his life; at this point in time, it was valuable in setting his work apart from the conventional production processes in New York. This created an ethos of a distinctive aesthetic rigour, perhaps further enhanced by Copeau's role as a cultural ambassador from a beleaguered Europe. Donahue argues that, despite the various pressures

> in New York he did hold true to his course. He had the backing of a very rich man, Otto Kahn, and that gave him the freedom to do what he wanted to do, along with having a rather large subscriber base at the time. Most theatres in the United States didn't do that sort of thing.[131]

Not only did Kahn's financial backing give Copeau some general artistic freedom, it also enabled him to progress ideas that he had not had time, or resources, to explore. He was given access to the Garrick Theatre in New York, and enabled to completely refashion it to his needs and interests. These experiments did not at first meet with universal approval from the New York critics:

> I think they didn't understand what he was trying to do. As we said earlier, the American critics were stuck within a Realistic frame. He broke the fourth wall. You don't do that! That was the first sin. [...] It was not a spectacle in any way, maybe they were expecting that as well. The critics at the time thought he was going to do something else. That's all. [...] This was being presented in a major theatre in the United States and supported by a man like Otto Kahn. And so, I think, critics expected to see something else in that context and he was going completely against the grain.[132]

As the company settled in to the rhythms its work in New York, the process of living and working together started to help the company to cohere.[133] The summer break between seasons in New York would have been the first chance since Le Limon to have rested from the generation of productions and to go back to something like first principles again. The company sojourned for the summer at Otto Kahn's wife's estate in New Jersey, where their existence was somewhat monastic. 'The mansion was beautiful [...] But they were just sleeping on regular little beds not in complete luxury, taking all their meals in common. That to Copeau was very, very important.'[134] This idea of a company living, working and learning together clearly looks forward to the future and the setting up of Les Copiaus in Burgundy, but it might also be seen as presaging the move towards the kinds of communal practice that inspired a whole generation of theatre-makers later in the twentieth century, for example Living Theatre, Gardzienice and Footsbarn. Such an approach would have been unusual in America at this time, however:

There was a small group of people who were involved in the theatre at the time who eventually created the Group Theatre about ten years later in 1928. They were a split off from the Theatre Guild; they were younger actors and they did the same thing [as the Théâtre du Vieux-Colombier had done previously], they went off to Connecticut to get their play together before it was produced under the aegis of the Guild and in a different theatre.[135]

The Group Theatre and the Theatre Guild were inspired by Copeau and the Théâtre du Vieux-Colombier in a number of ways.

The whole idea was that [Theatre] was an 'Art' and these were practitioners had an influence on younger actors. And I think eventually you see that in the very early years of the Theatre Guild. Remember that the Theatre Guild moved into the Garrick Theatre right after Copeau took his baskets out! These were young actors who knew what Copeau was doing and were influenced by that. [...] Harold Clurman, who was in Paris in the early 1920s studying French, went back and continued to work first with the Theatre Guild and then with the Group Theatre. So, he knew what was going on. He saw every play presented by the Théâtre du Vieux-Colombier, and attended every lecture, according to his account; so he was much influenced by their work. And then when Copeau came to New York in 1927, to do *Les Frères Karamazov*, Clurman was his right-hand man. Copeau said, 'Oh, when my English fails he's there to help me.'[136]

The way in which knowledge of this later work came to the UK was through the Compagnie des Quinze's tour to London and the work of Michel Saint-Denis and the British actor Marius Goring, who had travelled over to France and had worked with the Compagnie des Quinze at one point. Les Copiaus was in all sorts of ways, including geographically, quite isolated as an experiment during Copeau's lifetime. Despite its later significance, knowledge of the nature of the work was slow to disseminate and the influence of Les Copiaus was strongest through the later work of its key members:

Saint-Denis [...] worked in various theatre schools, helped to found the theatre section of the Julliard here in New York and so it had some influence then. But the Copiaus *qua* Copiaus, I don't think that really had any influence in the United States, not that I am aware of.[137]

The exchange of ideas and influence during the New York tour was, as we have seen earlier in this chapter, not just one directional. Bing was carrying out important experiments with Margaret Naumburg, and with aspects of the Montessori Method, in New York, and that was clearly a significant moment for her in terms of her own development. In America, she had a prolonged and important period to explore some of those ideas and techniques in practice, at length and in a sympathetic environment, rather than the shorter term, ad hoc experiments she and Copeau had undertaken previously.

> Copeau would go to The Children's School and see what the children were doing when they did their end of year presentations or even during practice sessions. [Bing] spent a lot of time there, at that school. And I think he was quite stunned actually by what he saw and what they were able to do with these young children, in terms of movement and expression. And then, of course, once they were back in Paris, and the school there was established, Copeau understood that they had to continue with those experiments that Bing had used so well. So, I think the main influence of the exchange between Bing and Naumburg was really understood at the school in Paris in the 1920s.[138]

Assessing any other longer-term influence of Copeau's work in America is complex. The general growth of interest in mime, masks, movement and devised performance in the second half of the century can be traced back through the impact of Decroux, Marceau and Lecoq to Bing and Copeau. Although the mime and mask work rarely achieved high status, it can be seen directly reflected in the work of practitioners such as Julie Taymor (who studied with Lecoq in the 1960s). This influenced would have chimed well with the general interest since the 1960s in the body as a site and source for devised performance work. Donahue argues that part of the problem with tracing this lineage lies in the way that Copeau and his collaborators's ideas have been subsumed into theatrical practice:

> One of the problems of dealing with the influence of Copeau is that I think that much of what he proposed and then carried out, both in his theatre and at the theatre school, was then carried on by others, and it sometimes disappeared. I mean it was so prevalent, people didn't even think that all this belongs to Copeau. The 'unit set', you see it everywhere and – that's Copeau! No one recognises that as an invention of Copeau and Jouvet, but there they are.[139]

By the time that mime became more widely acknowledged as an art form in its own right, it was no longer associated with Copeau and Bing, but rather with their students and collaborators and those that they had taught in their own turn. This cascade of attribution tended to prioritize the most recent and most visible. Copeau, Bing and Jouvet are today not generally recognized in America; outside of academia, they are best understood as part of the wider history of physical and devised theatre and of the theatrical artist community, bound together by a commitment to rigour, physicality and play.

The influence on French theatre

In early sections, several aspects of Copeau's influence on the development of twentieth-century French theatre have been outlined or described, including the impact of the Cartel des Quatres (established in 1927) by Jouvet, Dullin, Gaston Baty (1885–1952) and Georges Pitoëff (1884–1939); former pupils such as the Dastés, Jean Dorcy (1898–1978) and Léon Chancerel (1886–1965); and the French mimes (Decroux, Marceau and Lecoq). Copeau's ideas also influenced later directors and teachers such as Jean Vilar (1912–71). This chapter aims in particular to (re)examine the trajectory of Copeau's work and influence through reference to female practitioners. With this in mind, the next section will look in particular at Copeau's influence on the practice of Ariane Mnouchkine (1939–) and the Théâtre du Soleil. Mnouchkine remains a major figure in contemporary French theatre. She trained with Lecoq and established the Théâtre du Soleil in 1964. Since that time her productions with the company have toured widely and received international critical acclaim.[140] Significantly, the ensemble company is a theatre collective, and they have a permanent base to the southeast of Paris.

> Ariane Mnouchkine has repeatedly acknowledged her debt to Jacques Copeau as a forerunner of the kind of popular theatre she does and had been searching for when she came back from a year of traveling in Asia and China in the mid-60s determined to find a new formal solution for making stunning theatre that would also be popular. Anne Neuschäfer tells us[141] that Mnouchkine actually plunged into Copeau's methods and thought through discussions with the theatre critic Alfred Simon, at the point where the young Théâtre du Soleil was about to embark on rehearsals for what became *l'Age d'Or*, a collective creation (1974) that was comprised of a series of *commedia*-influenced sketches critiquing the treatment of immigrant workers, capitalist greed, dysfunctional families (a 'comedy for our times', as Mnouchkine called it, after Copeau's own framing of the work he sought to do.) His quest for a form to convey contemporary history has marked her own theatrical questing at least since then.[142]

Mnouchkine also shares Copeau's commitment to a popular theatre. For both, this emphasis on the popular does not mean ignoring the classics or creating cheap entertainment for the masses. Mnouchkine also understood the importance Copeau and his collaborators had placed on commitment and community in creating the right working environment in which to make popular theatre.

> Mnouchkine ranks Copeau with Jean Vilar as someone whose commitment to theatre 'for the people' spoke to her as a young theatre

artist and as someone searching for the way to marry clear and well-defined forms of theatricality with political consciousness. Copeau to her means 'ethical commitment'. While Jean Vilar, was, in her opinion, the most savvy and passionate theatre man of the twentieth century in terms of making theatre available to what he termed the 'non-public', and has been a guide to her in setting up her theatre in the Cartoucherie[143] as a 'public service' (pricing, publicity, communal meals, discussions), reading Copeau helped her imagine the kind of fraternal [sic] and actor-centred work that she has pursued ever since the early 1970s.[144]

The location of the Théâtre du Soleil at La Cartoucherie, in the Bois de Vincennes on the edge of Paris is also significant – it represents a similar desire to that of Copeau's, not to be contaminated by the pressures of urban, metropolitan culture. As we have discussed previously, Copeau had located his first rural retreat in Le Limon and later, in 1924, had taken his new company to Burgundy in order to avoid the distractions of the theatre industry and focus on creating the kind of performances he dreamed of. This idea of the 'retreat' has subsequently informed the work of several significant practitioners: Grotowski's various work centres; Gardzienice in rural Eastern Poland; Odin Teatret in Holstebro, Denmark; Peter Brook's work in Iran, Africa and India; and Footsbarn's work in rural Cornwall and then rural France). These projects all sought to react against mechanization, urbanization and their perceived dehumanizing effects. These retreats can also be seen as connected to an increasing interest in notions of the natural body – a concept already critiqued earlier in this chapter and elsewhere.[145] Mnouchkine was aware of Copeau's work in Burgundy.

> Interestingly, before delving fully into Copeau's writings, she had, as he had, moved her company to Burgundy (she for a short time: the summer of 1968) to reflect on what kind of theatre the Soleil would wish to do, to improvise before 'regular' people from the region who came by to see what was happening, to develop expertise in clowning and prepare *Les Clowns*, the collective creation that queried what the role of theatre could be, given the generalized depression after the failed 'revolution' of May 1968. The company installed itself for several months in Claude-Nicolas Ledoux's Les Salines in Arc-et-Senans and their discussions and readings also helped indirectly prepare what would be their breakthrough productions on the French Revolution and on the rise of the bourgeoisie: *1789* and *1793*.[146]

Mnouchkine's training with Jacques Lecoq in the 1960s was a formative experience for her and that helped her to develop the underpinning aesthetic of the company. Apart from any direct influence via Copeau's writing, working with those who had worked with Copeau and Bing, and her general knowledge of his vision for theatre, her time with Lecoq is obviously

another way in which this influence has taken place. Lecoq's work on masks
and on what he calls 'dramatic territories' enabled Mnouchkine to introduce
these practices and approaches to the company and into the creation of new
work.

> Most of her approach to making theatre in the earliest phases of her
> work was through masking; and she continues, even today, to use masks
> in her productions but now more in the form of make-up. Masking
> encourages her actors to think with their bodies, something that Copeau
> (and Lecoq) taught as well. It is also interesting to note that in 1969
> the company worked for a time with Catherine Dasté and Marie-Hélène
> Dasté. Catherine Dasté had directed them in a children's play, *Jérôme et la
> Tortue*, which they performed at the Avignon festival in 1969. Something
> of Copeau's practice must have rubbed off during that period.[147]

This direct link to the women who form part of this lineage and to
Mnouchkine is important to note here, particularly as Marie-Hélène Dasté,
like Bing, did not produce extensive written accounts of her work with
Copeau, Saint-Denis and their other collaborators.[148] Indeed, Mnouchkine
may be unaware of her debt to Bing's earlier work and contribution
because of the lack of documentation and discussion about the work of
these women, and Naumburg and Howarth, in Copeau and Saint Denis's
personal published accounts, as well as in many of the early-twentieth-
century historiographies of this area of theatre practice.

Copeau, Bing and Lecoq all shared an interest in the theatre practices
of Asia and East Asia earlier in the twentieth century. During the 1960s
and 1970s access to these cultures became increasingly easy, and popular
interest grew as a result of cheap travel and a wider interest in non-
Western traditions of making and performing theatre. Unlike Copeau
and Bing, Mnouchkine travelled to Asia and experienced Asian theatre
forms first-hand. She may well also have been aware, through her contact
with Marie-Hélène Dasté, of Copeau and Bing's work on Japanese Nō
dramas. Her own work, since the Théâtre du Soleil's Shakespeare revivals
in the early 1980s, has been deeply influenced by Japanese and Indian
theatre practices, and these have continued to inform her own aesthetic
principles.

The Cartoucherie has provided the kind of blank canvas that has enabled
her to explore the use of space in ways surely also influenced by Copeau.

> In a series of interviews with Fabienne Pascaud,[149] Mnouchkine also
> speaks with enthusiasm of Copeau's notion of a *lieu unique* (a form of
> sacred and unchangeable theatre space where anything can be performed.)
> Her playing space at the Cartoucherie has evolved in that direction and
> represents the kind of great 'empty space' Peter Brook named as essential
> to doing/making theatre. She 'geometrises' her huge thrust stage with

highly symbolic set pieces and/or props; but the cavernous and visionary feeling stays the same – a space of work emerging from the space of imagination.[150]

This is an example of how Copeau and his collaborators' work after 1924 impacted on practitioners such as Mnouchkine. In distancing herself slightly from Paris, emphasizing the ensemble and collective creation, and drawing on intercultural influences, Mnouchkine's work can be seen as a contemporary radical extension of Copeau's project and Bing's pedagogic and devised theatre-making innovations.

The impact on contemporary UK practice

This 'Importance' section concludes by considering the influence of Copeau's work on UK practice. A few of Copeau's productions had toured to the UK, and his work with both the Théâtre du Vieux-Colombier and Les Copiaus was known to those in the UK theatre industry at the time with an interest in European theatre. The most significant impact came however with Michel Saint-Denis's arrival in London in the 1930s. Saint-Denis's two highly influential drama conservatoires, both heavily based on his experiences with his uncle and with Bing, together with his collaborations with George Devine and his role as one of the three original directors of the Royal Shakespeare Company, ensured that awareness of Copeau's work reached into important and influential elements of the UK theatre establishment. Most UK drama conservatoires would now freely admit the debt they owe to Saint-Denis in respect of the design of their curriculum, the role of movement in particular within their training and the inclusion of mask-work.

Much of the influence identified above has already been covered in other sources.[151] Therefore, in this section we have chosen to examine Copeau's influence on a contemporary UK practitioner, Suzy Willson. Willson studied drama at Manchester University and then trained at the Ecole Jacques Lecoq in Paris. She founded the Clod Ensemble in 1995 with Paul Clark; and the company creates innovative performance work for a range of environments and contexts. A major long-term project has explored the relationship between performance and medicine. Willson's training at the Lecoq School places her at the relatively recent end of the genealogical line from Copeau and Bing, and enables her to offer some interesting reflections on the relationship between Copeau and Lecoq's pedagogies and on their value both within and beyond theatre practice. It has been indicated earlier that Lecoq's pedagogy has several points of connection with the work of Copeau and Bing. After the Second World War, Lecoq worked with the Dastés's company and he met Copeau in Grenoble in 1948. Lecoq also references Copeau in his own writings, even though he did not openly refer to Copeau or Bing while teaching.[152]

As a student, Willson's own initial understanding of the lines of influence was, she admits, fairly limited:

> At Ecole Jacques Lecoq the teaching was practical; there [were] no theoretical classes. I knew that Lecoq had been involved in sport and physical education, but I didn't really understand his place in a French tradition of movement. I didn't hear Lecoq say anything about the relationship of his work to Copeau while I was at the school (although my French wasn't that good so he may have done!).[153]

This echoes the situation for many students training in theatre performance – the practice takes precedence. Although Copeau and Bing ensured that the Vieux-Colombier School included classes on the historical context of theatre and key principles of their practice, subsequent training regimes have tended to minimize this kind of curriculum content. Willson reports that when she left the School, she knew about Lecoq, Decroux, Marceau and Saint-Denis, 'but I didn't know anything about Copeau, and certainly nothing about Suzanne Bing!'[154]

Willson became more aware of Copeau's work and the connections with Lecoq's teaching and practice after she left the school and started doing more research into neutral mask. She identifies one of the problems in transmitting this kind of historical knowledge as embedded in the nature of the subject:

> It is notoriously difficult to capture performance [...] It is particularly challenging to write about physical practice in words – so it is not surprising that this 'lineage' is perhaps under-represented in history. The exercises and knowledge are passed on through practical teaching and shift and evolve in this process, from generation to generation. I would say, there is a kind of embodied philosophy that he developed, a way of seeing, that you learn through moving. A theoretical underpinning or knowledge of history is not necessary in order to experience that.[155]

For Willson, the heart of Lecoq's work lies in his emphasis on play, on the neutral mask and on embodying nature. The system of *auto-cours*[156] within the training emphasizes and encourages the creation of new theatrical work in response to the provocations offered by the teachers. As we have discussed previously, this notion of self-led learning had of course originally been used by Bing and Copeau at the schools in Paris and Burgundy. Like Copeau, Lecoq dreamed of his students creating the theatre of the future. Willson explains that 'he talked a great deal about being the "the neutral point through which you must pass in order to better articulate your own theatrical voice",[157] like the point through which things flow'.[158] Lecoq's school has been in operation for sixty years now and his approach has inspired many UK companies including Footsbarn, Moving Picture Mime

Show, Complicite, Hoipolloi, Theatre O, Jammy Voo, Theatre Ad Infinitum, and Rhum and Clay. Like Copeau and Bing before him, Lecoq's legacy is equally defined, at least in part, by the successes and achievements of his students and collaborators.

Willson also recognizes, through her own experience of Lecoq's training and in relation to her own interest in creating work within community contexts, the value of Copeau's encouragement to Les Copiaus to devise performances as a direct response to the contexts and environments within which they were based:

> This idea [...] clearly comes from Copeau [...] that the techniques can be used more broadly in society has been important. Lecoq says, 'We hope that our students will become livers of life, not just on the stage, but in their lives'. And I suppose this is a key principle when using these techniques, to encourage people to fully inhabit their physical being in life, not just on the stage. Like Copeau, I make and direct performances *and* I am also very interested in education. The Lecoq training that I undertook informs all of this work, incredibly deeply, and without having had that education I would not be making the work I am now.

Willson's work, in line with the ideas of Copeau and Lecoq, reacts against what Lecoq saw as the cultural atrophication of people's physicality. In the development of courses for healthcare professionals she has often reflected on the relation between physical education and movement practices in theatre, drawing on the practices of both Copeau and Lecoq:

> It seems to me that what Copeau did, and Lecoq after him, was take those ideas about Physical Education, but make them much broader to reveal a general potential for physical expression, and you could say well-being. They used Hébert's system of natural gymnastics, a form of physical education, but in relation to wider educational goals than just sport. It has the rigour of the technique of sport, in terms of efficiency or economy of movement, without it being about athleticism – and you can see the need for that in life generally. When I work with healthcare professionals it is the same principle: how can their movement be much more economical, so that they are not wasting energy, so that they are using this incredible resource of their own body more fully, and understand how their own body relates to space.[159]

Evans[160] discusses the complexities of this relationship between sport, performance and notions of efficiency and points out the ways in which such notions draw together some of the complex operations of power which circulate around efficiency and the body. As Willson warns:

I am always cautious about 'programmes' and 'systems' of movement in relation to physical education – you only have to think of the Nazi emphasis on gymnastics and physical fitness to understand that these ideas about movement and well-being can easily be employed to promote a dangerous utopianism, body fascism or dogma. I don't think Hébert was doing that, but it's worth remembering how easily ideas can tip over into evangelicalism. My impression was that Lecoq was also cautious about this too and resisted systematic thinking.[161]

Copeau passionately believed in training but he was also a director and his work was always bound up with his own directorial identity. Bing probably represents a more direct lineage to Lecoq's approach, because she was the primary pedagogue of the School and she mentored young artists to take the techniques into new types of work. She spent many years looking at how they could blend techniques and how to facilitate play, how to observe and how to hand it over. Handing it over was possibly to her detriment, in that she has been largely ignored and/or written out of the popular history of this strand of French practice. As Willson argues:

I think it is good to remember that most good ideas are the cumulative result of many people's thinking often over many years and not a flash of genius from one individual – as much as contemporary culture tries to keep us caught up in a somewhat reductive cult of the individual. Sadly, it's not surprising that Suzanne Bing has been largely forgotten. The lack of acknowledgement of the work of women in history is one of life's great sadnesses.[162]

Finally, Willson eloquently outlines how she perceives the influence of Copeau and Lecoq operating on her work. It is worth quoting her at length, as she weaves together the ways in which Copeau's work still operates to support and inform the work of contemporary UK theatre performance.

I have always had a love of the 'workshop' as a process of creation and have always applied this in lots of different settings, for very different people. I work a lot with neutral mask, or ideas around neutrality; and that is part of the Copeau lineage. The thinking behind neutral mask is to try to help performers free themselves from inscribed codes of movement and physical habit. I would say you can see those inscribed codes in musicians, dancers, and doctors – in all walks of life – and sometimes they are getting in the way and causing unnecessary conflict or limitation. I also love the idea of the 'poetic body' – that the performer can embody movement dynamics in nature and transpose these into dramatic or poetic movement (e.g. the movement of volcanic larvae transformed into a choral scene of mass exodus, or the dynamic of an ice cube melting transposed into a portrait of surrender).

Then, there is the broader theatrical influence. The idea of the ensemble or the chorus, which came from Greek tragic chorus, is central to my work and very much influenced by Copeau and Lecoq's work in this area. But I think the word 'ensemble' in the arts is a term that can be confusing. Is an ensemble about a collective, where politically the decisions are made together? Or is it about a way of playing together? They are not always the same. Within Clod Ensemble we do not have a permanent company and there is no collective in terms of the infrastructure of our organisation. It is an ensemble that comes together, for the particular project or event whether that is a workshop in a school or hospital or for a production. I would describe our method of creating performance as an ensemble process, there is no one star performer. And it is an ensemble not just in terms of the people on stage, but also in relation to the music, lighting and design. Different elements playing together on stage, and that the actor is just one of those elements, and the director is also just one of those elements – it is a collaborative ensemble process.[163]

These are some of the same issues that confronted Copeau nearly one hundred years ago, and that he sought throughout his working life to address and resolve: how to work collaboratively, but with a director; how to bring the actor to a full awareness of their physicality and potential for expression through the body; and how to address the purpose of performing – for whom do we perform and how should that knowledge shape the way we perform?

Conclusion

Copeau has been an inspiration for theatre-makers across Europe and the United States. His work, and that of his key collaborators (Bing, Dullin, Jouvet, Saint-Denis, Jean and Marie-Hélène Dasté) has been passed down through the bodies of generations of theatre-makers. Copeau himself recognized the value of rediscovering the practices of the past in order to rejuvenate the theatre of the present for the future. But his focus was always on what worked in addressing problems they faced in the present – a consequence of the success of this approach is that, ironically, history has not paid him, and his collaborators, the recognition that they deserve. Their spirit, and Copeau's vision for a theatre based on openness, self-knowledge, collaboration, creative play and sincerity, informs much of what is now taken for granted in European and American theatre practice.

Understanding the rich web of relationships which circulate around Copeau, which he sometimes held together and also sometimes disrupted, is a necessary part of understanding why he is so significant. In celebrating the diversity of his achievements, we should also understand how the contribution of others that made his success possible has been obscured by subsequent cultural inflections that have prioritized the achievements of some over others, and deserves to be brought into the light. Without Copeau, there would have been no Vieux-Colombier theatre invigorating Paris theatre, no New York success, no innovative theatre school, no Burgundy experiment and the birth of devised physical theatre – his energy, single-mindedness and commitment made these things happen. But equally, none of these could have been achieved without the dedication and talent of his collaborators, actors, students and family. In this simple sense, Copeau embodies many of the artistic, political and interpersonal tensions and dynamics of twentieth-century theatre.

2

Theodore Komisarjevsky

Jonathan Pitches and Claire Warden

Introduction: The many professional lives of Komisarjevsky

Theodore Komisarjevsky (1882–1954) occupies a shifting position in twentieth-century theatre history, aesthetically and geographically. Designating him as a 'director' at all proves difficult, though it seemed to be his preferred title. In his 1929 autobiography/theatre practice guide *Myself and the Theatre*, he plays this term off against the 'commercial manager', a figure embedded in the vacuous, profit-focused theatre scene he so hated.[1] The conviction that the director figure should challenge financiers who engaged with theatre simply as an industrial scheme for economic return remained with him throughout his career. In this same volume, however, he also uses 'producer' to describe his practice. This was a role he clearly understood as distinct from similarly designated figures in the West End or on Broadway. He elaborates on this moniker in *The Theatre and a Changing Civilisation* (1935) when he notes that the English translation of 'producer' connotes 'a farmer, a husbandman, an agriculturalist, and *not* an artist who interprets plays on the stage and directs all concerned in the interpretation'.[2] Rather than reject the term out of hand, though, Komisarjevsky appears to be rejuvenating it. His vision of the producer here is purposefully detached from commercialism and consumption, and instead re-imagined as a figure of the stage who 'directs' and 'interprets'.

FIGURE 2.1 *Komisarjevsky in 1923. Photo by Nickolas Muray/Conde Nast via Getty Images.*

In the same book, he employs another naming device to describe his craft: the *régisseur*, a 'spiritual leader, a kind of magician, psychologist and technical master'.[3] A *régisseur* has a broader role, in charge of overall artistic interpretation. The term is historically more readily associated with ballet or opera, suggesting Komisarjevsky's enduring interest in inter-artistic performance methods; music and movement were as important to him as dialogue and stage proxemics. This is not the only French word used to define Komisarjevsky's directorial role. In his 1954 obituary, actor John Gielgud referred to him as a 'great *metteur en scène*'.[4] The title is more often employed in film rather than live performance, and suggests a degree of technical proficiency and an awareness of skilled crafts such as lighting design and set building. The use of a French term to describe a Russian director working predominantly in Britain and the United States is an interesting decision, perhaps nodding to Komisarjevsky's cosmopolitan identity as an émigré Russian as well as to one of Gielgud's own influences: the French actor and director (and later co-founder of the London Theatre Studio) Michel Saint-Denis. In fact the word *régisseur* (or *rezhisseur*) is also used in the Russian language. Komisarjevsky was always interested in the practice of creating theatre; Simon Shepherd refers to him as an 'actor-trainer', which illustrates his commitment to teaching as part of his directorial role, a theme we pick up later in this chapter.[5] Yet, apart from during his brief time at the Komissarzhevskaya Theatre, he never led his own company of actors, so this designation, too, needs careful thought. The fellow Russian director Vsevelod Meyerhold used this issue of role definition to criticize Komisarjevsky's practice. In a disparaging article for the 1910 *Apollon* about Komisarjevsky's version of George Bernard Shaw's *Caesar and Cleopatra*, Meyerhold said 'we are witnessing the birth of a new kind of director, the director-compiler'.[6] As a director figure, Meyerhold believed Komisarjevsky was capable only of cherry-picking the practices of others and fusing them together. Gielgud, by contrast, considered him 'one of the very first directors to exist, and certainly the first ever to free his cast from the simple instruction to learn their lines and not crash into the furniture'.[7] For Gielgud, Komisarjevsky rejuvenated and re-imagined the role and responsibilities of the director. There is clear disagreement, then, as to whether Komisarjevsky was simply a gatherer of existing directorial ideas or a true, path-breaking innovator, a dispute which this chapter will help mediate.

Komisarjevsky himself seemed unable really to settle on one term, referring to his own role in various places as a designer (of scenery, theatre buildings and costumes), a decorator and a writer, as well as a director. When he decided to move to the United States in the late 1930s, Komisarjevsky (who, incidentally, first trained as an architect) wrote a document for the authorities that listed all these professions.[8] His letterhead for his New York-based Komisarjevsky Drama Studio refers to a 'director', yet also mentions his roles as professor, instructor and actor-trainer (in voice, speech, expressive movement and musical interpretation). It also includes acknowledgement of the three countries he had lived and worked in; it would seem that his broad artistic and geographical experiences went hand in hand.[9] This ability to engage in all aspects of the theatre is recognized by Michael Billington who claims him as 'a draughtsman and designer as well as director. His was the entire and total concept', an auteur.[10] In fact, his very name has a certain transnational fluidity. When he arrived in Britain in 1919 he anglicized his name from Fyodor Komissarzhevsky (Федор Комиссаржевский) to Theodore Komisarjevsky. This semantically separated him from Russia and embedded him in a more Anglophone context. Even then, as with many Latin alphabet transliterations of Cyrillic words, this anglicized version is not fixed, spelt in numerous different ways, particularly in newspaper reviews of his productions. Many co-workers referred to him simply as 'Komis', a nickname that almost entirely concealed his Russian heritage. Due to his reputation as a womaniser, actor Edith Evans (one of the few who refused to succumb to his charms) pronounced a different anglicized version: 'come and seduce me'.[11]

This brief analysis of his name and role reveals the complexity of understanding him as a 'director' at all, notwithstanding the intrinsic fluidity of the role in the first place. He is difficult to pin down, though this opening analysis also means he can be read alongside many other directors of the period who are equally difficult to define – Edward Gordon Craig, André Antoine and Jacques Copeau to name but three. All seemed to understand the role of the director in an extremely broad, expansive way: as scenic designer, as actor-trainer, as dramaturg, as creator of entirely new performance methodologies.

Komisarjevsky's Life

Komisarjevsky's position in theatre history becomes even more complex when recognized as part of distinct theatrical dynasties and genealogies. He was born into an undeniably theatrical family in Venice in 1882. His father, Fyodor Petrovich Komissarzhevsky, was a noted opera singer, who trained in Italy and became a lead tenor at the Mariinsky Theatre in St Petersburg, creating many of the lead roles in the Russian opera. After his retirement Komissarzhevsky Senior taught at the Moscow Conservatoire where he trained Konstantin Stanislavsky (later head of the Moscow Art Theatre and one of the twentieth-century's most influential directors) who originally hoped to be an opera singer.[12] Theodore Komisarjevsky's half sister Vera Komissarzhevskaya was a celebrated actor, creating the role of Nina in Anton Chekhov's *The Seagull* (1896). She became a theatre manager, working with both Stanislavsky and Meyerhold (among others), and running her own, highly innovative theatre in St Petersburg until her early death in 1910.

While the three theatrical family members differed in their methodologies and practice, illustrating general changes and trends in nineteenth- to twentieth-century theatre, Victor Borovsky focuses on some of the traits that united them: 'indomitable determination and indestructible hope in striving for a theatre of their dreams. What matters in such a theatre is not personal success in a performance, but the success of the performance itself as a whole.'[13] Although Borovsky's eulogizing description is a little flowery, it is interesting to note that he unites the three through the notion of ensemble;

FIGURE 2.2 *Vera Komissarzhevskaya in the 1900s. Photo by Getty Images.*

while all three adopted positions of leadership – or directorship – actually they understood that success depended on the way this role integrated with the ensemble as a whole.

Theodore Komisarjevsky lived in Russia until 1919. He began his theatrical work in 1903 with his sister's company, becoming a design assistant for Meyerhold, before taking over as artistic director in 1907. He worked at a variety of theatres, including the Gay Theatre (with the symbolist playwright and director Nikolai Evreinov), the Nezlobin Dramatic Theatre, the Imperial Grand Opera and Sergei Ziminne's Moscow Opera House. His portfolio during this period was eclectic, ranging from Russian opera (*Prince Igor, Boris Godunov*) to plays by Shaw, Ibsen and Wilde. He also established his own Free School of Scenic Art, which became the Komissarzhevskaya Memorial Theatre in honour of his half sister. The American traveller Oliver Sayler, who incidentally also refers to Komisarjevsky as a *régisseur*, witnessed the work of the Free School of Scenic Art during his trip to Russia. He described the Russian's intentions as he saw them:

> At his theatre, Kommissarzhevsky has had this principle for his *mise en scène*: to achieve a harmony between the interpretation of the actors, the ensemble, the forms and the colors of the scenery and costumes, the music and the light – the harmony between all these and the idea and style of the dramatic author.[14]

Even early in his career, while still in Russia, Komisarjevsky seemed to display a talent for understanding the whole theatrical experience. Similarly to other modernist directors, Komisarjevsky was not content to change just one aspect of the theatre; every element needed an overhaul and these new methodologies had to combine together to produce harmony and artistic synchronization. Though Komisarjevsky's practice changed and developed throughout his career, the sort of innovations Sayler witnessed remained central to his vision.

Working in Moscow, Komisarjevsky can, therefore, be understood with reference to the burgeoning theatre art scene in Russia, both before and after the Revolution. These theatrical networks were not always harmonious. While his father trained Stanislavsky, Komisarjevsky did not always agree with the influential director's processes. While acknowledging Stanislavsky's shifting ideas as important, Komisarjevsky questioned their usefulness on the imaginative stage: 'acting is a result of the processes of *creative assimilation* and not of ordinary *associations*, which Stanislavsky recommends to actors when on the stage'.[15] In addition, he admired Meyerhold's 'artistic individuality' while disagreeing with some of 'his methods and philosophical outlook.'[16] [**For Stanislavski, see Volume 1; Meyerhold, Volume 2.**] His time working with Meyerhold (on three of the founder of biomechanics' most important early productions – Maurice Maeterlinck's *Sister Beatrice*, Alexander Blok's *The Fairground Booth* and Leonid Andreyev's *The Life of*

Man (1904–6)) – certainly taught Komisarjevsky 'an important lesson in how to push forward an agenda of reform in the theatre'.[17] Despite Meyerhold's acrimonious split from Vera Komissarzhevskaya's company, Komisarjevsky remained fairly sympathetic to Meyerhold's grand revolutionary project.

Komisarjevsky's decision to leave Russia was partly political and partly aesthetic, though, of course, these two concepts overlapped considerably in 1919, two years after the Revolution. His letter to the Commissar for People's Enlightenment, Anatoly Lunacharsky, dated June 1919, reveals some of the central issues. Komisarjevsky bemoaned the lack of innovation on the Russian stage, a space still dominated by establishment figures, despite the dramatic changes the Revolution engendered. However, he was equally resistant to the new bureaucracy which he deemed poorly organized and run by officials with little understanding of the true nature of art. He sums up the predicament by referring to it as the 'almost tragic situation in which the Russian theater in general is about to find itself'.[18]

Arriving in Britain via Paris after escaping from the increasingly turbulent political and aesthetic situation at home, Komisarjevsky would have found a substantial Russian émigré community. During the first decades of the twentieth-century British artists often looked to their Russian compatriots for inspiration; Rebecca Beasley and Philip Bullock refer to this as 'British zeal for Russian culture'[19] while Caroline Maclean's recent book describes such transnational intellectual exchange as a 'vogue for Russia'.[20] It was a trend that had both political and artistic motivations. The ideas of Russian writers and theatre-makers appeared in journals and magazines. Texts (plays, novels and poems) were also translated in what Beasley terms '*the* translation project of British modernism'.[21] Despite this, Russian techniques and ideas appeared rarely on the British stage during the first two decades of the twentieth century, and, when they did they often 'proved baffling and alien' developing a 'reputation of being emphatically highbrow'.[22] There were exceptions, of course – the Ballets Russes' tours around Britain, and early versions of Chekhov plays which, though confusing for British audiences, received some positive reviews – but, mostly, British theatre proved resistant to Russian methods prior to Komisarjevsky's arrival in 1919.

Komisarjevsky's first production on British soil was the 1919 *Prince Igor* for Covent Garden. During the 1920s, he worked with some of the premier experimental theatre companies in Britain, including the Stage Society and the Barnes Theatre. His productions were, again, eclectic, ranging from large-scale operas to versions of Chekhov's *Uncle Vanya* (1921) and *The Cherry Orchard* (1926) to avant-garde modern plays such as Luigi Pirandello's *Six Characters in Search of an Author* (1922). In the 1930s he dedicated himself to writing: *Myself and the Theatre* (1930), *The Costume of the Theatre* (1931), *The Theatre and a Changing Civilisation* (1935) and, with designer Lee Simonson, *Settings and Costumes of the Modern Age* (1933). His major practical projects during this decade took place at the Shakespeare Memorial Theatre (SMT), Stratford where he produced highly innovative versions of Shakespeare's plays. But he also remained committed to directing modern experimental works such as *Le Cocu Magnifique* (The Magnanimous Cuckold, 1932, written by Belgian Fernand Crommelynck and published in 1921). In addition, he designed the interiors of a number of theatres and cinemas during this period, including the Phoenix Theatre in the West End which still acknowledges Komisarjevsky's contribution as 'art director' (yet another potential label) on its website[23] and the Granada Tooting cinema, the 'high point of the extravagant fantasy cinema interior in Britain'.[24] While in London he worked with many prominent British actors, including John Gielgud, Edith Evans, Peggy Ashcroft (his wife for a time) and Charles Laughton. Although accepted and even celebrated by many in the theatre community in Britain, he remained a dangerously experimental and even scandalous figure with a 'reputation of a radical modernist and an *enfant terrible*'.[25] In 1939 he moved to the United States and lived the rest of his life in Connecticut. He directed on a freelance basis in New York and at the Montreal Festival but, by and large, restricted himself to teaching and lecturing, through his own New York-based drama studio (with Ernestine Stodelle) and at Yale between 1940 and 1942.[26]

Komisarjevsky lived, then, in three different places – Russia, Britain and the United States – and, although he travelled and worked elsewhere (including Paris in the 1920s) this tripartite geography might initially seem a useful way of arranging his practice. However, this would overlook the complexity of Komisarjevsky's career and innovations. Actually, Komisarjevsky's life and work reveal a more intricate layering of identities and aesthetics. He worked in an era of increasing globalization; more people than ever appeared to be moving, whether in search of new adventures, or due to coercion or war. Komisarjevsky embodied this increasing sense of transnationalism, less a figure with a threefold national identity and more a human expression of what Rebecca Walkowitz refers to as 'entanglement'. Her two kinds of entanglement – 'the literal knotting together of cultures and experiences that seem to be disparate' and 'the effect of ethical discomfort or embarrassment that is generated by incommensurate or unconventional associations' – can both be applied to Komisarjevsky's life and theatrical work.[27] Like so many others creating work in this early- to mid-twentieth-century period of travel, transnational exchange and cosmopolitan aesthetics, Komisarjevsky represented an amalgam of identities and practices. It is this mixing ('entanglement') that makes his work so fascinating and dynamic.

Uncritically adopting the three-way model of Russia, Britain, United States also sets the trap of reading Komisarjevsky's work through cultural centres (Moscow–London–New York, for example). While these spaces clearly influenced (and were influenced by) his directorial practice, actually this typical capital-centric model occludes many aspects of Komisarjevsky's work. His innovative re-imaginings of Shakespeare's canon in Stratford are the obvious examples of a more regional impact. But there are many other cases that move beyond this reading; after all, Stratford rapidly became a cultural centre even if it was outwith England's geographical capital. His productions of Edward Knoblock's version of A.J. Cronin's *Hatter's Castle* at the Lyceum Theatre, Edinburgh (1932) and Beverley Nichols's *Mesmer* at the King's Theatre, Glasgow (1935) illustrate his willingness to travel north of the border when approached by producers. His work in Holyhead, Wales for the 1927 Eisteddfod (the annual Welsh festival of the arts) provides an even more expansive example here. In *Myself and the Theatre* he describes taking the train to Bangor, North Wales, every Saturday to rehearse *The Pretenders* (in Welsh, *Yr Ymhonwyr*) with a group of amateur actors. Initially they struggled to successfully execute Komisarjevsky's instruction. However, gradually they made progress. In Komisarjevsky's own words:

> As the rehearsals proceeded and I managed to make them less conscious of what they were doing and saying, and more interested in the *meaning* of what they had to say and do, they began to 'feel' their parts and gradually and successfully assimilated to my directions.[28]

Komisarjevsky encouraged his amateur actors to move beyond the systems of the stage and the mechanics of acting towards something more organic and character centred. The actors presented the play (in Welsh) in a pavilion by the cliffs overlooking the Irish Sea. Komisarjevsky reflected on the success of this enterprise:

> The sincerity and power of the actors took the audience. At the finale there was at first a long silence and then loud applause which lasted so long that we thought the audience would never leave unless we gave the whole play over again.[29]

Geographically this production occurred far away from any conventional cultural centre-point. Indeed, *The Pretenders* appeared right on the edge, literally and figuratively. Examining Komisarjevsky's work through a static tripartite structure, then, leaves less space for discussing directorial experiences such as this one.

This initial discussion of Komisarjevsky's life reveals deep transnational and aesthetic complexities. He is difficult to define professionally – is he a director, designer, producer, trainer or all of these? In terms of identity, Komisarjevsky is a layered presence, moving between spaces, carrying various theatrical approaches and identities with him. In a sense he embodies the artistic and geographical cross-fertilization typical of the period. This chapter seeks to take this complexity as a challenge and a stimulus, juxtaposing well-known examples of Komisarjevsky's practice with the less familiar, the decidedly avant-garde with the more conventional, the triumphs (artistically or commercially) with the less successful, the celebrated with the obscure. In order to address these dichotomies, we examine four different facets of Komisarjevsky's practice: the commercial and the avant-garde;

rhythm and musicality; universality and synthesis; directing and training. These pillars of Komisarjevsky's *practice* provide a fourfold way of focusing on the progression and lineage of artistic ideas. They enable an inclusive study of Komisarjevsky's diverse body of work, permitting a way of reading, say, his versions of Chekhov plays alongside his later foray on to Broadway, or his innovations at the SMT in parallel with his commitment to actor-training studios.

This approach to understanding Komisarjevsky differs from Victor Borovsky's valuable *A Triptych from the Russian Theatre: An Artistic Biography of Komissarzhevsky,* which analyses him in a genealogy of theatre-makers and is structured in a linear, biographical manner and expands on studies such as David Allen's *Performing Chekhov,* which focuses on a single facet of Komisarjevsky's practice, in this case his versions of Chekhov's plays. Robert Tracy's chapter 'Komisarjevsky's 1926 *Three Sisters*' in Patrick Miles's *Chekhov on the British Stage* similarly (and singularly) examines the Russian's innovations using Chekhov. In its broad aesthetic scope this chapter also builds on co-author Pitches's previous chapters in *Russians in Britain* and in John Britton's *Encountering Ensemble*, which focus on actor-training and ensemble work, respectively.

In the current chapter these four important elements of Komisarjevsky's practice are read through the topographical landscapes of the twentieth century in which he worked or resided to produce a multi-dimensional image of Komisarjevsky as transnational importer and exporter of diverse practices, as connective intersection between geographical spaces and disparate theatre-makers, and as challenger of orthodoxy, inspirer of actors and vehement opponent of the commercialization of theatre.

Komisarjevsky's Art

The commercial and the avant-garde

In one sense Komisarjevsky can be understood as a figure deeply embedded in the higher echelons of the theatrical hierarchy, first in terms of family connections and collaborations in Russia noted above and, later, after moving to Britain and the United States working in premier venues and with some of the twentieth-century's most illustrious actors. He could in fact be regarded as an establishment figure. He taught at the Royal Academy for Dramatic Art (RADA) during the mid-1920s, for example, and, while it is tricky to determine the exact content of his training courses (the archives having been lost in a fire), he almost certainly introduced ideas of pantomime and *commedia dell'arte* to RADA students.[30] In terms of aesthetics Stuart Young even refers to him as 'conservative, both in his choice of Russian plays and in his approach to their mise-en-scène of the English stage'.[31] Given this, why was he also regarded as frighteningly experimental and foreign, as supplying 'a modern avant-garde kick', as one of his *Macbeth* cast members recalled?[32] In this regard he can be read alongside a number of other directorial figures, especially in a British context, who seemed to walk a line between the experimental and the more conventional: people such as Basil Dean, who worked on a 1939 expressionist version of J.B. Priestley's *Johnson over Jordan* as well as the more conventionally linear tragedy *The Constant Nymph* (1928), and André van Gyseghem who directed Agatha Christie plays, but also highly original foreign works such as *Miracle at Verdun* by Hans Chlumberg (Embassy, 1932). What united these three directors (and others) was a total rejection of the commercial stage and its managers who, in Komisarjevsky's words, were 'merely experts at "stage business" in addition to "box office business"'.[33] The three moved between different aesthetic choices during their careers, but they were resolute in this commitment to art rather than economic profit, though all three did venture successfully into the West End at times; Komisarjevsky's 1936 *Seagull* with Gielgud and Ashcroft (two actors who were equally interested in avant-garde aesthetics as West End successes) provides a case in point here. While, in a sense, he transmuted from émigré experimenter to feted director at Stratford, Komisarjevsky, we suggest, consistently oscillated between the popular and the unpopular, the celebrated and the ignored, the familiar and the dangerously experimental. But his conviction to free theatre 'from the clutches of the commercial manager' remained a key facet of his directorial work.[34]

In 1926, for example, Komisarjevsky directed a production of *The Government Inspector* at the Barnes Theatre. Written by Russian Ukrainian Nikolai Gogol in the mid-nineteenth century, it is one of the classics of the Russian theatrical canon.

But it also became one of the most important post-Revolutionary plays, with productions by Stanislavsky (1921), who introduced more satirical elements, and Meyerhold (1926) who transported the play to the urban centre and used stage trucks to move the characters around the playing space.[35] The latter production, in particular, caused a great furore when it first played in Moscow, as it was felt that Meyerhold took too many liberties with the text. In essence, as director, he became a new author.[36] Four years earlier Meyerhold had produced Crommelynck's *The Magnanimous Cuckold* with set design by the constructivist artist Lyubov Popova. With its kinetic elements, platforms and clowning, this production is often understood as the high point of Soviet constructivist stage aesthetics. In 1932 this play reappeared in Britain, directed by Komisarjevsky for the Stage Society under the French title *Le Cocu Magnifique*. Neither of Komisarjevsky's attempts to bring these decidedly Russian plays to Britain proved particularly successful economically, and caused significant confusion for reviewers, but both say something important about his commitment to experimental, anti-commercial aesthetics.

FIGURE 2.3 The Government Inspector *at the Barnes Theatre, 1926. Photo courtesy of Cadbury Library.*

The Government Inspector was clearly a play that contained a wealth of latent potential for a director such as Komisarjevsky. The play narrates the expected arrival of a government inspector in a small Russian town, an event that causes significant alarm for the mayor. Khlestakov arrives; the mayor and his officials presume he is the feared government inspector and set about ingratiating themselves. Eventually it is revealed that Khlestakov is not the official but, by then, the mayor's corruption has been uncovered. It is a highly satirical work about petty bourgeois dishonesty that might have appealed to Soviet Russian and early twentieth-century British audiences in different ways. The journalist from *The Observer* described Komisarjevsky's set:

> Against a formalised panoramic background, and occupying most of the stage, stands a brightly-painted roundabout, with door and window frames where the horses and what not usually prance. This revolves to suit the action of the play, becoming indoors or out of doors in a twinkling, and thus permits swift continuity.[37]

The design could be compared here to Meyerhold's constructivist ideas; the revolving stage, for example, resembles the rotating 'windmill' in *The*

Magnanimous Cuckold. The Observer's journalist appears to notice this connection and acknowledges a particular Russian feel:

> He has given the Russian kaleidoscope a very racy twist, and the new pictures he presents have nothing in common with the old. They are as impudently fin-de-siecle [*sic*] as their theme is timeless.[38]

There is the sense of nineteenth-century Russian origin here (unsurprisingly for such a classic Russian play that was simultaneously disturbing audiences in Moscow), but also a clear acknowledgement of an avant-garde approach: the newness, a (notably semantically French) fin-de-siècle decadence and vibrancy. While 'fin-de-siecle' was clearly a little old-fashioned by 1926, the reviewer seems to be using the term here as synonymous with the 'new'. For this reviewer, at least, the foreign and the experimental seem almost inextricably linked.

While *The Magnanimous Cuckold* was written by a Belgian, a haunting sense of Russianness still seemed to appear in the British version. Crommelynck's play is about the consequences of marital jealousy and is, in essence, a farcical (though to modern eyes, decidedly problematic) analysis of relationships. Meyerhold's version created a playground for his biomechanical-trained actors, with slides, steps and a rotating wheel upstage. Komisarjevsky's 1932 version maintained a similar feel:

> When M Crommelynck desires that somebody shall write, M Komisarjevsky first makes that scribe mount a pylon like the exalted contraption used for mending overhead tram-lines and then dip an outsize goose-feather into some monstrous, inky carboy, thereby endowing an everyday feat with Grock-like infeasibility.[39]

Comedic constructivism defined Komisarjevsky's design; the mention of Grock, a contemporary Swiss clown who transferred from the circus to the theatre and used a variety of props for comic effect, is particularly noteworthy.[40] Again, as with *The Government Inspector*, reviewers observed its distinctly Russian aesthetics. In fact, the reviewer from *The Observer*, acknowledging the constructivist set, condemned it as 'a fad much favoured by the plodding anti-realists of the Soviet Theatre' before sarcastically concluding, 'I wish I could understand the deep spiritual significance of putting up the furniture and then omitting the upholstery.'[41]

Reflections on both plays seem to intertwine avant-garde aesthetics with Russianness, whether to praise or criticize. This double-edged observation may well have suggested an awareness of previous Russian productions of these plays. Or, perhaps, it was just the directorial presence of Komisarjevsky that compelled reviewers to make these transnational connections. Either way, it is interesting to note that aesthetics and national identity (in this case avant-garde constructivism and Russianness) seem to coalesce in the reviewers' reflections. These two productions illustrate Komisarjevsky's commitment to producing difficult, international work, at least in the eyes of contemporary British reviewers.

In 1929 Komisarjevsky directed a new play by British playwright Hubert Griffith: *Red Sunday*. On first reading, the script, which narrates the history of Lenin's rise to power in three acts, seems fairly conventional. However, its performance history was less than straightforward, initially banned by the censor after complaints from the *Times*, the Russian émigré community and even the Royal Family.[42] Griffith responded in his published introduction to the play, in which a character from the fictional Ping-Pang-Bong questions the decision to ban the play by suggesting that the British public is being kept in delusional ignorance about Russian history.[43] Komisarjevsky took on *Red Sunday*, producing it at the Arts Theatre Club, a private subscription theatre that could avoid the dreaded censoring pencil of the Lord Chamberlain. Despite its focus on real-life characters (and the actors do look remarkably like the historical figures they are playing[44]) and its political overtones (Vera Figner's speech about the history of Russian revolutionary principles is the most overtly political moment) which allow this play to be understood alongside declamatory theatrical methods such as agitprop and verbatim, *Red Sunday* seems an orthodox, linear rendering of Russian history, albeit tinged with melodrama, the gothic and the tragic. However, Komisarjevsky's directorial presence casts doubt on this easy demarcation, as evidenced in a review in *The Stage*:

> There is little we can congratulate M. Komisarjevsky on in the production. For example, he makes a surely unpardonable mistake in these advanced days – putting a red 'spot' on Lenin on his first entrance in scene 1. There was nothing in that cellar that could possibly have flung that halo of light on the wall of a steep staircase, nothing to switch it off immediately the character began to speak.[45]

The problem here is that Komisarjevsky's rather more symbolist directorial choices (the red spot) disturbed the naturalist linearity in the reviewer's expectations. There is no logic, cries the critic; where is the light switch? Komisarjevsky's concern, however, was about mood and atmosphere, about enabling his actors to discover the emotional content of the character. In the same year as *Red Sunday*, Komisarjevsky published *Myself and the Theatre* in which he wrote of the need for the 'imaginative actor': 'nothing on the stage can be called "natural", because the Theatre is a form of art, and is therefore inventive'.[46] While the characters of Trotsky, Lenin, Rasputin, the Tsar and others seem, at least visually, to be mirror images of their real-life counterparts, based on his writings of this time, actually Komisarjevsky encouraged a far more, in his words, 'inventive' approach to acting. Even in such a realist (or perhaps 'realistic') play, he committed to creating a more visually nuanced and experimental piece of work.

Komisarjevsky's reputation for avant-garde experimentation rests predominantly, however, on his work at the SMT. Before presenting his series of six plays at the Theatre between 1932 and 1939, Komisarjevsky told *The Daily Telegraph* he was 'not in the least traditional'.[47] This anti-establishment intention defined the rest of his work in Stratford, illustrated by his second production which he designed and directed: *Macbeth* (1933). His version created a controversial and experimental adaptation of Shakespeare's classic Scottish play, freeing it from the familiar and expected, and, instead, presenting it as a psychological drama (unlike, say, *Red Sunday*), the stage world created through Macbeth's increasingly unstable imagination.[48] Using aluminium screens, symbolist lighting denoting moonlight and storm clouds, a recurring red leitmotif (comparable to that used in *Red Sunday*), steel helmets and grey cloaks for the soldiers, and presenting Banquo as a partially visible shadow transformed this play into a moody, though historically non-specific, piece.[49] Expressionist in one sense, Komisarjevsky's collaborative rendering of *Macbeth* (working with Lesley Blanch) could also be read through contemporary history as a stark warning of the oncoming war and a reminder of the one past.[50] Reflecting on his design elements, Komisarjevsky said, while they might have 'looked "like nothing on earth" and have "no meaning" ... for me those elements, the material they were made of, their composition and their lighting, had a most important meaning; they assisted the spectators to re-create in their minds the creative work of my irrational self'.[51] Here Komisarjevsky's description of the piece as a reinterpretation through the psychological turmoil of the central character recalls the similar intentions of other avant-garde theatre-makers, such as Ernst Toller, Sophie Treadwell or Antonin Artaud. *Macbeth* clearly illustrates his deep commitment to challenging the conventional.

So, was Komisarjevsky an establishment figure or an avant-garde experimenter – a conservative or a modernist, a welcome bringer of new ideas or a dangerous (and frankly incomprehensible) spoiler of the modern stage? In a sense, the examples above reveal him as potentially all of these things. Ultimately, however, Komisarjevsky's aesthetic choices and directorial decisions were united by a single conviction: economics should not be the driving factor of the stage. 'Commercial managers', he was convinced, 'although they make pretence of giving the greater public what it wants, merely guess at *everybody*'s taste and of course in most cases wrongly'. 'The commercial theatre', he goes on to say, 'resembles a huge factory, backed by eccentric capitalists, which goes on producing a poor assortment of cheap stuff for the masses which no one really wants'.[52] Stylistically Komisarjevsky was eclectic, refusing to affiliate to any particular modernist school of thought. In intention, however, he remained firm: to challenge the dominance of the mercantile profiteers who valued theatre for profit rather than artistic merit.

Rhythm and musicality

Written by Ronald Mackenzie, *Musical Chairs* (Figure 2.4) seems, in many ways to be a fairly conventional linear play with a tragic ending. Its original cast list included luminaries such as Margaret Webster, Frank Vosper and John Gielgud, and was produced by Komisarjevsky in 1931 at the Haymarket in London before transferring to the Criterion in 1932. It tells the story of a Polish family, the Schindlers, who are trying to strike oil. The pragmatic, profit-driven brother Geoffrey is played off against the artistic, piano-playing war-invalid Joseph, who, it turns out, may well have killed his own fiancée in an air bombing. There are two further American characters – Irene, Geoffrey's fiancée who falls for Joseph, and the oil man Plagett who, like Geoffrey, is more comfortable discussing drilling techniques than listening to Frederic Chopin. As might be imagined from the title, *Musical Chairs* is infused with music.

The play begins with Joseph playing J.S. Bach's *Prelude and Fugue in C Minor* and concludes, after Joseph's death, with the father Mr Schindler turning towards the quiet piano – 'He closes the lid and as he passes from R to L he draws his hands along it lovingly'.[53] Throughout the play, the piano acts as another character, a feature developed by Komisarjevsky in his advice to Gielgud who played Joseph:

> At the first rehearsal he [Komisarjevsky] led Gielgud to the middle of the stage and said: 'There is your piano, and there on it is the photograph of that girl who was killed. Build your performance around those two things'.[54]

The piano constantly intervenes in the action; Mary inadvertently plays some notes as she dusts it, Joseph's gentle version of *Tell me the old, old story* is an incongruous accompaniment to Plagett's financial wrangling, the piano stool represents the absent player. Further, the piano seemingly plays a duet with other noises: thunder, the explosion as the workers hit oil, the gong rung for dinner.

This illustrative example introduces a key element of Komisarjevsky's theatrical aesthetic: musicality. While only a prop or narrative device in *Musical Chairs*, Komisarjevsky used music and, vitally, musical *rhythm*, throughout his career, particularly as a way to free the stage (especially the *British* stage) from its unwavering devotion to realism. Notions of rhythm can, of course, be discerned in other Russian director's work, namely in Meyerhold's biomechanics, or Alexander Tairov's choreographic dance rhythms in his innovative 1914 *Shakuntala*.[55] Komisarjevsky's sense of rhythm seemed to emanate not from the factory or the dance studio per se, but, rather, from his deep understanding of music. This important facet of his aesthetic shaped every part of his theatre-making. In a sense, Komisarjevsky created a *Gesamtkunstwerk*, a form of theatre that reunited

FIGURE 2.4 *John Gielgud and Carol Goodner, in Komisarjevsky's production of* Musical Chairs, *1932.*

the sister arts, including music; he called this the 'synthetic theatre'.[56] This innovation was embedded in the multiple rhythmic elements of the stage: 'the rhythm of the music must be in harmony with the rhythm of the words, with the rhythm of the movements of the actors, of the colours and lines of the decors and costumes, and of the changing lights'.[57] In this sense Komisarjevsky's synthetic theatre can be described as the interaction of separate yet intertwined theatrical rhythms.

Musical rhythms affected all aspects of his stage and rehearsal practice. For example, he viewed his actors in musical terms:

> I begin to hear each actor as a series of notes. And all together the actors form a fugue, running concurrently or in opposition, in harmony or discord – a fugue, which I must never allow myself to lose.[58]

Komisarjevsky enabled his actors to understand themselves in the same way. Music became a vital tool for his actors to discover character; in rehearsal he encouraged them to play a piece of music of their choosing and invent a story to fit around that music. This improvisatory technique, he believed, could open up the intricacies of character. This sense of musicality was just as vital to the physicality of the actors:

> His acting must always be music ... He must become neither a restrained God from Olympus nor a mere beast who surrenders himself to his instincts ... He must know the limits of the scale of his instrument ... he must have a light and sensitive touch for every stage of transition from *piano* to *forte* ... His words and movements must appear from the front as if coming instinctively in harmonious accord.[59]

Body and mind exist in a melodious relationship. Such an approach, says Komisarjevsky, would free the performer from the usual pitfalls of acting: pretense, affectation and fakery.

While his actors discovered their innate rhythmic musicality, Komisarjevsky would search for the musicality embedded in every play. 'I try to convey to the audience not only the story and ideas contained in the play (if there are any!)', he said, 'but the music and rhythm (which can be discovered in any play) which is expressive of its emotional content'.[60] A number of Russian directors would have, at least partly, agreed with Komisarjevsky's musical approach to the stage: directors such as Stanislavsky, who used different tempos and timbres of music to enable his actors to discover their characters, and Tairov, who understood the actor as 'an enchanted Stradivarius', that is as a beautiful harmonious instrument.[61] This musical theatre aimed to affect the spectator, to draw her into the *Gesamtkunstwerk* synthesis.[62] For Komisarjevsky, then, music acted as an accompaniment to action, a creator of atmosphere, a driver of narrative structure, a way for actors to tap into character traits, and, ultimately, as an intrinsic part of any play.

Such a focus on musical rhythm is unsurprising when one considers Komisarjevsky's background. His father's talents as an opera singer and his own early work in Russia with opera companies provided a foundation that would affect his body of work even after his moves to Britain and the United States. In fact, it is interesting to note that one of Komisarjevsky's final productions in Russia and first productions in Britain was an opera: Alexander Borodin's *Prince Igor* for the Moscow Opera House (1914–18) and at Covent Garden (1919).[63] Borovsky suggests that the Moscow Opera House production was seminal in the development of his ideas; ideas about rhythm, pace and structure, 'the precise scoring of individual roles and the performance as a whole', came directly out of this production.[64] Moving to Britain, Komisarjevsky was invited to direct this opera again for Covent Garden. He did not have a particularly high opinion of this grand London opera house, saying that it 'presents the kind of anecdotes you would find on a provincial stage in a hick town like Tsarevokokhaisk'.[65] Again, his criticism of Covent Garden rested on its decision to produce shows that would simply make money rather than display true artistry. British audiences generally admired his Covent Garden production of *Prince Igor*. Interestingly reviews mention the choreographer, Alexandre Gavrilov, and the conductor, Albert Coates, but, like so many opera reviews of the period, do not seem to refer to the newly arrived Russian director.[66]

Clearly music was a required element of opera, but Komisarjevsky's commitment to musicality – as part of his rehearsal process, as embedded in play narratives and as an intrinsic facet of his synthetic theatre – remained. Komisarjevsky produced layered soundscapes throughout his career; referring to his work in Stratford he said, 'the world beyond the acting area and its influence on the *dramatis personae* had to be suggested in my theatre by the *acoustic perspective* and by the *light perspective*'.[67] The acoustic (and acousmatic) became a vital part of his character development and scenic atmospheres. In *Musical Chairs* this was achieved through the regular musical interventions. But the 'acoustic' in this play is actually broader, consisting of all sound interventions, including the thunder and explosions offstage. The complexity of sound in this play recalls the breaking string in *The Cherry Orchard*, a famous acousmatic device that has been analysed in myriad ways.[68] Komisarjevsky's versions of Chekhov plays, produced in the 1920s, revolutionized British understanding of the great Russian playwright's most important works. Chekhov, of course, is so often regarded as a highly musical playwright; the early-twentieth-century British theatre critic Desmond MacCarthy said 'Chekhov makes a work of art which moves us and exalts us like a beautiful piece of music'.[69] British audiences at first received Chekhov's plays with a mixture of admiration, bemusement and boredom; Chekhov was regarded as the 'spokesman of bewhiskered melancholia', as Laurence Senelick puts it.[70] But increasingly, during the 1920s, Chekhov plays were more readily regarded as capturing the disillusioned post-war mood in Britain. Komisarjevsky presented versions of Chekhov's plays that were more accessible (linguistically and formally) to British audiences not used to the Russian playwright's symbolism or distinct Russian themes. For example, he set up romantic leads (such as Tuzenbakh in *Three Sisters*, who is described as ugly in Chekhov's original play but was transformed into a dashing hero by Komisarjevsky), and altered the period or settings of plays. As Robert Tracy suggests, 'he kept his actors almost constantly in motion, often having one deliver a line, cross the stage, then recross [...] Komisarjevsky apparently stressed movement to combat the notion that Chekhov's characters were passive, lethargic'.[71] In effect, he discovered new rhythms in Chekhov's work, rhythms that were, perhaps, more in keeping with the playwright's intentions than Stanislavsky's slower-paced productions. Komisarjevsky's version of *Ivanov* for the Barnes Theatre (1925), for example, was praised by critics for the excellence of the acting and the subtle comedy, but also for the sense of appropriate musicality. One reviewer confirmed 'as a producer Mr Komisarjevsky has the power no English one has: he is the master of tempo, of piano and forte, especially of the piano'.[72] His *Three Sisters,* produced in the following year, also captured the musicality of Chekhov's work; Borovsky suggests that 'this production preserved the depth and richness of Chekhov's writing, a result achieved by a special method of working with the actors called "musical analysis"', breaking down roles into rhythmic constituent parts and enabling actors to feel a stronger sense of emotion, intention and character.[73] Musical rhythms could be used both to enable the actor to interpret and internalize character and, as music so often does, to create a sense of united ensemble.[74] Norman Marshall, in his 1947 reflections on British theatre, praised Komisarjevsky's Chekhovs by focusing on his move away from factual realism:

I have seen nothing more lovely in the theatre than the stage pictures Komisarjevsky created on that cramped little stage at Barnes. His productions were as satisfying to the ear as they were to the eye. His use of subtle variations of tempo, modulation of tone and delicately timed pauses was far in advance of anything in the English theatre.[75]

Musicality and rhythm, so intrinsic to Chekhov's playtexts, remained a central, abiding focus of Komisarjevsky's work. For Marshall, as for many of the theatre critics, Komisarjevsky's musical adaptations at the Barnes were as much a challenge to British styles of directorship (which Marshall and Komisarjevsky largely regarded as dictated by economics rather than art, by the desire for crowd-pleasing lucrative hits rather than a sustained actor-focused process) as artistic triumphs in their own right.

Komisarjevsky's interest in music remained even towards the end of his career after his move to America. In 1940 he directed the musical *Russian Bank* at the St James Theatre in New York, although it failed to capture the imagination of the Broadway audience, closing after just eleven performances. The story, written by Komisarjevsky and Stuart Mims, moves from St Petersburg to Long Island and is an odd tale of a Russian prima donna, a love triangle, a Communist commissar and, in the words of a reviewer, 'comedy Bolsheviks'.[76] Reviews were scathing, with most referring to it as an incomprehensible messy mix of Russian history, comedic tragedy and melodrama. The one positive comment was reserved for the Russian music of the piece which, Brooks Atkinson in the *New York Times* noted, was 'wholly enchanting'.[77] Mostly these songs are unidentified, but certainly were arranged by Komisarjevsky and collaborator Zinovy Kogan, and included the Russian ballad 'Dark Eyes'.[78] While clearly unsuccessful in terms of reviews and audiences, Komisarjevsky still revealed his ability to include striking musical elements in his theatrical work.

Music and rhythm, in their broadest senses, remained a key facet of Komisarjevsky's aesthetic from his earliest opera work to his appearance on Broadway. Music infiltrated every contributor to the theatrical process, from the director, whom he compares to a conductor, to the actor who must learn, he said, to move 'his tone and actions from the "life key" to the "key of the play"'.[79] All plays have an intrinsic sense of musicality that needs to be unearthed, he maintained, and any music used in a theatrical production 'must be dynamic, to act with, and express the moods of the characters, the rhythm, the tempi, the crescendo, the diminuendi, and every point and accent of the action'.[80] Komisarjevsky's productions were full of sounds but, more than this, were constructed around the very notion of sound. The actor Warren Jenkins, who received training from Komisarjevsky, recalled the director pausing in the middle of rehearsals to play to piano, then turning to his actors saying, 'This is the mood.'[81] The very feel, atmosphere and intention of the theatrical event were, for Komisarjevsky, musical elements. Music, therefore, became a vital access point into the production for director, actors and audience members.

Synthetic theatre and the universal actor

Komisarjevsky's sensitive understanding of musicality clearly informed his vision of what he called a 'synthetic theatre' and this latter term threads its way through this chapter as much as it does through Komisarjevsky's own *Myself and the Theatre*. But there is one more complementary term introduced in his most practically illuminating book: 'universality'. He explains the relationship between the synthetic – 'combining all the various branches of the actor's art' – and the 'universal' in Chapter Six:

> An actor who played in such a synthetic show would have to possess a knowledge and practice of music, poetry, singing and dancing, and would have to be master of every means of theatrical expression and, therefore, a perfect performer, a *universal* actor, as I call him.[82]

Later in this section Komisarjevsky goes on to clarify what those 'various branches' are in his thinking, citing a harmony of emotion, voice, movement and surroundings while bemoaning the fact that the actors of his day lacked the skills to effect such a harmonization.[83] Without this harmony of elements, he argued, the seeds of ensemble cannot begin to grow and the stage becomes devoid of atmosphere. In Komisarjevsky's mind, this problem was not confined to the theatre, but extended to dancers and opera singers, accounting for the sense of disconnectedness he often experienced as a theatregoer at the time (in the late 1920s). Even Wagner, the über-theorist of 'total theatre' and a significant influence on Komis as we have seen, is guilty of a separation rather than a synthesis of the performing arts disciplines. Wagnerian performers merely illustrate movements already evoked by the score, Komis suggested, taking 'the music out of the infinite region of time and drag[ging] it down into the narrowness of three dimensional space'.[84]

In spite of his ambition to be a director of multi-skilled, 'universal', performers, Komis did not achieve this level of synthesis very often in his own practice. The pinnacle of his success, according to his own self-assessment, was during his last year in the new Soviet Union in 1918, working at the private Soviet Opera House on pieces such as *Lohengrin, Fidelio* and *Barbiere*.[85] The harmony of a synthetic theatre, it seemed, was most obviously realized in the inherently synthetic art of opera. Later, though, Komis cites some examples from his time in Europe and the United States when he 'tried to put some of [his] synthetic theories into practice': *Cosi Fan Tutte* in Turin, *Peer Gynt* and *The Tidings Brought to Mary* in New York and *King Lear* and *The 14th of July* at the Oxford University Dramatic Society.[86]

Reviews of the season in New York in 1922, at the Theater Guild, reveal something of what Komisarjevsky was describing and highlight some of the conditions his 'universal actors' experienced. Somewhere between the repertory system on the European continent and the 'devastating long-run system of the London theatres',[87] the Theater Guild organized six shows a season, including one purely experimental production with no commercial imperative at all. 'For the actor who cares for his art', the *Manchester Guardian* correspondent opined in 1923, such a context 'means salvation'.[88] Working with Lee Simonson as set designer, forsaking his role as overall auteur, Komisarjevsky's *Peer Gynt* and *The Tidings* borrowed heavily from the expressionist tradition heralded by Leopold Jessner [see **Volume 4**]. 'Whenever an American production attempts to be ultramodern in its settings there are whispers of "Jessner" abroad. With *Peer Gynt* they are more than whispers,' the *New York Times* correspondent, Henrietta Malkiel, observed.[89] This influence from Europe is clearly in evidence in the sharply choreographed tableaux of *The Tidings* scenes, arranged atop expansive steps typical of Jessner's designs and reproduced in *Myself in the Theatre* (though with no mention of Simonson as designer).[90]

The sense of artistic synthesis and harmony is a feature of the reviews of *Peer Gynt,* in contrast to an earlier outing of Ibsen's play in Munich. Malkeil describes the latter production as 'part glorious fantasy, part incongruous realism', whereas 'the Guild production is more unified in conception'.[91] Another respondent a few days earlier, while finding some of Simonson's designs 'horrible to behold', still notes: 'the beautiful thing about the Theatre Guild production seems to me to be the working together and harmonizing of all the elements in Ibsen's chaotic play for the sake of the play itself and of Ibsen himself'. This harmony was achieved in spite of the dramaturgical challenges the play set for the production team:

The presentation gives us a kaleidoscopic view of the exotic creatures and their doings, together with the influence of these upon a central figure, with as nearly a unity of purpose and action as it would seem possible to extract from such a play.[92]

That 'unity of purpose and action' is central to the idea of a synthetic theatre. Despite the multiple sources of creativity that are at play, there is at the same time a cohering directorial vision, drawing the threads together. In *Settings and Costumes of the Modern Stage*, Lee Simonson recounts how this synthesizing vision worked in his collaboration with Komisarjevsky, explaining how good theatre design needs to be embedded in the 'general pattern of action that a director can invent'. 'A stage setting', he observed 'is, essentially, a plan of action', and 'inseparable from the method of acting' espoused by the director.[93] Perhaps to argue for design as an integral element in the theatre, woven into the director's interpretation of a playwright's voice and complementary to the chosen style of acting, is not so radical in the twenty-first century, after the rise of the more holistic practice of scenography. But the parlous state of American theatre design (and writing), as it is described by Simonson, suggests that this European and Russian[94] philosophy of integrated theatre-making was yet to impact widely on the United States in the 1920s.[95] 'American designers seem to be marking time', he contended, and 'in setting many recent plays, or in acting them, nothing more is required than an adroit imitation of surfaces'.[96]

While Komis chose to highlight his suite of opera productions as exemplars of a synthetic theatre in *Myself*, he strangely overlooked his production of *Three Sisters* at the Barnes Theatre in 1926 (and revived in 1929). Later, however, he does allow himself a self-congratulatory paragraph, one which indicates that this important piece bore all the hallmarks of a synthetic theatre:

> The big success of my production of 'The Three Sisters' in London at the Barnes Theatre was largely due to the fact that I evolved the way to convey Chekhov's inner meaning and made the rhythm of the 'music' of the play blend with the rhythm of the movements of the actors, giving the necessary accents with the lighting and the various outer 'effects'. If this synthesis had not been completely harmonious the play might have seemed thin and even meaningless to the audience.[97]

As we have noted above, this is evidence of Komisarjevsky's 'musical analysis' in action, that is musicality extending to the dynamic manipulation of the scenographic environment and to the actors' work.[98] But how was this harmonious synthesis achieved? And what did it mean in practice? As one of Komisarjevsky's most celebrated productions – there being 'nothing more lovely in the theatre'[99] than his *Three Sisters* – there are many accounts of the production explaining how, as we have noted above, Komis pampered his English audiences and romanticized Chekhov for a generation of British theatregoers.[100] Important as Komisarjevsky's editing choices were in the construction of a 'chocolate box reproduction of life' (ironically Komisarjevsky's own scathing words to describe the state of British theatre),[101] the aim here is briefly to examine the staging choices he made through the lens of synthetics and universality. Using evidence drawn directly from the original prompt copy of *Three Sisters*, now housed in the Houghton Archive at Harvard, it is possible to examine the directorial choices Komis made to effect the sense of harmony which was widely felt by his audiences. In doing so it is worth returning to the formula Komisarjevsky himself offered in defining his synthetic theatre: a harmony of emotion, voice, movement and surroundings.

Chekhov's play ends with an off-stage duel in which Baron Tuzenbakh is killed by the maverick Solyony and the Doctor, Chebutykin, who remains curiously indifferent, is tasked with breaking the news to the Baron's fiancée Irina: 'It doesn't matter. It doesn't matter.'[102] It is a layered and complex ending which combines several theatrical devices to communicate its melancholic message of unrealized aspiration and domestic entrapment. Komisarjevsky exploited all these devices to maximize the atmospheric synthesis of Chekhov's finale. The off-stage march Chekhov uses to signal the garrison leaving was, in Komis's *Three Sisters,* Joseph Wagner's composition *Under the Double Eagle*.[103] This set a rousing and upbeat tempo to contrast radically with the mood on stage as Tuzenbakh's death in the duel is confirmed and the three sisters are all forced to reflect on their inaction and frustrated hopes. Komisarjevsky manipulated the dynamics of this musical backdrop carefully, with the band being cued in on page 93 of the prompt copy, just as Natasha, the prowling interloper now in full control of the house, screams at the Maid: 'why is there a fork lying about on this seat?'[104] On the next page the instruction 'FLICKER BAND' appears echoing Chebutykin's rather out of place rendition of 'Ta-ra-ra boom dee-ay. It's all the same. It's all the same'. On the final page, 'the Music sounds more and more distant' and Chebutykin is now quietly humming while reading his paper. The instruction 'FADE MUSIC FLICKER' accompanies a 'SLOW curtain'[105] as Kulygin comes back onto stage with his wife Masha's hat, underlining the moribund existence to which she is returning after the briefest of respites in her flirtation with Vershinin. The musical noises off, then, in Komisarjevsky's production worked to create an atmosphere of parting, of loss and of progressive alienation for those left behind, a set of surroundings which harmonized with the emotional direction of Chekhov's play.

The scoring of light was executed with similar attentiveness, deft touches of projected candlelight in Act 3 for instance, and the seasonal shifts so important to the play's development captured subtly with the minimum of fuss, a shadow of a maple branch standing in for the fir trees Natasha has lined up for felling. The actors' movement, too, was carefully arranged, so much so that Gielgud playing the Baron later reflected on their 'intricate patterns' and on the precision of 'groupings, entrances and exits', all marked out on the rehearsal floor in chalk.[106] Indeed, Gielgud's general assessment of Komisarjevsky's skill in this area of theatre directing was unequivocal:

> Some extremely skilled directors (Granville-Barker, St Denis, Komisarjevsky) who have their plan worked out in great detail in advance, can bring an almost perfect scheme, prepared in every detail, to the early rehearsals, and the movement of the play can then be rehearsed and set in the first weeks, leaving two weeks or more for the development of detail, pace, character, and the finishing touches.[107]

Three Sisters illustrates compellingly how the extrinsic conditions of music, sound, light and movement can be built up in harmonic complexity by a director to give the actors the most stimulating, affective context for their playing. As Komis said in an interview conducted the same year as the production: 'finding the rhythm was a way of reaching the emotion of a scene or role',[108] returning us to the inherent musicality of his directorial practice outlined earlier. In this 1926 production Komisarjevsky was sensitively underscoring Chekhov's writing with rhythmic cues for his actors, building on the signifiers in the text to immerse his actors in a holistic experience of sound, light and action. This was the synthetic theatre in microcosm, as critics of the production were quick to point out, not because the actors were universally adept at 'music, poetry, singing and dancing' but because they were inescapably embroiled in a harmonic score of Komis's making, one which exploited all the elements of the theatre, organized under a controlling directorial eye. Though the elements of a synthetic theatre are considered in equal relation to one another, there is no doubting who is responsible for their arrangement: the director or régisseur. Late on in his career Komis crystalized this idea in highly economical terms in unpublished notes put together for a lecture course in the United States. Entitled *Play Direction*, the notes capture the enduring lessons he had learnt and suggest how his model of directing had matured and solidified:

> My methods of directing a play. Harmony of visual and oral interpretations. 'Interpretation of a play'. The idea on which the production of a play is based. The style of the play. The rhythm of the play. What is rhythm. The harmony of arts on stage. The interrelationship of arts on the stage. Necessity of one directing mind.[109]

The director-trainer

The five words Komis used to describe the function of the director in his *Play Direction* lecture notes – 'Necessity of one directing mind' – hide a multitude of complexities. As is already clear and further elaborated below, Komis was at times a very good collaborator and happy to cede elements of artistic control to other artists (Lee Simonson, Lesley Blanch, Valdemar Bernadi, for instance), even if the historic record does not always make these collaborations visible, as we shall see later.[110] At other times he was altogether more dogmatic about his role as the singular directorial force in a production. Writing to the chairman of the Board for Sloane Productions in 1927, while he was working on a production of Arnold Bennett's *Mr Prohack*, Komis was unambiguous, to say the least:

> When we had our preliminary discussions of my proposed season at the Court Theatre, I made perfectly clear to you and to Miss Cheston (and to Mr Bernstein also), that my main condition in starting the affair was – that I should be the sole and autocratic artistic director and producer of the company. You all agreed to it. It is clear, that according to this agreement, there could be no other artistic conception of the theatre during the above mentioned season, than my personal conception, and no law on the stage except my personal law.[111]

Komisarjevsky had been irritated by the actress Dorothy Cheston, Bennett's lover and mother to his child, who had not been adhering strictly to his movement score. But special circumstances aside, the emphases in his letter ('sole and autocratic', 'personal conception') are telling and speak more generally to Komis's underlying assumptions of the role of the director as he had experienced it in Russia – from his sister Vera, from his sister's short-term collaborator, Meyerhold, and from his long-term inspiration and nemesis, Stanislavsky. All three figures represented a particular model of directorial single-mindedness that counted the task of training actors among the many functions of a director. Komis was no different. As Simon Shepherd notes in *Direction*:

> The director as actor-trainer begins most famously with Stanislavski and his contemporaries, Meyerhold and Komisarjevsky and [...] some directors still regard the development, if not training, of their actors as the most important part of the directorial role.[112]

It is an important distinction, the difference between training and development, and Komis moves between the two across his career. But the question remains as to *how* a director serves a role as trainer, particularly in contexts where there is not an institutional backdrop to help meet this aspiration. One might also ask *why*? Given all the other functions a director fulfils, what is the need for them also to act as an actor-trainer? This section will look at both these questions in relation to Komisarjevsky's practice, reviewing first his school in Moscow, modelled on his sister's idealized vision of a nursery for actors, before looking at some of the techniques he used to develop his actors during his time working in Europe. Finally we will examine the limited evidence that exists concerning the training he devised for his students in New York, in order to examine the effectiveness of his final phase as director-trainer, working alongside his third wife Ernestine Stodelle.

The Vera Komissarzhevskaya Theatre Studio

As the section on Life indicates, Komisarjevsky's formative time in Russia was spent working with his sister until her death in 1910, before he developed his own practice as a trainer and a director. Interestingly it was in that order, his formation of the Vera Komissarzhevskaya Theatre Studio in 1913 coming a year before his founding of the Komissarzhevskaya Theatre, which ran in parallel with the teaching studio from 1914. In *Myself* he reveals his motivation for doing things that way, talking in eulogistic and nostalgic terms about the pedagogical aspirations of his sister. Vera had closed her own theatre in 1909 to enable her to generate revenue from yet another provincial tour and it was her intention not to reopen it before establishing a training space for actors where 'every student could become a healthy joyful, cultured artist'.[113] But she died suddenly in 1910 on that tour and left Komis with barely enough money to bury her. Turning her wildly idealistic plans for a studio 'in the country, near the sea', where actors would be encouraged to find themselves,[114] into a clearly defined and progressive teaching institution was the choice Komis made to mark Vera's legacy, though he retained his sister's commitment to developing 'cultured artists'. This was achieved by blending what might now be called classes in 'cultural studies' with sessions on practical acting skills. Thus, Borovsky tells us, the 'pupils wrote essays on various aspects of culture and took part in seminars. At discussion time (conducted by Fyodor himself) the students had to defend their arguments against experienced professionals.'[115] This approach then complemented classes in acrobatics, dance, fencing and stage speech, arguably a more familiar range of disciplines in the context of conventional training.[116]

There is little concrete evidence in English of the curriculum designed by Komisarjevsky for his Moscow studio[117] but one passage in *The Theatre and a Changing Civilisation* helps clarify a vital aspect of the approach, helping to explain further the sections on musicality and synthetic theatre above. 'To train the students and actors of my Moscow theatre', he notes:

> I used to teach them music [...] I showed them that if a piece of music is rightly *felt* by them, they can express its emotions in rhythmical movements produced to it [...]; and that by taking a piece of music and 'living through' it and afterwards performing it, by synchronizing his movements with his rhythm, an actor can make a much stronger impression than acting without the assistance of music.[118]

It is important to remember when reading this that Komis was recounting a period just before the First World War, over two decades before Stanislavsky's *An Actor Prepares* (1936) was first published and fully forty-five years before very similar ideas like these were described in the chapter on tempo-rhythm in the delayed accompaniment, *Building a Character* (1949). Indeed, even at the time when Komis published *The Theatre and a Changing Civilisation* in 1935, the concept of 'living through' an experience – Stanislavsky's now familiar concept of *perezhivanie* – was only known to those who had first-hand experience of the System in development or had been schooled in it by one of the tributaries of Stanislavskian training, Vakhtangov, or Michael Chekhov, for example. Viewed in isolation it might be tempting to consider this statement of Komisarjevsky's as a piece of pragmatic plagiarism from the better-known stable of Stanislavsky but it should be clear now that harmony, musicality and the synchronizing of movements to a score are all essential components of Komisarjevsky's directorial approach. Seeing how he helped prepare actors to achieve this synthesis in the early days of his career puts flesh on the bones of the claim he makes many years later in the *Play Direction* lecture notes that to 'know how to direct acting one must know [...] how to teach acting'.[119] Time and time again teaching comes first in Komisarjevsky's thinking.

The director-trainer in Britain

Though fleeing poverty and revolutionary chaos was one of his major motivations in leaving Russia, practising as director in Europe still came with sacrifices. Chief among these was the absence of a theatre and an accompanying studio, the model he had found to be so beneficial in developing 'cultured' performers in Moscow. The years between 1919 and 1939 were spent in continuous reinvention with casts from London, Glasgow, Paris, Turin, Holyhead, Leeds, New York, Edinburgh, Stratford and Oxford and unsurprisingly it was impossible to achieve anything like the conditions his sister had called for – when actors are able to spend long periods together and develop a 'feel [for] each other'.[120] Of the directorial projects he took on at the time, perhaps the closest to that Russian model of ensemble was the Barnes season in 1926, where, in addition to *Three Sisters*, he directed four other plays – *Ivanov*, *Katerina*, *Cherry Orchard* and *The Government Inspector* – and was able in small but influential ways to achieve a training of sorts for his casts. That training was, as Pitches has argued elsewhere, 'a creative synthesis of Russian ideas from the early twentieth century peppered with some important singular innovations'[121] and as such it shared many characteristics with Stanislavsky's System. But Komis was working in an entirely different context from his countryman's, one in which the very word 'ensemble' was alien and viewed with suspicion and he therefore needed to find a more pragmatic and flexible approach which focused on small gains with quick results.

In the space available to us here it is worth summarizing the flexible approach Komis took to directing-training in Britain and describing in brief his key philosophy.[122] Put succinctly, Komis preached a form of textual scrutiny, character depth based on research and ensemble performance founded on an acute sensitivity to the surroundings. As we have seen, these principles were underpinned by his belief in musicality and theatrical synthesis. In practice this meant that he demanded his actors gathered intelligence on their characters' histories and contexts to deepen their connections to the role. Gielgud, Peggy Ashcroft and Charles Laughton all report the impact of this demand on their preparation, and the private student Phillada Sewell, who we will meet more closely, later, was inspired for life by this new-found commitment to textual analysis. Layered and allusive texts such as Chekhov's could not have been performed with integrity and nuance without such preparation. Interestingly it was the Russian realistic school to which Komis turned when working in Britain, a repertoire very different from his portfolio in Moscow[123]; he was clearly confident that he could inculcate the skills needed for such a genre and quickly came to be a recognized expert in the field, a teacher of quasi-Stanislavskian practice before Stanislavsky had been heard of in the UK.

In terms of his development of ensemble skills, he used a number of strategies: collective readings of the text by the cast to share the absorption of the playtext; movement sequences and stage pictures built up over time and with the full engagement of the cast, as Gielgud identified above; a holistic vision of the stage 'conditions', designed to stimulate the actors' imaginations as much as the audience's; and an overarching appreciation of the importance of *atmosphere*, the unseen but strangely tangible influence which binds actors together in rehearsal and performance. As the *Times* theatre critic in 1921, reviewing Komisarjevsky's *Uncle Vanya*, observed: 'Here it is the atmosphere that constitutes the unity of the play – its preservative from the mere haphazard incoherence which English disciples mistake for Chekhovism.'[124] These core ensemble skills Komis had identified as givens for his success as an interpreter of the Russian realist school in Britain and he managed to embed them in his directing *during* preparations for the Barnes season, not as an independent activity. In doing so he was recognizing both the strengths and weaknesses of the British theatre tradition at the time, exploiting the possibilities of a particular kind of make-do pragmatism and a historic belief in on-the-ground apprenticeship.

The Komisarjevsky Drama Studio

Given the regard Komisarjevsky had for training as much as directing actors, it is perhaps not coincidental that he ended his life working with (and married to) an exceptional teacher, the modern dance practitioner, Ernestine Stodelle. Stodelle had been in Doris Humphrey's dance company in the late 1920s, where she partnered José Limon with whom she also collaborated as a choreographer. Later, after Komisarjevsky's death, she turned to academic writing and dance reviewing and produced a biography of Martha Graham, *Deep Song* (1984) as well as a study of Humphrey. In 1990, as first-hand witness and dancer in Humphrey's original company, she reconstructed dances by Humphrey and Charles Weidman for teaching and scholarly purposes and is noted for carrying on her teaching well into her eighties: 'Ernestine at 85 could make dancers in their 20s ashamed they couldn't move so well', her *New York Times* obituary reads.[125]

While there is little evidence available of the details of their curriculum, it is clear from documents in the Houghton Archives in Harvard that Stodelle and Komis taught alongside each other beginning their collaboration with lecture demonstrations in which Komis played the historian and Stodelle the practitioner: 'Demonstrations of Dance and Movements to illustrate Mr Komisarjevsky's lecture [Expression in the Theatre] will be given by Miss Ernestine Stodelle' a press release from 1937 declared.[126] By the time they formed the Komisarjevsky Studio in 1940 they had planned a mixed economy of sessions: 'Group courses in acting. Day or Eve. Private coaching. Public performances. Summer theatre.' Stodelle was enlisted to teach movement and composition and 'special lessons in posture'.[127] Later still, a more even split of responsibilities seems to have been devised, a one-page handwritten note entitled 'Group Courses in Drama: Curriculum' giving a hint that the kinds of classes Komisarjevsky had developed in Moscow were being revisited in the United States:

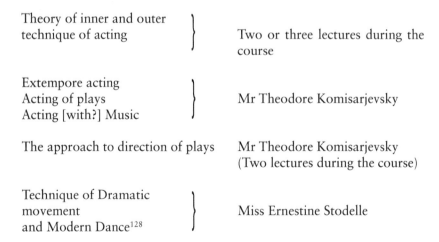

Theory of inner and outer technique of acting	Two or three lectures during the course
Extempore acting Acting of plays Acting [with?] Music	Mr Theodore Komisarjevsky
The approach to direction of plays	Mr Theodore Komisarjevsky (Two lectures during the course)
Technique of Dramatic movement and Modern Dance[128]	Miss Ernestine Stodelle

Cryptic though it may be the document gives us one of the few indicators of Komisarjevsky's teaching in the United States. Unlike other émigré actor-directors who moved to the United States to teach – Michael Chekhov and Richard Boleslavsky, for instance – ex-students have not gone on record to claim Komis as their master teacher, although many of Stodelle's dance students name *her* as an inspiration after the Komisarjevsky Drama Studio ceased.[129] In Moscow Komisarjevsky luxuriated in the context of a theatre and an accompanying studio and was able to incentivize his student actors by offering them early access to the theatre (if they were good enough). This was the high point of his director-trainer days, during which he developed a suite of ideas that became fundamental to his understanding of theatre after he left Russia. In Europe the ground was never stable enough for him to build the infrastructure for a training studio but that did not stop him *developing* the actors he worked with (to return to Shepherd's phrase), many of whom have gone on record in memoirs, in reviews and in obituaries to capture the impact Komisarjevsky's ideas had on their practice. On the surface of things, the United States represented a return to an ideal context of director-training, with an expert teacher at his side in Stodelle and the glimmerings of a deliverable curriculum underpinned by the pivotal concepts he first developed in his youth (musicality, improvisation, scored movement). But his teaching offers were too diverse and the student body too fluid to build momentum. The professional outlets for his students were also much less defined than in Russia and the rich interaction of preparation, rehearsal and performance he achieved at moments in the UK was never possible stateside. Komis may have begun and ended his career running a studio to train actors in a major capital city but Moscow and New York were two very different kinds of studio, the first inspired by the artistic ideals of his sister and the second by the economic realities of survival.

Komisarjevsky's Importance

Writing for the *Oxford Dictionary of National Biography*, Norman Marshall offered his assessment of Theodore Komisarjevsky's impact on the British theatre, drawing on Gielgud's experience working with him:

> During his twenty years working in the English theatre Komisarjevsky had more influence than any other producer on methods of direction, acting, setting, and lighting.[130]

Marshall quotes Gielgud's description of Komisarjevsky when he died as 'a master of theatrical orchestration'.[131] But the full obituary published in the *Times* offered a more balanced evaluation of the Russian director's strengths and weaknesses:

> Technically he excelled in lighting, grouping, striking scenic ingenuity and fine musical taste. He loved young people and knew how to encourage them and bring them out; but his disdainful attitude towards men of business prevented him from gaining their confidence, and so he never

came to manage a theatre of his own in England, or to create, as he should have done, a group of actors following a definite policy dictated by him.[132]

The common ground between the two commentators is clear: Komisarjevsky was a theatrical polymath and his contribution extended over many complementary functions in the theatre. His impact was felt not just in the orchestration of the actors on the stage but in the development of their scenic environment – in lighting, setting and, by implication, sound – his 'fine musical taste'. It was to be measured as much in his teaching as it was in his directing, and both training and production methods in English theatre at the time (1919–39) were given a well-needed shake-up by his approach. As Marshall argued later in his biographical note: 'At a time when English acting had a glossy veneer which concealed its shallowness, Komisarjevsky demanded from his actors a new intensity of feeling and a deeper understanding of the characters they were playing.'[133]

Yet as Gielgud identifies, this 'intensity of feeling' was not a product of a sustained and strategic approach by Komis, nor did he have the requisite people skills to deliver fully on his innovations. As we have seen, his time in England was characterized by short-term contracts, shotgun theatrical weddings and frustrated plans for a school which *could* have offered training along the lines he developed in Moscow in 1913 and in the United States from 1940. Marshall's timeline in the opening quotation – '*during* his twenty years working in the English theatre …' – in fact betrays a conspicuous lack of legacy which haunts much of Komis's output. He was influential as a teacher, director and scenographer at the time but how many of his ideas endured beyond the interwar period in English theatre history?

This is a principal question for this section of the Komisarjevsky chapter, evaluating his **Importance**. But before we can attempt to answer it there are some larger questions which lurk behind the two opening contributions by Marshall and Gielgud, questions of a historiographical bent. The most fundamental question is of course: importance to whom? Both Gielgud and Marshall represent a particular elite audience, as theatre directors themselves and as men with established cultural value operating predominantly in the capital city of London, both coming to prominence in the interwar period. But what of Komisarjevsky's influence on theatre beyond the capital? What, if any, imprint did he make in regional theatres, what story is there to be told beyond England – in Wales and Scotland for instance, building on the sections above and on notions of 'entanglement'? What, relatedly, was the significance of Komisarjevsky's work in Russia and in the United States? And how did the impact of these separate geographical locations on Komis's work leak into one another, explicitly and implicitly? What about all the women who worked with Komis, as actors, designers, co-directors and co-teachers (Margaret Webster, Phillada Sewell, Lesley Blanch, and the aforementioned Ernestine Stodelle)? And how can one foreground what, beyond the emphasis on Komis's second wife, Peggy Ashcroft, has often been a marginalized set of voices? Finally, following Dennis Kennedy's lead, what are the measures of impact *beyond* those of an individual personality? Is it possible in the interest of historiographical rigour to 'de-emphasise essentialist biography', eschewing narratives of nationhood[134] to ground the analysis in the smaller picture?

What follows, then, is a series of contrasting perspectives on Komis's 'importance', an attempt to avoid a causal grand narrative and instead to present several micro-histories, as Thomas Postlewait calls them, 'focus[ing] on specific individuals and communities'. 'In this way', Postlewait argues, 'the historian hopes to reformulate the relation between everyday life and the public world.'[135] The micro-histories in this section are arranged thus: Komis's impact on actors and acting; Komis's impact on design and stage aesthetics; Komis's impact on education and training; and Komis's impact on theatre directing cultures. Echoing Postlewait, these are organized to move from personal, everyday life histories to their reflections in the public world.

Actors and acting

Komisarjevsky began working with actors at the theatre of his half-sister, Vera Komissarzhevskaya, in 1903. His last production (Alban Berg's *Wozzeck*) was staged in 1952 in New York City. In the intervening fifty years, as is already evident, Komisarjevsky worked with some of the most talented actors of his generation in Russia, Europe, across the British Isles and in North America. Many of these figures have spoken in their own memoirs and publications about Komisarjevsky's approach and from these accounts it is possible to gain an insight into his modus operandi as a director and, by extension, into the acting methodology he adopted with his performers. Komis was well known for his use of subtle and allusive suggestion in the rehearsal room, a characteristic which Margaret Webster, co-starring with Gielgud in Ronald Mackenzie's *Musical Chairs* (1931), captures in illuminating terms. The Russian director, she recalls,

> allowed the subtle relationships between the characters to develop gradually, with a hint here and a comment there, until we had absorbed the play into our blood, into our skins. It grew together organically. We all trusted him and each other and the script. There was a good deal of progress by 'feeling it out', but not by chopping and changing, which is a very different thing.[136]

Gielgud observed something similar about the ensemble at the Barnes Theatre:

He let them find their own way, watched, kept silent, then placed
the phrasing of a scene in a series of pauses, the timing of which he
rehearsed minutely. Very occasionally he would make some short but
intensely illuminating comment, immensely significant and easy to
remember.[137]

Both accounts testify to a rigorous, if understated, actor-director
dynamic in the rehearsal room yet this subtlety did not restrict the
decisive influence the Russian director had on the new wave of acting
talent in the 1920s and 1930s. Komis's impact on Gielgud's inclination
for histrionics, on Ashcroft's facility for play analysis and on Laughton's
visibility in his early career, is well documented[138] and forms an important
part of his reputation as a sensitive reader of actors. But if we are to be
true to the spirit of micro-history outlined above and really value the
everyday stories of those not already in the limelight, then a different
focus is needed. Here and in the next three sections below the focus
is primarily on lesser-known figures whose lives were caught up with
Komisarjevsky's in varying ways, people who were clearly influenced
by him but may also have had an influence *on* him, people, in short,
whose stories have not yet been heard in accounts of Komisarjevsky's
importance as a director.

Phillada Sewell

To describe Phillada Sewell simply as an actress, even though she
performed in the theatre, on radio and in films for six decades, is to
deny the extraordinarily wide range of creative roles she fulfilled from
the early 1930s to the 1990s (she died at the age of eighty-eight). She
did her formal training at RADA and at the Webber Douglas Singing
School but counted her very short time as a private acting student
with Komisarjevsky as infinitely more important to her professional
development. Witnessing the famous Barnes Theatre season first-hand
when Komisarjevsky was at the helm inspired her to write to him to
ask for tuition and the handful of classes she enjoyed with the Russian
cemented a twenty-five-year relationship, which was only curtailed by
Komisarjevsky's death in 1954 in the United States. This relationship is
documented in her journal and in an extensive series of letters between
her and Komis that span the entire period, a correspondence of some
300 letters, mostly from him to her.[139] The letters chart the development
of Sewell from a star-struck naïf to an assured, experienced artist and a
highly capable project manager.[140] The first exchanges between the two
set the tone for the next twenty-five years: he, relentlessly on the move,
demanding and mercurial; she, constant, pragmatic and determined to
improve herself:

1 Bernard Mansions
Russell Square, WC1   17th June 1930

Dear Miss Sewell,

I had your letter forwarded to me by Heinemann's. Yes, I still take students, but only for private lessons & not into classes. The fee for a lesson is one guinea.

  If you are interested, come and see me, but write before for an appointment.

Yours truly,
Th. Komisarjevsky[141]

1 Bernard Mansions
Russell Square, WC1   13th July 1930

Dear Miss Sewell,

I have to go unexpectedly abroad & will be back in three week's time. I hope you will be in town then, & we will start our work again. I am sorry that I have to break this up [?], but I *must* go.[142]

1 Bernard Mansions
Russell Square, WC1   14th September 1932

Dear Miss Sewell,

I came back from abroad a few days ago, but I wrote you [*sic*] during the last winter. Of course you can have your lessons – I believe I owe you two or three hours.[143]

Sewell's journal fills in the gap between Komisarjevsky's last two missives:

10th August 1930

Last term a simply wonderful thing happened. I had a lesson from Komisarjevsky! Then another lesson and then a third!!! – then he had to go away for three weeks and he hasn't come home yet – I never enjoyed any lesson like these lessons though I didn't do much good because I was so terrified – not of him exactly but of being stupid, and that made me stupider than ever – I studied the part of Anna in Ivanoff with him but never got as far as acting it. Everything Anna says – I must know why she says it – I must find out all her thoughts and know all her past. Komi's brain seems to work about ten times quicker than anyone elses – and the queer thing about him is that you can follow his thoughts quite easily and know what he is feeling at once – in fact his is a wonderful example of his own theories of acting. If he will have me I want to go on learning from him in the Autumn – I feel that if he cannot teach me to act then nobody will.[144]

There is the same echo of an intuitive, understated pedagogy here as we have seen with Gielgud and Webster above, the same attention to detail and implied overarching methodology. For Sewell these few lessons sparked an enduring relationship with the Russian which resulted in her acting under Komisarjevsky's direction;[145] taking on the role of secretary for his acclaimed production of *The Seagull* in 1936; acting on his behalf as a skilled broker with publishers and money-lenders; and, ultimately, becoming a kind of dramaturg-at-a-distance for him, once he had migrated to the United States but still needed theatre intelligence from the UK. Fourteen years after being formally recruited as a secretary-cum-stage manager for *The Seagull*, Sewell seemed still to be performing the same role, 3,500 miles away and with no remuneration:

Darien, Connecticut Monday   [24th April 1950]

[...] Could you get me some pictures of 1) an English soldier (Khaki) 2) an English officer of the Army (Khaki) 3) a Yeoman in uniform (full view from toe to top, 4) a modern traditional costume of a Lord (with wife etc.), 5) a costume of a male Court dress, 6) a picture of the old Queen Mary, wife of George V (for her dress), 7) a French fashion magazine for ladies with all sorts of afternoon & morning dresses, the latest fashions (for Imogen), 8) a picture of a modern English Country girl (poor worker on a farm) for Imogen in disguise 9) a uniform of a French officer, 10) of an Italian officer, 11) Dress of a maid at Buckingham Palace. The next thing is would you let me know the accents on the names in Cymbeline & their right pronunciation. I want to be perfectly sure, as the Americans argue about anything that is English [...]

Please do all this at once for me. The pictures should be sharp & the costumes on them viewed from toe to top.

Lots of love[146]

Within a few days, Sewell had clearly already responded to the brief as Komis replied on 12 May saying how much material he now had for his coming production of *Cymbeline* at the Montreal festival, thanks to her research.[147] The production, Komisarjevsky's last Shakespeare piece before his death, was praised in the Montreal Gazette as 'singularly beautiful and very discreet'[148] and later was credited with marking the end of 'half a century of theatrical experimentation that allowed *Cymbeline* to be freed from the Victorian pictorial tradition'.[149]

At other points in the correspondence Komis relies on her to broker discussions about a new version of *The Theatre and a Changing Civilisation* with his publishers in London, Bodley Head: 'Could you find from them personally would they be interested in my doing that & would they be ready to come to a financial arrangement with me?'[150] He even asks Sewell to find out loan terms to cover the costs of setting up the acting school in New

York already examined above: 'Do you know some good soul (a business soul too!) who would see a "proposition" in lending me the money, let's say from next August or July & until February 1940? To be repaid with 10% interest?'[151] As we have seen, the venture was ultimately funded as the Komisarjevsky Drama Studio, running from 1940 until 1952.[152]

These snapshots of Phillada Sewell's industry and creative labour between 1930 and 1954 reveal the extent to which Komisarjevsky relied on her as a troubleshooter, researcher and confidante and how influential she was in the three fundamental areas of his life: his directing, his teaching and his publishing. Komis in turn had inspired Sewell to become an actress in just a handful of private lessons charged at a guinea a time, a career she pursued for six decades, even though she never broke into the mainstream, playing small and supporting roles for much of her career. The letters reveal an alternative view of Komisarjevsky's successes – his groundbreaking work with Shakespeare, for instance, or his work as a theatre academic – and although his voice is dominant in the archival record, with the majority of Sewell's corresponding letters lost or unavailable, her unspoken competence and dogged professionalism are palpable.

Design and stage aesthetics

As Norman Marshall identified in the opening biographical note to this section, Komis was as much celebrated for his contribution as a scenographer as he was for his directorial work. Indeed, given the nature of cultural transmission and its inevitable dependence on documentary records, images of productions tend to endure more than the embodied experiences of performers, even if the latter are often translated into prose in memoirs and transcribed interviews. Along with his co-author, Simonson, Komisarjevsky added to the historical record of theatre design himself with *Settings and Costumes of the Modern Stage* (1933), published just a year after Leon Moussinac's much more celebrated *New Movement in the Theatre* (1932). The study is restricted to stage designs from Europe and America but his introductory essay reasserts the synthetic approach discussed in the **Art** section, prompted by the early days with Vera Komissarzhevskaya's theatre:

> The ideas of simplified realistic productions expressed by Vera Komisarjevsky [*sic*] before and after the disappointment in Meyerhold's symbolic experiments establish the main principles of my Synthetic-Realistic theatre, with a stage space, and without the scenic paraphernalia of the old theatre.[153]

It is the practical realization of this synthesis that has been noted by critics, where, Komisarjevsky argues, 'the décor must be in dynamic harmony with the acting and should be made to change, if not always its forms [...] at least the colours and effects of light and shade'.[154] In very different ways, this was true both of his Chekhov work and his productions of Shakespeare. As Richard E. Mennen notes of Komisarjevsky's tradition-breaking *Merchant of Venice* at the SMT in 1932, 'the internal eclecticism [...] worked in several ways – sometimes simultaneously – to create movement, and to stimulate associations, to comment on or satirise the action (and the traditional staging), and to stimulate comic invention'.[155] To illustrate, Mennen references the Venetian setting with 'drunkenly crooked houses' and 'obvious fairytale "make-believe" associations'.[156] As a foreigner with little or no cultural baggage, Komisarjevsky had been hired by the festival director, William Bridges-Adams, explicitly to redefine the SMT's approach to Shakespeare and this was exactly what Komis did, marking what the *Times* critic of the day called a 'fundamental shift in attitude to the play'.[157] This shift was, according to Mennen, 'primarily a product'[158] of Komisarjevsky's synthetic eclecticism, 'mixing historical periods and styles'.[159]

Lesley Blanch

Thirty-one critics reviewed this production, an unprecedented number for the SMT. But how many of them mentioned Komisarjevsky's collaborator on this production, Lesley Blanch, who co-designed the sets and costumes for the production and must surely be credited with some of the innovations that drew such praise? In Mennen's detailed account of the production Blanch does not get a single name-check nor does she appear in the most comprehensive and detailed of all Komisarjevsky accounts, Borovsky's *Triptych from the Russian Theatre*.[160] Sybil Rosenfeld recognizes Komis as 'the most experimental' of the modern designers who centred on Stratford in the early 1930s, citing the 'expressionist style' of *Merchant* but again failing to mention Blanch.[161] Even Komis himself omits to name Blanch's contribution in any of his books, even though he had known her from an early age and had, in addition to the *Merchant* design, contributed to his production of *Macbeth,* a production Komis discusses in *Settings and Costumes of the Modern Stage*.[162] More recent scholarship is similarly myopic in terms of Blanch's contribution.[163] Like Phillada Sewell, Lesley Blanch seems to have been overlooked in the established narrative of Komisarjevsky's history.[164]

Opening her famous travelogue, *Journey into the Mind's Eye* (1968), Blanch made a confession:

> I must have been about four years old when Russia took hold of me with giant hands. That grip has never lessened. For me, the love of my heart, the fulfillment of the senses and the kingdom of the mind all met here. This book is the story of my obsession.[165]

That obsession is personified in her book in the character of the Traveller, an enigmatic visitor to the family house who acts as the stimulant to Blanch's slavophilia, full of mysterious tales and alluring accounts of the Trans-

FIGURE 2.5 *Lesley Blanch in the 1960s. Photo by Henry Clarke/Condé Nast via Getty Images.*

Siberian railway. Remaining a family friend for Blanch's entire childhood, the Traveller slowly transforms from an itinerant and erratic faux-uncle to her central love interest, even though at Blanch's own admission such a development was 'deplorable'.[166] It wasn't until the recent publication of her lost papers by her goddaughter, Georgia de Chamberet, that the true identity of the Traveller was revealed and it was, of course, Komisarjevsky:

> In 1921 Lesley was 17 and, Komisarjevsky was 39. [...] An older, worldly-wise man, he was sustaining not only emotionally, but also by way of her eventual collaboration with him as a scenic and costume designer. Yet she never talked about him, choosing instead to immortalize him as 'The traveller' in her autobiography.[167]

Blanch was much better known for her writing than her design. An author of ten books,[168] she became the features editor for *Vogue* in 1937, shortly after her unsung collaboration with Komis in Stratford. She travelled extensively, had a fierce intellect as well as a lively and engaging writing style and was, along with her husband Romain Gary, incredibly well connected. In her writing she specialized in lavish views of the East, inspired by the first dreams of the Trans-Siberian railway implanted by Komis/The Traveller. But her ability as an artist should not be overlooked. She trained at the Slade School of Art from 1919 and worked as an illustrator for *Tatler,* producing several book covers on the side. Her status as a theatre designer in the 1930s was confirmed when her designs were chosen to represent England in the New York Museum of Modern Art's (MOMA) Theatre Art International Exhibition in 1934, organized by Lee Simonson.[169] Blanch, like Sewell, had seen Komisarjevsky's Chekhov productions at the Barnes and as early as 1923 had produced designs for him for his production of *Le Club des Canards Mandarins* (The Club of Mandarin Ducks) at the Champs Élysées theatre in Paris, although playbills only cite Komisarjevsky as the designer.[170] By the time she worked on the Stratford productions she had international visibility and a demonstrable track record as a designer.

The extent to which her influence can be seen to have impacted on the Komisarjevsky productions in Stratford is not easy to establish, mainly because of the effacement of her name from so many records. But also because the share of responsibilities in the design process, as with so many artistic collaborations, is not spelt out in any documents, even those which *do* name Blanch as co-designer. What is clear from a comparison of designs held now by her executor de Chamberey with those published in Mennen's account is that the expressionist style he celebrates in the *Merchant* production, attributing it solely to Komis, is consistent with Blanch's designs for the earlier production of the Italian opera *Giannina et Bernardone,* a little-known production by Komis produced in 1931 at the Pigalle theatre in Paris. There are the same distorted bridges and towers, identical juliet balconies, bent and warped in Gaudi-style; there are even echoes in both designs of the characteristically striped venetian mooring poles, leaning over at dangerous angles.

As the two most developed set designs in Blanch's portfolio at the time (see Figures 2.6 and 2.7), it is likely that these two designs, alongside those for *Macbeth* in 1933, would have formed the centrepieces of her submission to the MOMA Theatre Art Exhibition in 1934. Ironically, for this event she is *solely* attributed as designer, at least in the 1934 press release: 'England is represented by scene and costume drawings by Mrs Lesley Blanch', alongside Oliver Messel's designs for *The Miracle* and those by six other designers.[171] No mention is made of Komisarjevsky in this release, even though Russian designers were very well represented with thirteen designers, including Golovin and Akimoff, featuring.

It is impossible to know how much the oft-referenced distortions and the overall 'fanciful celebration of theatricality'[172] of the *Merchant* designs are attributable to Blanch and how much they are part of Komisarjevsky's vision. The truth is clearly somewhere in between. But what does come out of a scrutiny of the recently released Blanch design portfolio is that the enduring connection between the two was not simply based on Blanch's juvenile infatuation with the Russian and her ultimate rejection by him for another woman – 'Peggy Ashcroft took him off me', as Blanch fumed late in her life.[173] In fact, it was her professional relationship with Komis, dependent on her skill as an artist and theatrical imagination that complemented some of the most important work

FIGURE 2.6 *Scenic design by Lesley Blanch of* The Merchant of Venice, *1932. Copyright Georgia de Chamberet.*

FIGURE 2.7 *Scenic design by Lesley Blanch of* Giannina et Bernadone, *1931. Copyright Georgia de Chamberet.*

Komis produced in his career. If he was the unnamed 'Traveller' in her most renowned artistic contribution, she was the unnamed designer in his.

Training and education

As we have seen in the **Art** section, Komisarjevsky's importance as a trainer mixed the personal and the institutional. It was often through his efforts with individual actors, both in private lessons and in the rehearsal room, that he was best able to communicate his ideas and effect subtle change in his actors' approach to preparing for a role. The training studio in New York (funded with help from Phillada Sewell, as we have seen) had little impact. There were simply too many competing studios run by Russian émigrés at that time (the early 1940s) for Komisarjevsky's particular brand of pedagogy to take root[174] and, as Gielgud has identified, for all his personal charisma Komisarjevky did not have sufficient business nous or corporate charm to build a network of influential advocates who could embed his influence institutionally. As he rather pitifully remarked to Sewell of his time in England: 'I have been perpetually an alien in that Country, alien physically & alien spiritually, in spite of the truly great work I have done for the English Theatre & the English commonwealth.'[175]

From an educational perspective, however, there is one unlikely example of Komisarjevsky having an impact, not in England, nor in the United States or Russia but in Wales, emerging from research done by W. Gareth

Jones in relation to Anton Chekhov's absorption into the country's cultural landscape. Jones hails the commissioning of Komisarjevsky by Lord Howard de Walden for the 1927 National Eisteddfod as the 'foundation stone' for the development of a serious cultural offer in Wales, one which looked further than London's West End for its inspiration.[176] As we have referenced in the **Life** section, it was not in fact Chekhov which provided this impetus but Ibsen's play *The Pretenders* in a Welsh translation by J. Glyn Davies and D.E. Jenkins of Liverpool University.[177] Surveying the status of Welsh drama at the time, the *Manchester Guardian* correspondent, E.M.H., described it as nascent and in 'crisis', marking the inclusion of serious drama into the Eisteddfod in the form of Komis's *The Pretenders* production as a potential flashpoint for influencing the entire dramatic movement in Wales.[178] Doubtful before the production that this could be achieved, E.M.H. praised *The Pretenders* after it was performed, in a later review, singling out Komisarjevsky's 'simplicity of scenery', the exciting intrusions of the cast into the audience and the excellence of 'all the women', heralding the Ibsen production as 'an important point in the history of Welsh Drama'.[179]

That importance was not to be measured in return trips to the National Eisteddfod for Komisarjevsky, as it had been for him with the repeat summer contracts at the SMT. Instead, the lasting effects of the 1927 *The Pretenders* were to be felt in the Higher Education sector, as Jones narrates:

> Until then, drama in Welsh had been perceived as a didactic tool or sociable pastime with little of the prestige that the chapel, Eisteddfod, and University had bestowed on music making. If the Eisteddfod had been forced to acknowledge the artistic power of Komisarjevsky, the University was now pressed to give it due academic status.[180]

Within four years of the production the first dedicated Drama lecturer in Wales was appointed to the University College of North Wales, now Bangor University, a certain Albert Evans-Jones or Cynan, as he was known, a senior figure in the National Eisteddfod movement and the only man ever to be elected twice as its Archdruid.[181] The appointment, the first academic recognition of Drama as an independent subject in Wales was, W. Gareth Jones argues, 'prompted by Komisarjevsky and his "theatre theatrical"', a judgement based on the extent to which the status of Drama as a subject was buttressed in Wales by this pivotal event.[182]

Directing culture

Writing in his introduction to *Modern British Theatre*, Simon Shepherd identifies two methodological lineages of theatre direction. The one, coming out of 'suggestions [glances, small movements, tentative tones exchanged between actors]', he ascribes to Tyrone Guthrie.[183] The other, arriving at rehearsals with 'all the positions and moves worked out', he identifies with

Michel Saint-Denis [see **Volume 1**], and to Komisarjevsky's early collaborator George Devine.[184] It should be clear by now that Komisarjevsky occupied both camps, at particular moments in his career, and the testimony included in this chapter highlights this ambivalence: the director-trainer offering incisive and off-the-cuff suggestions in the *Musical Chairs* rehearsal room, alongside the detailed prompt copy evidence looked at in the *Three Sisters* analysis, for instance. These two poles of activity do not cover all the bases of directorial practice of course and it is perhaps more illuminating to think beyond pragmatic influence, that is the *means* of directing, to the cultural influence Komis wielded, on directing as *an institution*. In doing so this section must inevitably move towards the more conventional territory of macro-history to 'deal with events between one point in time and another'.[185]

Placing Komisarjevsky at 'one point in time' unavoidably demands a consideration of before and after: What models of theatre direction did he draw upon for inspiration and who in turn followed in his footsteps? In terms of the former, Komisarjevsky's commitment to Wagner and more specifically to notions of the total artwork or *Gesamtkunstwerk* is clear. Indeed, as we have seen, he calls in strident terms for the birth of the Total Actor in *Myself and the Theatre*[186] and his own multi-disciplinary facility with all the media of the theatre contributed to this idealized pursuit of theatre as an integrated art form. His debt to previous directors may also be read in his work for the SMT in collaboration with Lesley Blanch. As Cary DiPietro points out in *Shakespeare and Modernism*, '*Macbeth* appears to have drawn inspiration from Edward Gordon Craig's design for the play' originally conceived in 1906, and drew also on Leopold Jessner's signature use of steps.[187] Along with Appia and Fuchs, Craig figures significantly in Komisarjevsky's *The Theatre and a Changing Civilisation* where the Russian recounts witnessing the famous but flawed production of the Englishman's *Hamlet* at the Moscow Art Theatre in 1911–12.[188] Of course the founder of that theatre, Stanislavsky, also features in Komisarjevsky's 'before-time', even if Komis spent considerable time denouncing Stanislavsky's ideas. In many ways Komisarjevsky was the same evangelizing force for Anton Chekhov in London in the 1920s as Stanislavsky had been in Moscow between 1898 and 1904, and their respective productions shared the praise for atmospheric density and subtle theatricality. But if Komis himself is to be believed, all of these creative precursors are irrelevant when compared to the influence of his sister. Indeed Vera Komissarzhevskaya, Komis argued in *Myself and the Theatre*, was the progenitor of the Russian theatrical avant-garde itself:

> All the modern Russian tendencies in the theatre have resulted from and evolved directly or indirectly from my sister's theatre.[189]

It is worth looking beyond the familial bias in this statement to consider if there is anything more enlightening here than confirmation of Komisarjevsky's devotion to his own theatrical dynasty. In fact, the identification of his sister's theatre as the model for the twentieth-century revolution in the theatre is as good an indication as any of the predilections he harboured as a practising director in Russia, Europe and the United States; hers was a theatre operating outside of the mainstream, balancing its commercial needs with a non-commercial, artistic repertoire; a theatre unafraid to experiment scenographically, albeit with sometimes very limited resources; a theatre which recognized the need for rigorous training to achieve its ends, even if the infrastructure to deliver that training was never fully realized. Above all, even though she began life as a state-sponsored Imperial Theatre actress, Komissarzhevskaya's importance was as a tradition-breaker and innovator, in Catherine Schuler's estimation, devoting 'all of her material, emotional, and spiritual resources to promoting post-realist modernism in Russia'.[190] This was the radicalizing role Komisarjevsky himself adopted when he worked in a similarly antique and tradition-laden context in England, in Stratford upon Avon. In life and in death, Komisarjevsky did not enjoy the same mythical artistic status as his sister (a status no doubt enhanced by her early demise), and this was clearly a frustration when he was looking to return to England during and just after the Second World War.[191] But he was charged with a similar revolutionary remit when appointed by Bridges-Adams to direct Shakespeare at the SMT and he achieved equally radical results with the then-unknown Chekhov at Barnes. As such his work kick-started reform in two extremes of British theatre society, prompting both Peter Brook to position his own work in an 'unbroken line' of Shakespearean innovation going back to Komis[192] and George Devine to claim long-term inspiration from him both for the London Theatre Studio and later for the Royal Court.[193]

While his importance as a director in the United States is more difficult to gauge, and he was certainly less productive stateside, there was still the residue of his sister's revolutionary spirit in productions like *Cymbeline,* which, as we have seen, Phillada Sewell fed into at a distance. In Russia, Komisarjevsky was always playing second fiddle to the more established 'mafia' of theatre directors: Stanislavsky, Meyerhold, Vakhtangov and Tairov. Not a single one of his productions is listed in Konstantin Rudnitsky's definitive: *Russian and Soviet Theatre: Tradition and Avant garde,* for instance, which sketches in detail the period Komisarjevsky was active in Moscow and Petersburg. Unlike his more feted contemporaries, Komis's challenge to tradition (and his importance as a director) was mainly achieved as an émigré.

Conclusion

It is fitting in the section above to have shifted attention once again to another significant female influence in Komisarjevsky's life and work, for while the main thrust of the section was to evaluate his impact and enduring legacy, it should now be evident that to make such an assessment without looking offstage to some of the figures who have not been given attention in the historiographies of Komisarjevsky is to misrepresent that legacy. The women in this chapter – Phillada Sewell, Lesley Blanch, Ernestine Stodelle, Margaret Webster, along with the indelible imprint of Vera Komissarzhevskaya – reveal a parallel set of histories to those alluded to by Norman Marshall in his biographical note: Komis as 'a great *metteur en scène*, an inspiring teacher, and a master of theatrical orchestration'.[194] Focusing on their micro-histories is not to devalue this assessment or to overclaim the influence of these lesser-known figures. That would simply return us to a causal tendentiousness that has been critiqued by many of the theatre historiographers quoted here. But to consider his directing, his scenography and his teaching *in the context of* the lives of a handful of female creative artists helps stress that cultural value and artistic impact are not achieved in a vacuum, nor are they best articulated in the essentialist biographical terms decried by Dennis Kennedy. Many of the women in Komisarjevsky's life, so often characterized as figures of untrammeled desire and unable to resist the 'come-and-seduce-me'[195] magnetism of the Russian director, were in fact implicated in the art works he was making in much more interesting ways.

Beyond the focus on these figures, Komisarjevsky is revealed in this chapter as an artist who was unafraid to champion the 'smaller' causes of regional and amateur theatre (in Leeds and in Holyhead, for example) while simultaneously occupying influential positions in the theatre establishment – in Moscow, at Stratford's soon-to-become Royal Shakespeare Company, in London's West End and in New York. He used this dual position (or it was used by others) to influence several arenas of related theatre activity – in mainstream education, in actor training, in modernist theatre design and in theatre philosophy and history. His legacy is clouded by his often caustic and sometimes volatile working relationships but still there remains a deep affection for him in the available literature – in the biographies of the many actors he influenced, for instance. Culturally, geographically and amorously 'entangled' as he was, there are several parallel narratives, some explicitly contradictory, which need to be constructed to capture his significance as a director and our approach in this chapter has been designed accordingly. But, influential complexity aside, there is a consistent thread running through Komisarjevsky's multifaceted career: the view that the director's responsibility, if not raison d'être, was to advance the cause of theatre as a medium of artistic invention. That belief informed his approach to the preparation of the actor – in both the formal and informal contexts of training he established. It defined his work as a designer or 'conductor' of the stage picture, sometimes stretching tradition to breaking point. It informed his multiple written outputs and it is threaded through the vast network of collaborations he fostered in his near-fifty-year career. That some of those collaborations were problematic bordering on the internecine, just as others bred lifelong creative relationships is a reminder that the affection people hold for directors is always conditional and the working relationships which surround them are at times as transitory as the art form itself.

3

Tyrone Guthrie

Roberta Barker and Tom Cornford

Introduction: The life and legacies of Tyrone Guthrie

FIGURE 3.1 *The main entrance to Jean Nouvel's 2006 Guthrie Theater, Minneapolis, MN. Photo by Craig Lassig, courtesy of AFP/Getty Images.*

From the first, William Tyrone Guthrie (1900–71) lived at the crossroads between multiple worlds. Depending on one's perspective, he was born into the last year of the nineteenth century or the first year of the twentieth; he grew up in the final days of the Victorian age, and in the early days of the modern era. On his father's side, he came from a long line of Scots Presbyterians, including numerous ministers of the Scottish Kirk; on his mother's side, he was descended from the popular nineteenth-century Irish actor Tyrone Power.[1] Guthrie himself was born in Tunbridge Wells; educated at Wellington College in Berkshire; and went up to St John's College, Oxford, in the final months of the First World War.[2] By the time he was knighted in 1961 and made an Honorary Fellow of his alma mater in 1964, he might have been said to embody the English establishment. By his own report, however, he had from boyhood 'an exaggerated regard for "originality," an exaggerated dislike of English upper-middle-class routine'.[3] His own closest identifications were with his Scots and Irish forbears, and in the very first pages of his autobiography he describes himself as a rebel.[4] These tensions – between English and non-English, between traditionalism and rebellion, between conservation and innovation – were to define his identity and his vocation as a director.

In the pages that follow, we argue that Guthrie's foremost contribution to the modern theatre lies in his elaboration of the complex position we now call that of the 'Artistic Director': the director who is also an administrator and leader of institutions. Over the course of his career, Guthrie served as Producer at the Old Vic Theatre, London (1933–4 and 1936–46) and later also as Administrator of the Old Vic and Sadler's Wells companies (1939–46), as well as being the founding director at the Stratford Festival in Ontario and the Guthrie Theatre in Minneapolis. His work at these and other major theatres was praised for its invention but also disparaged as 'gimmicky',[5] for Guthrie was a self-conscious innovator who longed to rethink and put his stamp on established classics and entrenched organizational models. Such choices were, we shall argue, nevertheless governed by a fundamentally conservative agenda: conservative insofar as Guthrie made such choices primarily to preserve the relevance, popularity, and cultural status of the dominant dramatic canon and of the theatres associated with it. He was an organizer as well as an artist: a theatre-maker who defied time-honoured norms to keep time-honoured norms in place. By making such choices, he helped both directly and indirectly to shape the policies of the subsidised, festival, and repertory theatres that still dominate the Anglo-North American scene.

Our analysis of Guthrie's career takes its cue from Ric Knowles's 'materialist semiotics',[6] which reads directing as a branch of middle-management working within a theatre shaped by a 'hermeneutic triangle' that encompasses the 'performance text', the 'conditions of [its] production', and the 'conditions of [its] reception'.[7] Knowles suggests that this methodology 'can complicate, intersect with, and enrich historical and historicized analysis':[8] an approach, we believe, that will prove particularly beneficial to those striving to understand Guthrie's working life. As we analyse his output, we consider the material conditions that helped Guthrie first to develop and then to consolidate many aspects of the director's and artistic director's role that have now become so established in the Anglo-North American theatre as to seem almost self-evident. We also offer in-depth case studies of specific, key productions in his career, showing how his directorial process both shaped and was shaped by the institutions and situations in which he worked.

A few preliminary words may serve to introduce the reader to the main milestones of this career, which we will analyse in more depth in the pages that follow. Tyrone Guthrie gained his first theatrical experience as an actor under the director James B. Fagan (1873–1933) at the Oxford University Dramatic Society: then, as now, the door into many stage careers. Though he went on to play some roles in the professional theatre, his physique and personality alike worked against a successful life as an actor: not only was he exceptionally tall (six feet five inches), but by his own report he had a 'cutting voice and an incurable tendency to emphasize the grotesque'.[9] Like many theatre-makers of his generation, he gained much of his early professional experience working in radio, taking on jobs as a writer, director, and administrator with the BBC in Belfast and in London, as well as with a Canadian National Railway-sponsored radio project in Montréal. He also worked as a director with the fledgling Scottish National Theatre Society, at the Festival Theatre in Cambridge and at the Westminster Theatre in London. His successes in these experiences led to his first key appointment: his ascent in 1933 to the position of Producer (that is, director of plays) at the Old Vic Theatre.

From this moment onward, though never uncontroversial, Guthrie's career as a theatrical producer, director, and administrator would be one of the most influential and wide-ranging of his generation. He directed in the West End, for the Royal Shakespeare Company (RSC), on Broadway, for the Habimah company in Tel Aviv, for the Swedish Theatre in Helsinki, and for the Edinburgh Festival. His close association with the plays of Shakespeare began in earnest in 1932 with his 'gossamer' production of *Love's Labour's Lost* at the Westminster Theatre,[10] which caught the attention of the Old Vic's Lilian Baylis (1874–1937). It continued at the Old Vic through critical successes such as an austere *Measure for Measure* (1933) and popular hits such as a picturesque neo-Victorian version of *A Midsummer Night's Dream* (1938). He directed multiple *Hamlet*s, with star actors such as Laurence Olivier (1936–7) and Alec Guinness (1938) as well as with young performers like George Grizzard (1963). He also brought new attention to lesser-known Shakespearean plays like *Henry VIII*, which he directed to great acclaim in Stratford-upon-Avon in 1949–50; *All's Well That Ends Well*, with which he helped to christen the Festival Theatre in Stratford, Ontario, in 1953; and *Troilus and Cressida*, which he offered in an excoriatingly sardonic modern dress version at the Old Vic in 1956. Still, he was not solely – or even primarily – a Shakespearean director. His career's highlights also included multiple masked, ceremonious productions of Sophocles's *Oedipus Rex* (Habimah Theatre, 1947–8; Helfingors Theatre, Helsinki, 1948; Festival Theatre, Stratford, Ontario, 1954); and numerous tender, witty productions of Chekhov's plays, from an early *Cherry Orchard* for the Festival Theatre in Cambridge (1930) to a string of lyrical late-career stagings in Minneapolis (*Three Sisters*, 1963; *The Cherry Orchard*, 1965; and *Uncle Vanya*, 1969). He directed successful premieres of new plays, including notably J.B. Priestley's *Dangerous Corner* (Lyric Theatre, London, 1932) and Thornton Wilder's *The Matchmaker* (Assembly Hall, Edinburgh, and Haymarket Theatre, London, 1954). He also helmed some famous flops, the most spectacular of which was the first production of Leonard Bernstein and Lillian Hellman's *Candide* (Martin Beck Theater, New York City, 1956). He directed operas, masques, operettas, and radio plays; his interests were wide, and his influence prodigious.

That influence, moreover, stretched well beyond the impact of specific productions, for Guthrie was a writer and mentor as well as a director. His numerous books, including among others *Theatre Prospect* (1932), *A Life in the Theatre* (1959), *A New Theatre* (1964), *In Various Directions* (1965) and *Tyrone Guthrie on Acting* (1971), affected the views of generations of theatre artists and critics. He collaborated with, and often nurtured the careers of, many of the greatest actors of his time: Sybil Thorndike (1882–1976), Edith Evans (1888–1976), John Gielgud (1904–2000), Laurence Olivier (1907–89), Flora Robson (1902–84), Alec Guinness (1914–2000), Charles Laughton (1899–1962), Jessica Tandy (1909–94), and many more. He also formed lasting partnerships with numerous designers and technicians, foremost among them the great English designer Tanya Moiseiwitsch (1914–2003), with whom he worked not only at the Old Vic and in Stratford-upon-Avon, but also in Canada and the United States. During the final decades of his career, Guthrie created perhaps his most permanent legacy by helping to found two new North American theatres: the Stratford Festival in Ontario and the Guthrie Theater in Minneapolis. In the last year of his life, he travelled to Australia to direct two of the plays that had meant most to him: *Oedipus Rex* in Sydney and *All's Well That Ends Well* in Melbourne. A traveller almost to the end, he nevertheless died at home, sitting in a wooden chair in his study on his estate at Annagh-ma-Kerrig in County Monaghan, Ireland. 'A great tree has fallen', remarked a family friend.[11]

Some efforts have been made to understand Guthrie's career in biographical terms, especially with reference to his sexuality. The actor Anthony Quayle, for example, declared that Guthrie preferred spectacle and facetiousness to sentiment and intimacy – 'Any demonstration of love between a man and a woman, or a boy and a girl, this embarrassed him. He couldn't direct such a scene' – because of his own personal inhibitions.[12] In the most sophisticated and convincing scholarly reading of Guthrie's career to date, Robert Shaughnessy links Guthrie's directorial practice not only to his hybrid Anglo-Scots-Irish identity, but also to his own conflicted sense of masculinity and his intimate relationship with his mother.[13] As Shaughnessy notes, this reading stretches back to James Forsyth's 1975 *Tyrone Guthrie: A Biography*, in which Guthrie is described in maternal terms 'not as a creative radical opposed to the forces of order and the law of the father, but as a diplomat and a conciliator':[14] a 'leader of men', but also 'a good listener, a good audience'.[15]

If biography can link Guthrie and his practice to the mother, however, it can also underline his paternalism. As a young director at the Festival Theatre in Cambridge, he programmed his friend James Bridie's play *Tobias and the Angel*; having done so, he gave it to Evan John to produce, choosing himself to play the part of the Archangel Raphael.[16] That decision was both personally and professionally revealing: Guthrie was in love with the young Flora Robson, who was making the transition from an amateur earning her living in a Shredded Wheat factory to professional acting in the Festival company.[17] It is tempting to see Guthrie positioning himself in a semi-paternal role as the producer-cum-Archangel looking adoringly down on the undiscovered actress, for whom he reportedly told Bridie to write another play during rehearsals for *Tobias and the Angel*. This same paternal strand would surface frequently throughout Guthrie's career. He was fond, for example, of retelling the story of successfully disciplining the star Marie Tempest during rehearsals for a 1935 production Robert Morley's *Short Story*.[18] By contrast, he rarely discussed such encounters with men, to whom he was, in any case, much more likely to defer. His tendency towards paternalism chimes, as we shall see, with his attitude towards North American culture, which he loved but also regularly and unthinkingly patronized.

Perhaps it is truest to say that in romance and sexuality, as in so much else, Guthrie was conflicted and contradictory. He proposed to Robson in 1930, but received an ambiguous response and the news that she would want children. Despite going on to become the 'father' of numerous theatres, Guthrie seems to have been uninterested in biological paternity, and the relationship did not develop. Nevertheless, the two would work together consistently for many years and Guthrie would name Robson, alongside Peggy Ashcroft, John Gielgud, Alec Guinness and Laurence Olivier as one of the greatest actors of his generation. In 1931, he married his sister Peggy's childhood friend, Judith Bretherton, and by his own account 'lived happily ever after'.[19] On the one hand, Guthrie emerges from this tale as a man whose love of the stage could easily overcome romantic disappointment; on the other hand, he also appears as a man who longed to escape the metropolitan cut and thrust of his working life and retreat to a home safely beyond its reach. Both of these attitudes – the love of the gifted 'star' and the desire to escape the metropolitan rat race – would shape Guthrie's professional practice.

To anyone wishing to understand that practice, an understanding of Guthrie's personality is even more crucial than a knowledge of his biography. He was intensely charismatic: charming, funny, energetic, authoritarian, sympathetic and commanding. He was also generous, a great listener, an astute observer of others and a genius when it came to instilling confidence in the insecure. His Canadian friend and collaborator, Robertson Davies, wrote that his 'greatest gift was not specifically theatrical; it was that power to discern what was best of each one of a group of widely differing people and to use them in a common cause, which is characteristic of great leaders in politics and the church'.[20] Guthrie's particular form of directorial greatness, for these contemporaries, consisted not only – perhaps not even primarily – in inspired artistic choices, but above all in the ability to build a vision based upon the gifts of his collaborators and then to convince them of their own ability to put that vision into practice. Born between eras and between nations, he would be a builder of bridges: an imaginer of new artistic roles and a preserver of old canons. For better and for worse, this powerful personality helped to shape twentieth-century theatre on multiple continents, and has left a legacy with which we are still grappling today.

Among theatre scholars and practitioners today, Guthrie is remembered above all for his contribution to theatre architecture. In 2011, the Association of British Theatre Technicians (ABTT) published a booklet entitled *The Guthrie Thrust Stage: A Living Legacy* for the Prague Quadrennial of Scenography and Theatre Architecture. It identifies Guthrie as one of the 'few geniuses [in "the rapidly evolving world of theatre architecture and scenography"] who have recast the theatre experience'.[21] The document was created with principal sponsorship from the ABTT and the RSC who, that year, opened their own remodelled three-sided auditorium in Stratford-upon-Avon. Its opening pages position a portrait of Guthrie opposite plan drawings of various three-sided auditoria, implicitly identifying him as their progenitor. The featured auditoria range from the 1948 layout of the Assembly Hall in Edinburgh (created for Guthrie's production of *Ane Satyre of the Thrie Estates*) through Stratford, Ontario (1957); Chichester (1962); Minneapolis (1963); the Vivian Beaumont Theater in New York City (1965); Perth, Australia (1969); the Young Vic in London (1970); the Sheffield Crucible (1971); the Olivier Theatre in London's National Theatre (NT) (1976); the Swan in Stratford-upon-Avon (1986); Shakespeare's Globe (1997); and the Royal Shakespeare Theatre (2011). Relatively few of these theatres, however, were founded directly by Guthrie; moreover, any viewer who thinks beyond a very basic notion of the 'thrust' stage will realize that their shaping principles differ wildly. The featured theatres represent a loose and multifarious movement in twentieth-century theatre architecture in which Guthrie played a part, rather than a singular legacy. We argue, therefore, that a focus on architectural impact as the defining characteristic of Guthrie's career is a flawed approach to his life and influence. Any account of Guthrie's status as a director that assumes that the thrust stage represents his major contribution will necessarily overlook his sophisticated use of other forms of staging, not to mention his work in other media, and his consistent dedication not only to staging plays, but to managing and administrating theatres.[22]

One key factor underpins not only all of the theatre buildings with which Guthrie was associated, but also, we argue, almost everything for which Guthrie strove in his professional life: the almost constant experience of existential crisis in which the mid-twentieth-century theatre found itself. Practitioners of many art forms experienced crises of representation during the years between the Great Depression and the cooling of Cold War relations in the late 1960s. In the case of the theatre, these were amplified by the incursions first of film and later of television into the availability of audiences for theatre and the careers of performers, writers and directors, as well as by the considerable expense of maintaining theatre buildings and mounting productions. Consequently, Guthrie (who was professionally active between 1926 and 1971) spent almost all of his working life attempting not so much to reform auditoria as to reconstruct theatre organizations to make them artistically vibrant and economically viable. This is not to assert that Guthrie's commitment to redesigning auditoria was insignificant, but that (as Gay McAuley has argued of theatrical space more generally), the rebuilding of theatres should be considered not only as the production of an 'aesthetic object', but as 'a complex social process'.[23] The social processes that produced, and were produced by, the building of the theatres listed above were indeed complex, but they were also underpinned by a simple project, to which Guthrie was consistently committed: the effort to preserve what he and his contemporaries saw as an intelligent and artistic, as opposed to opportunistically commercial, theatre from extinction. Ironically, this attempt is part of the reason for publications such as the ABTT booklet claiming to represent 'Guthrie's living legacy': capital projects to secure support for the physical reconstruction of theatres (such as the RSC's remodelling of its main house) have proved an effective way of sustaining the organizations they contain. Guthrie's role in the construction of theatre buildings must, then, be considered within the wider context of his work to construct sustainably funded, well-managed theatre organizations in order to secure the future of the art form, which he perceived as threatened by a combination of artistic negligence, market forces and the creation of new media for performance.

So, too, must Guthrie's work as a director of specific theatrical productions be recognized: work that was commonly described in his time as 'superbly inventive'.[24] Among those for whom the inventiveness of Guthrie's directing was self-evident were perhaps the two pre-eminent English theatre directors of the twentieth century: Peter Brook and Joan Littlewood. Guthrie was the only mainstream English director for whom

Littlewood ever expressed admiration,[25] and Brook describes respecting him 'almost to idolatry'.[26] He was also the only director named by Brook as an inspiration in a 2007 interview, where he placed him alongside Beckett and Shakespeare. In that interview, Brook lauded Guthrie's masterly handling of large groups in rehearsal at Covent Garden, as well as the pace and rhythm of his productions, specifically recalling his 1944 *Hamlet* starring the dancer Robert Helpmann: 'Suddenly *Hamlet* was the most exciting play.'[27]

Excitement was central to Guthrie's conception of the director's role: his cardinal rule was that one must not bore one's audience, a pitfall he associated strongly with productions that moved 'too slowly'.[28] He considered that the director used actors 'like a sculptor uses material' to generate both physical groupings and musical scores. In an uncontroversial articulation of the work of a director, Guthrie suggested that stage groupings should be arranged with characters 'in a meaningful relation to one another that says something about their situation and them'.[29] Less conventionally, however, he described using 'musical terminology [in rehearsals] all the time [...] to remind them that acting is music [... and] the spoken dialogue of a play is the score of an opera'.[30] Guthrie's assertion that the play-text should be considered a unified score whose rhythm, tone and dynamic are determined by a single vision was not unique, and indeed was shared by the other directors explored in this volume. However, given that he began his career as a director when the role was often not publicly recognized in the English theatre and worked in a mainstream Anglophone theatre that was (and often still is) conspicuously unwilling to see itself as a 'Director's Theatre', Guthrie's stance was unusually autocratic.

In fact, Guthrie repeatedly showed himself to be perfectly willing to assert the benefits of directorial control. In considering how to run a theatre, it would be 'better', he wrote, 'to risk the dangers of autocracy than of democracy or oligarchy; at worst there is always the sanction of the box office; at best there is hope of a Granville Barker, a Jacques Copeau, or a Diaghileff'.[31] The name of Max Reinhardt, the early twentieth century's most prominent European director, could be added to this list since Guthrie considered his productions the best he had seen.[32] Although all of these four directors functioned relatively autocratically, the inclusion of Barker and Copeau is revealing, as both sought at key points in their careers to establish ensemble companies and thereby to create theatre if not democratically then certainly collegially. Guthrie was not committed either politically or pragmatically to the idea of an ensemble, saying that 'I don't think committees can create anything'.[33] Even as he acknowledged his admiration for the autocratic Reinhardt, however, Guthrie professed himself unable to replicate Reinhardt's method of creating his highly patterned productions in isolation, notating even minute details in his *Regiebücher* (director's books). 'I have to work with the people,' said Guthrie; 'almost in every production I've done, I think most of the really best and most interesting ideas have been suggested by other people'.[34]

This was not a case of modesty (false or otherwise); Guthrie's biographer, James Forsyth, described him as a man with 'a gift for administration', and this is borne out by Guthrie's reflections on the work of directing.[35] He commonly described rehearsals as a matter of organization and management, asserting, for example, the fundamental importance of knowing that 'you've got the whole thing covered at least a week before the production', and emphasizing the director's responsibility for maintaining a good working environment: 'the atmosphere of the rehearsal must stem from the director'.[36] These observations anticipate a more recent turn, in academic studies of directing, towards a consideration of the director not so much as an artistic autocrat but as a branch of middle-management, responsible for mediating between industrial imperatives on the one hand and artistic instincts on the other, and for organizing, ideally by consent, the work of a large number of collaborating workers. In the words of Dennis Kennedy:

> Trade issues like systems of finance, theatre organization, actor training and unionization, along with shifting audience majorities and the incursions of mass media, all of these establish the base on which the superstructure of directing must operate.[37]

Following Kennedy, Simon Shepherd has suggested that 'perhaps [...] the most significant aim and impact of the newly emerged role of director were that it assumed to itself the duty of *organising theatrical activity*'.[38] It would be hard to find a director whose career is more thoroughly compatible with Shepherd's tentative definition of the role than Tyrone Guthrie.

Even at the very start of his directorial career, Guthrie was acutely aware of the crucial significance of organization as both the conceptual and practical basis for his work. His 1932 book *Theatre Prospect* has been described somewhat dismissively as a prediction of 'the impending demise of bourgeois civilisation', 'the death of naturalism' and 'a new avant-garde founded on [...] the classics', and it is indeed somewhat impetuous and declamatory in tone.[39] It may, however, be read quite differently. Guthrie begins by describing the stage as a fireplace: it illuminates the spectators and is illuminated by their attention. He asserts that 'it is this relation between the stage and the audience that constitutes the essence of "Theatre"' and that 'this relation is reciprocal'.[40] Even so, he moves very quickly on from theorizing to organizing, declaring that 'if an intelligent theatre is to survive it can only be by carefully planned organisation, not only behind the curtain but in front as well'.[41] Guthrie also rejects any idealistic separation of art and finance (with art organized 'behind the curtain' and finance 'in front'). Instead, he describes the purpose of organization 'in front' as both 'financial and artistic: to fill the house, and to fill it with the kind of people who want the kind of play that is being produced'.[42] From this moment on, 'organisation' becomes an operative term in the book, explicitly featuring in a third of its chapters, and driving its project:

Those who wish for the continuance of a serious theatre will be obliged to face the necessity for organisation; to face the fact that unless the public for serious plays organises itself to form some scheme for both the production and the attendance of such plays, the Theatre of Ideas will have to put up the shutters once and for all.[43]

By the 'Theatre of Ideas', Guthrie seems simply to mean a not-for-profit theatre committed to the staging of literary, canonical and largely classical, plays. His commitment to this ideal leads him to dedicate himself, in subsequent pages, to the analysis of various models for what would now be called 'audience development', which seek to mitigate the risk of a purely commercial venture. These models include subscriptions, the selling of season tickets and theatre clubs. Guthrie favoured season tickets and advocated reducing expenditure on marketing to limit costs and reduce pressure on their sale, proposing instead a more informal network of communication that would leverage existing networks of amateur theatrical societies and the British Drama League. Thirty years later, the Guthrie Theater in Minneapolis would adopt a similarly canny approach to publicity, depending upon what Guthrie called 'wealthy women with nothing to do' but to phone their social circles and nag them into purchasing tickets.[44]

Theatre Prospect's attitude to the artistic side of directing is similarly pragmatic. It proposes two alternatives for the production of classic plays, 'the most conscientious possible reproduction of the original' or the application of 'a contemporary viewpoint and the best available contemporary technique to the play', before concluding that 'in practice, of course, a compromise between the two must be adopted'.[45] Guthrie is also clear-sighted about the limitations placed upon experimentation by technique:

Any attempt to break wholly away from the current naturalistic convention requires on the part of the director, not only sufficient originality to invent a new means of expression, but sufficient executive technique to make a new means of expression intelligible to the public.[46]

Again, Guthrie moves quickly to organization, proposing 'no "star salaries"', 'long contracts', 'long association [...] with the same producer' and 'a school attached to the theatre' as well as 'the training of dramatic authors',[47] so as to create the conditions for successful experimental work:

It is only by familiarity with prevailing conventions that the foundations can be laid for experiment. And a theatre will only be able to achieve valuable experimental work when author, designer, director, and actors are all working in close co-operation in a technique that they have evolved together.[48]

This aspect of Guthrie's work aligns him closely with pioneers of the Studio movement such as Barker and Copeau.[49] It even echoes closely ideas that would be much more radically articulated in the UK by Joan Littlewood. She expressed admiration for Guthrie's work but stopped short of endorsing him, complaining that 'he didn't try to change the world'.[50] She was right: the fundamental conservatism of *Theatre Prospect* continued throughout his career.

Guthrie's conservatism was not simplistic, however. Robert Shaughnessy has argued persuasively that he was at his directorial best when plays' neglected or unknown status gave him the freedom to reform them.[51] He sought the freedom to be at least a little radical, but he used that freedom to fundamentally conservative ends. If he sought out abandoned plays, he did not do so to challenge or to overhaul the canon, but to broaden and sustain its appeal, and thereby to reassert its value and extend its reach. Recalling the appeal of working as director of the Old Vic in 1933, Guthrie cited two reasons: its 'classical repertoire' and its 'anti-metropolitan' situation (though it is hard to believe today, the pre-war Old Vic was certainly not a 'London theatre' in the same sense as those in the West End).[52] Opening the Guthrie Theater thirty years later, he followed the same principles, choosing Minneapolis, in part, because of its distance from the metropolitan hub of American theatre in New York, and creating a programme founded on the classics. The thirty years that separated these two directorial ventures had taught Guthrie a great deal. He had, in fact, used them to develop a modus operandi that continues to shape the work of almost all artistic directors in the Anglophone theatre today. The nature and scope of the role of the artistic director, and its imbrication with the structure and function of mainstream theatre organizations today, is, we will argue, Guthrie's most significant legacy.

In the two core sections that follow, we delve more deeply into Guthrie's work as it both influenced, and was influenced by, the social and theatrical world that surrounded him. We do not divide his **Art** from his **Importance**, but rather consider them side by side, for we agree with Knowles that the artistic choices reflected in a performance text are always shaped not only by the conditions of its production but also by those of its reception, and that '"meaning" in a given performance situation – the social and cultural work done by the performance, its performativity, and its force – is the effect of all of these systems and of each pole of the interpretative triangle working dynamically and relationally together'.[53] A similar logic determines our division of the analysis that follows into two main parts: 'Guthrie in the UK' and 'Guthrie in North America'. Because the conditions of production and reception that shaped Guthrie's work in Britain were so different from those that affected it in Canada and the United States, we consider these periods of his career separately, focusing on his negotiations with emerging UK institutions and funding bodies in the first section, and on his fraught relationship with the legacy of settler colonialism in the second. The key productions we analyse in depth are not always the most exquisite – or even the most celebrated – examples of Guthrie's work in each place and period;

rather, we focus upon works that exemplify the inextricability of Guthrie's *mises en scène* from the theatre institutions in which they were staged and the audiences for whom they were performed. Whether helming the Old Vic during the Second World War or building a new theatre in Cold War-era Minneapolis, Guthrie was formed by the material and historical conditions of the world into which he was born: a modern world struggling between old and new, between preservation and destruction, between values of commercial success and values of 'high' art. Guthrie embodied that world's contradictions, and in that embodiment remains richly worthy of our attention.

Guthrie's Art and Importance, part 1: The United Kingdom

Learning to produce, 1926–33

The years 1926 and 1933 saw Guthrie's first 'big breaks'. In 1926, he was offered a contract to direct for the Scottish National Theatre Troupe. This job, which he accepted as an inexperienced recent graduate, set him on a path to one of the British theatre's most prestigious roles. On 26 January 1933, he was offered the contract of Producer (that is, director of plays) to the Shakespeare Company at the Old Vic by the theatre's manager, Lilian Baylis. The terms of his engagement stipulated that 'the producer's whole time belongs to the Vic', and that he would be responsible for 'selecting plays and artists' and creating productions for a season that would run from September 1933 until June 1934. Guthrie was 32, and becoming well known as a producer, having already enjoyed a rather varied career. After graduating from Oxford, he had worked in radio, editing scripts and directing radio dramas for the BBC and the Canadian National Railways. He had also written plays for the radio, and had begun to make a name for himself in the theatre, directing first for the Scottish National Theatre Troupe (1926–7), and then, in 1929 and 1930, at the Festival Theatre in Cambridge before moving to the Westminster Theatre in London in 1931. Guthrie's work in this period was by no means always successful. His radio plays, in particular, had not been sufficiently well received to suggest that he had a future as a writer. But he had learned the ropes and served an informal apprenticeship, an approach he would later advocate for would-be playwrights, whom he encouraged 'to come and work in a theatre' because 'that's how all the great playwrights have learned their craft [...] without exception'.[54] Whether or not that final assertion carries any weight is less significant than what it tells us about Guthrie's own approach to his work. He regularly stressed the significance of technical knowledge in all branches of theatre, and his early career was characterized by its acquisition.

Guthrie's period at the Festival Theatre was inevitably influenced by what he described as the 'good dose of avant-garde theatre' it had already received under Terence Gray (1895–1986), whose anti-realist interventions into theatrical production had been strongly influenced by Edward Gordon Craig. Gray's ideas are recorded in his 1926 book *Dance-Drama: Experiments in the Art of the Theatre*, where he attempts to imagine into existence a theatre where,

> freed from all the trammels of bureaucratic interference and commercial competition, dramatic artists and all artists of the theatre would be at liberty under almost ideal conditions to practise their art [...] for the benefit of a public who knew where to go in order to satisfy its interest and who would increase in ever-widening circles until the drama became once more a national and popular enthusiasm.

Gray's utopian theatre is a product not only of symbolism and expressionism, but also of technology. He particularly notes the significance of early-twentieth-century developments in lighting for the theatre, which enabled producers of plays to think beyond the dominance of text and the spoken word and to consider the stage's plastic and dynamic possibilities as expressive means on a par with the script.

These ideas were clearly important to Guthrie's development as a producer. He recorded in *Theatre Prospect* that 'a great change was wrought in production by the fact that movement – crosses, exits, entrances, and all business – was now conditioned by the new stage settings'.[55] Guthrie quickly developed a reputation for his skilled and inventive use of movement, particularly that of crowds, that he would retain for the duration of his career. He also firmly believed that the future of the theatre would not be found in naturalistic dramas dominated by the spoken word. However, Guthrie was not required, while in Cambridge, simply to serve Gray's legacy. He reported having 'an almost completely free hand on the artistic side', and his memories of producing at the Festival Theatre focus largely upon the pragmatic realities of learning to handle the theatre's technologies:

> Professionally, I learned during this time how to put a performance together inside the limits of a very hurried schedule. [...] Technically, my range was being broadened, partly by the wide variety and style of the plays, partly by the design of the Festival Theatre ... [which] was almost unworkable for a realistic play. [...] Moreover, Terence Gray had bequeathed to us the services of a really brilliant electrician, Mr Steen, who taught me a great deal.[56]

In spite of his success while at Cambridge with, for example, the anti-realist *Six Characters in Search of an Author* (1929), it seems that Guthrie considered his experience there more valuable as practical training in what

Knowles identifies as the 'conditions of [theatrical] production'[57] than as an induction into the aesthetic ideologies with which the theatre had become associated.

Guthrie's success in Cambridge took him, in 1931, to London's Westminster Theatre, which was opened by Anmer Hall (1863–1953), who had also managed the Festival Theatre. Guthrie chose, for his London debut, James Bridie's *The Anatomist*, which had opened in Edinburgh in 1930.[58] It starred the established Edwardian actor Henry Ainley alongside Flora Robson, whose name was made in the press by her performance. The *Times* announced that she 'carries off all the honours'.[59] Guthrie was pleased but somewhat frustrated by Ainley, reporting privately that, in spite of being 'reasonable, patient and polite', 'he's not intelligent: he doesn't understand what things mean. He's carried through by a wonderful, wonderful God-given bel aire – and his voice is a fine organ'.[60] This implicit attempt to reconcile the legacy of grand, late-Victorian acting (in theatres that absolutely required a strong voice) and the pleasant demeanour of Edwardian style with the intellectual demands of the new, modernist theatre of the 1920s would run through Guthrie's career. His productions' skilled and dramatic handling of crowds and larger-than-life central performances harkened back to the Victorian theatre, while his willingness to make bold directorial interventions, his penchant for strikingly realistic touches and his experimentation with open stages all derived from the scenographic experimentation of the interwar period. Guthrie's next production at the Westminster, a return to Pirandello's *Six Characters in Search of an Author*, productively exploited that tension in his work, combining contemporary absurdism and the opportunity for inventive production with heightened theatricality and bravura performance. It gave both Guthrie and Robson another well-publicized success.

During this period, Guthrie was fortunate in having Hall as a manager. He later described his regime as 'a rich management which was not primarily interested in money but in doing something of significance'.[61] We might expect Guthrie to have considered this a benefit, but, in fact, his reflections in *Theatre Prospect* show that he was not satisfied with dependence upon beneficent patronage of the kind offered by Hall. Even when matched with a degree of box office success, he did not believe that it could secure the theatre's future. Nonetheless, it was thanks to Hall's support that Guthrie achieved his first commercial hit in the form of J.B. Priestley's play *Dangerous Corner*, which he directed in 1932, with Robson starring, at the Lyric Theatre in the West End, where it ran successfully.

All of these experiences combined, by 1933, to make Guthrie an obvious choice for Baylis's producer. He had a strong understanding of dramaturgical structure and substantial experience of both traditional and experimental stagecraft. He was young and energetic, but also an authoritative figure, not least thanks to his towering height and somewhat aristocratic bearing. All of this prepared him admirably for a job loosely defined in Brander Matthews's 1914 book *On Acting* by the need 'to know how the play should be acted in every part' and the ability to 'suggest to the several performers the various effects they are to accomplish'.[62] But the years between 1933 and the end of the war in 1945 saw Guthrie shift from this role towards a prototypical version of the position of 'director' that would come to dominate the post-war theatre. Even late in Guthrie's career the job title 'Director' did not have the secure meaning it carries today. In the early 1960s, for example, Peter Hall was 'Director' of the RSC in the sense that he might have been 'Director' of any business: he was ultimately responsible for the company's strategy, financial regulation, personnel management and so on. Even so, Guthrie's activities in the pre-war and wartime periods, mainly but not exclusively at the Old Vic, would set the mould for the role of 'Artistic Director' in the post-war subsidised UK theatre in which he would hardly work, but which he was instrumental in establishing.

From producer to director, 1933–45

Guthrie's 1933–34 season at the Old Vic was described by its previous producer, Harcourt Williams, as the opening of 'a kind of flood-gate': 'it was drastic, but, taking a long view, probably the best thing to do'.[63] Guthrie brought the film star Charles Laughton into the company with his wife Elsa Lanchester, to play alongside leading actors such as Leon Quartermaine, Flora Robson and Athene Seyler in productions of *Twelfth Night*, *The Cherry Orchard*, *Henry VIII*, *Measure for Measure*, *Love for Love*, *The Tempest*, *The Importance of Being Earnest* and *Macbeth*. At their best, Guthrie's productions contained the 'brilliant effects' of staging for which he was already well known, such as 'hosts of men armed with tall spears flooding over the built-up sides of his set' at the climax of *Macbeth*.[64] At their worst, they appeared opportunistic, as in Guthrie's attempt to profit, by staging *Henry VIII*, from Laughton's appearance in the film *The Private Life of Henry VIII*, which offered opportunities for character acting that Shakespeare's play was finally found to be lacking. In all, the season was markedly more commercial than had been the case in previous years at the Old Vic, attracting notably greater press attention and many more West End theatregoers, principally thanks to the presence of Laughton. But Baylis's opposition to the West End and its values, as well as the mixed reception of Guthrie's productions, led to the non-renewal of Guthrie's contract for the 1934–5 season. He returned to the commercial theatre, directing in the West End in 1935 and, the following year, on Broadway. Although Guthrie's productions of this period were for the most part frankly commercial, they had mixed success at the box office: on Broadway, *Call It a Day* by Dodie Smith ran for six months, while a revival of Jay Mallory's *Sweet Aloes* closed after only twenty-four performances.[65]

Guthrie had not abandoned the artistic theatre. In late 1935, he revived his staging of Auden's *The Dance of Death*, which he had directed for the Group Theatre (1932–9, 1950–6) for two performances in February and March 1934. Led by the actor Ormerod Greenwood and the dancer Rupert Doone (1903–66), the Group Theatre was a short-lived attempt to establish an experimental collective in the UK on a continental European model. Guthrie's conversations with Doone had informed his assertions in *Theatre Prospect* about the value of reviving English folk dance both in performance and training, and Guthrie had been involved with the Group Theatre from its beginnings in 1932.[66] He worked jointly with Doone, composer Herbert Murrill and a large chorus to bring what Michael Sidnell describes as Auden's '"epic" construction' to the stage, creating a 'strongly sequential choreographic, verbal and scenic montage ... without benefit of plot'.[67] Sidnell notes that 'Guthrie was in his element directing a large company in an intricate sequence of movement and song, though quite out of it as far as the political theme was concerned'.[68] Indeed, Guthrie never again returned to such an overtly political text as Auden's, which combined the agitprop techniques employed by companies such as Ewan MacColl and Joan Littlewood's Theatre of Action (the pre-war forerunner of Theatre Workshop) with the expressionist movement seen in London performances by companies such as the Ballets Jooss and Michel Saint-Denis's Compagnie des Quinze. He would, however, return to the morality play structure and pageant-like presentation of *The Dance of Death*, albeit in a far more conservative vein, in his 1947 production of *Ane Satyre of the Thrie Estates* at the Edinburgh Festival. Not only does this process of adaptation chime with Guthrie's brand of innovative conservatism, but it foreshadows the post-war phenomenon of the commercial exploitation of radical aesthetic tropes, as seen – for instance – in Sean Kenny's adaptation of the Brechtian aesthetic he had developed with John Bury at Theatre Workshop during the 1950s in his design for *Oliver!* (1960). But that trend was yet to come. At the end of 1936, Guthrie found himself caught between a commercial theatre he considered unreliable and of questionable value, and an experimental theatre whose politics were substantially more radical than his own and which was constantly threatened with collapse.

Ironically, given his 1933–4 Old Vic season that, in the words of Harcourt Williams, 'shook the traditions and outlook of the building to its foundations', the compromised position somewhere between the commercial and art theatres in which Guthrie now found himself was notably well aligned with the values of Lilian Baylis's Old Vic. Its policy of providing a socially diverse audience with high-quality productions of Shakespeare at an affordable price combined a traditional, conservative sense of canonicity with innovation and populism while also demanding dynamic productions, all of which resonated clearly with Guthrie's strengths as a producer. In 1936, then, he returned to the Old Vic, but, as Robert Shaughnessy notes, with 'extensive powers over the company organization and repertory system'.[69] These he used, in the first instance, to allow himself to continue to direct commercially and to commercialize the Vic's policies, in particular doing away with its repertory Shakespeare Company. These changes were summarized in an anonymous editorial for the *Vic-Wells* magazine in autumn 1936: 'Plays to run as long as they attract but not longer than eight weeks; the best available cast for each new production.'[70]

'Extraordinary flashes': *Hamlet,* 1936 and 1938

When Guthrie decided, in 1936, to stage the first of his four productions of *Hamlet*, he was indeed free to look for the 'best available cast'. Since Harcourt Williams's 1930 Old Vic production, John Gielgud had effectively owned the Prince's role on the British stage. Gielgud's Hamlet had been phenomenally successful with critics as well as with members of the acting profession and the public. James Agate called it 'the high water-mark of English Shakespearean acting of our time'; the foremost Shakespearean actor of the generation before Gielgud's, Dame Sybil Thorndike, described it 'Hamlet played as in one's dreams'; and its popularity with the public enabled a transfer to the West End's Queen's Theatre, where it played in a slightly abridged version.[71] Guthrie responded to this situation with characteristic brio, casting Laurence Olivier in the role. Gielgud's 1935 production of *Romeo and Juliet*, in which he had alternated the roles of Romeo and Mercutio with Olivier halfway through the run, had established the two young stars as polar opposites in acting terms. Where Gielgud, according to Agate, performed Mercutio's 'Queen Mab' speech 'exquisitely' and greeted his death with 'a smile which is all benison',[72] Olivier gave a reading of the part that W.A. Darlington described as 'full of zest, humour and virility'.[73] The opposition between their Romeos was similarly marked: Gielgud's 'romantic' rendition had 'a much greater sense of the beauty of the language' than Olivier's 'impetuosity' in the role allowed.[74] Later in life, Olivier would relate his comparative failure as Romeo positively:

> I was the outsider and John was the jewel, and a shining one, too – deservedly so. John still has the most beautiful voice, but I felt in those days he allowed it to dominate his performances. […] His voice, of course, was musical enough to sell his performance to the people on the old grounds. He was giving the familiar tradition fresh life, whereas I was completely disregarding the old in favour of something new. Somehow I feel that he was a little led by the nose by his audience and by his acolytes. He was greatly admired, in fact adored, and like all of us at some time in our careers he believed his publicity. So by the time we did Romeo, I was considered by the Establishment to be his opponent. Everybody was in his favour, while I might have been from another planet.[75]

Olivier's reputation as a reckless and virile modernizer must have occurred to Guthrie as he considered how to approach Hamlet; he decided to cast Olivier and to give the headstrong young star his head. Olivier recalled that Guthrie praised his make-up before the first night as 'every inch a Hamlet' (see Figure 3.2), warning his leading actor that 'they'll probably fault you for the verse speaking, and to a certain extent they may be right, but I expect you will come to your own decisions about that in your own good time'.[76]

This willingness to allow Olivier to follow his instincts defined the production much more than the preparatory work Guthrie and his Hamlet had done by visiting the psychoanalyst Ernest Jones to discuss his 1923 essay 'Hamlet and Oedipus'. Their discussions with Jones did set the pattern for Olivier's 1948 film of the play, which is obsessively Freudian in its scenography, with Hamlet probing the passageways and staircases of his own consciousness and mounting his mother on a conspicuously vulval bed.[77] Conversely, critics of Guthrie's 1936 *Hamlet* remained, as Robert Shaughnessy notes, 'universally unaware of the production's Oedipal dynamics and much more impressed by Olivier's astounding athleticism, vigour and masculinity'.[78] Later in life, Guthrie was caught between praise for Olivier's 'protean [...] attack' and 'displayey sort of art which I personally find endearing' and the nagging sense that this 'talent' was ill-suited for Hamlet: 'I don't think he was well cast as Hamlet, I didn't like his movie of *Hamlet* at all, but this was a performance of extraordinary flashes.'[79] In fact, the critic J.C. Trewin felt that Guthrie 'played up to' Olivier, allowing him exceptionally free rein: 'I don't say it was Shakespeare's Hamlet, but it was terrifically exciting.'[80] Some of the production's flourishes were considered excessive. Harcourt Wiliams thought Olivier 'a shade too acrobatic', and felt that Gertrude plummeting from a rostrum to her death was unnecessarily distracting.[81] Nonetheless, both Guthrie and his star would go on to repeat these tricks many times. Olivier appropriated the death-leap in his film of *Hamlet*, swinging from a balcony to kill Laertes, and in his 1959 Stratford *Coriolanus*, when his death was staged as a spectacular dive, head-first towards the stage, from which he was rescued by being caught by the ankles. Guthrie used the fall again in his 1963 Minneapolis *Hamlet*, with Laertes collapsing into the waiting arms of courtiers.[82]

The Guthrie/Olivier *Hamlet* is now best known, however, for its June 1937 transfer to a courtyard inside Kronborg Castle in Helsingør, Denmark. There, its opening night was threatened by torrential rain, leaving Olivier and Guthrie to restage it, at the last minute, in the ballroom of the Marienlyst Hotel. The success of this improvised staging, with the audience on three sides of the action, subsequently helped to shape Guthrie's arguments for the power of the open stage: 'at its best moments, that performance in the ballroom related the audience to a Shakespeare play in a different and, I thought, more logical, satisfactory and effective way than can ever be achieved in a theatre of what is still regarded as orthodox design'.[83]

FIGURE 3.2 *Laurence Olivier in Tyrone Guthrie's* Hamlet *(1936): the young star graces the cover of* Play Pictorial. *Image courtesy of Getty Images.*

In spite of that retrospectively narrated realization, Guthrie's next *Hamlet*, staged at the Old Vic in 1938 with Alec Guinness in the title role, betrayed no obvious interest in exploring an unorthodox relationship between audience and stage. Guthrie seems, instead, to have taken his cue from

Barry Jackson's 1925 contemporary-dress staging of the play in London and Birmingham, creating one of the earliest examples of the modern dress Shakespeare that would become a recurrent feature of his work. Later in life, Guthrie reflected that Guinness's talent was on a 'smaller scale' than that of Olivier and Gielgud, so perhaps the decision to use a contemporary staging was taken to play to his leading actor's strengths.[84] In any case, these two *Hamlet*s set the pattern for a career as interpretively pragmatic as it was theatrically inventive. Guthrie did not restage the play at Elsinore in response to a theory of the open stage, but as a practical reaction to weather conditions. He did not give the young Olivier freedom – or clothe the young Guinness in modern dress – because he thought it would produce a definitive Hamlet, any more than he staged Gertrude tumbling to her death because it provided the perfect climax to the character's development. He made these decisions in response to his audience's expectations, hoping to thrill but not to disconcert.

Guthrie and his funders: Forging alliances

A no less dramatic death than Gertrude's, that of Lilian Baylis on the opening night of Olivier's Old Vic *Macbeth* in November 1937, put Guthrie in overall control of the company. He officially became administrator of both the Vic and its sister opera and ballet companies at Sadler's Wells in 1939. Guthrie's period as administrator of the Vic-Wells companies would become most significant for his role in developing the close collaboration between the Vic-Wells organization and the Council for the Encouragement of Music and the Arts (CEMA), which had been established by a royal charter in 1940 to provide public funding for the arts for the first time. CEMA was quite open about its unusual commitment to the Old Vic as a vehicle for delivering its goal of 'the best for the most', a mission that underpins public funding of the arts to this day. In a short article included in the programme for Old Vic Tours during the war, Ivor Brown, CEMA's Drama Director, states openly that '[i]n the sphere of professional drama, CEMA has worked mainly through the "Old Vic", the reasons are obvious. The Old Vic's standards of performance are unquestionably high, and its policy has always been that of CEMA [...] a theatre that appealed to all and kept nobody out who had a few coppers to spend'.[85] The article goes on to stress both the quality of artistic experience and the value for money offered by this arrangement ('so economically and successfully does it work that the calls [on CEMA guarantees against loss] have so far been very small'), and concludes by presenting the success of CEMA support for Old Vic touring as a clarion call for a National Theatre:

> No theatre is really national or really popular unless it gives the nation
> and the people a chance to see if they like it. The essential conditions of

such a theatre are excellence, mobility and cheapness ... The 'Old Vic' has a tradition of the big achievement and the small price. The war has added mobility, and that quality, once discovered will not, I am sure, be abandoned. When the 'Old Vic' returns to its London headquarters after the war, it will remember to re-visit the friends it is now making. Having made an important production in London, it will not allow that to be wastefully thrown aside when a new piece is wanted, but will see that it goes on tour and is widely enjoyed. That, in my opinion, is the proper function of a truly National Theatre, to link the capital with the counties, while it links the present with the past by building a programme in which the modern drama is interwoven with the classic.

This rhetoric was echoed almost to the letter at the end of 1941 by the Old Vic's managing director, Reginald Rowe, speaking on behalf of the Old Vic's governors in the annual report of the Old Vic and Sadler's Wells companies who asserted that 'our work in the provinces must continue'. Quoting Guthrie, Rowe declared that

[t]he gifts that the Vic and Wells can bring must no longer be reserved for the metropolis, but scattered as widely as possible over a land that is evidently ready and eager to receive them. [...] [W]e are learning how to expand, so that in future London may see not less of our companies, but the provinces far more.[86]

Here, Guthrie the pragmatic administrator, already so evident in *Theatre Prospect*, is joined by Guthrie the visionary, anti-metropolitan conservative who would, only a decade or so later, be equally attracted to the idea of establishing a North American theatre away from the centres of power and influence on that continent.

From October 1942, Guthrie shared the role of administrator of the Vic-Wells Companies with the commercial manager Bronson Albery, who made it possible for both companies to use the New Theatre for London seasons, an arrangement that persisted until the reopening of the renovated Old Vic Theatre in 1947. Albery also took on the management of the ballet company. Again, we can see in this decision Guthrie's willingness to experiment in the name of tradition, an instinct that would go on substantially to shape the post-war title of artistic director that would be modelled substantially on Guthrie's activities during this period. It would, of course, also be true to say that Guthrie's position was fortuitous, and that the role of artistic director emerged more as a consequence of the matrix of influences from CEMA, the governors of the Old Vic and Sadlers Wells, and the public demand for consoling and fortifying renditions of dependable classics than as a result of his individual agency. Yet there was not a lengthy queue of highly qualified alternative candidates for the role. The actor Lewis Casson had produced plays at the Vic before the war, and was instrumental, along with his wife, the actress Dame Sybil Thorndike, to the success of the CEMA tours. But Casson was well into his sixties by this time and showed none of Guthrie's flair for leadership. Guthrie also noted himself that his priorities shifted during this period: 'I did a certain amount of production because man-power was so short, but as far as possible, I got other people to do the producing because I was occupied with the arranging.'[87]

Archival records from the wartime Old Vic provide clues as to Guthrie's success in 'arranging'. In his own introduction to the Vic-Wells Annual Report for 1941–2, Guthrie describes 'a period when values have had to be revised, old methods scrapped, new ones improvised'.[88] He is open about the challenges of touring, stating publically that '[t]hese tours have been difficult to organise, a tussle for the performers and they can never be commercially profitable'. Furthermore, in private correspondence with CEMA, he can be found arguing against touring to too many small rural venues on the grounds that it is excessively debilitating, and advocating longer contracts for 'a substantial nucleus of the personnel', as well as improved pay. In all, these documents show Guthrie as a skilled manager and political operator. On the one hand, he writes to company member Herbert Marshall to chastise him for expressing left-wing views in association with the Old Vic and CEMA, insisting upon steering 'absolutely clear of politics' rather than risking 'losing [the Vic's] Charity Commission charter'.[89] On the other hand, Guthrie was himself deeply embroiled in politics. He wrote to the governors in June 1942 to advocate closer association with CEMA so as to prevent exposing 'state-subsidy-to-the-theatre to the severe risk of being jettisoned in the first, enthusiastic economies of a post-war parliament' by building up 'CEMA's body of achievement'.[90] He is also regularly to be found in private correspondence with the highest officials at CEMA. He wrote to Ivor Brown, its first drama director, in July 1942 to congratulate him on being made Editor of the *Observer*, and ask 'who the hell will replace you at CEMA?' (his flattery disguised a genuine and urgent question), and to put on paper 'what I don't suppose I shall be able to say: thank you for much help and advice and backing during the period of our alliance'.[91]

Guthrie's close and informal relationships with CEMA went higher still. When he left the Vic in 1944, he left behind him, as requested in 'an informal conversation' with CEMA's chair, Lord Keynes, a 'Policy for Old Vic Drama', explicitly distinct from 'a plan or plans for individual productions'. The policy was broken down into five sections: Theatre, Repertory Policy, Staff, Company and Finance.[92] 'Theatre' describes the policy to install the Old Vic Company at the New Theatre, with a larger theatre or theatres being found for the Opera and Ballet companies. 'Repertory' outlines a plan based on eight productions per year, with three available for performance in rotation at any one time. The repertory should always include plays from the following categories: 'a Shakespearean or Elizabethan play', a British play of the period from the Restoration to the nineteenth century, a 'classical play of other nations' and 'a modern and, where possible, a new play'. In short,

Guthrie's plan charts a repertory that would characterize those of the large, subsidised theatres that emerged in the 1960s both in the UK and abroad, and that remains familiar to audiences at London's Royal National Theatre today. Under 'Staff', the plan names director John Burrell as the putative 'Director of Drama', supported by an 'Advisory Panel' including Laurence Olivier and Ralph Richardson. Again, this structure remains common today, with an 'Artistic Director' taking responsibility for the output of major, subsidised theatres with the support of 'Associate Directors' or 'Associate Artists', who typically direct or perform in certain productions and advise the artistic director about programming and artistic policy in general. The plan also stipulates a company of 'about 15 artists' employed for 48 weeks of each year and supported by other actors, engaged as necessary. Though this company is substantially smaller than the NT and RSC companies of the early 1960s, it offers the same model of employment that those theatres would go on to use. The plan concludes by acknowledging that 'the scheme would be expensive', while noting that 'CEMA is prepared for ambitious proposals'. Guthrie's success in arranging such proposals subsequently made him the obvious choice to advise the Australian government about a possible National Theatre, and, as we shall see, to establish major new theatres in post-war North America.[93] In Knowles's terms, Guthrie's plan also represents a brokered compromise between the expectations that condition the reception of plays by their audiences and the practical and financial pressures that shape the conditions of their production, one that has continued to influence the management and funding of theatres into the twenty-first century.

When Guthrie left the Old Vic in 1944, leadership of the company was handed to the actors Laurence Olivier and Ralph Richardson, who led productions that toured internationally. Despite their high-profile success, however, neither they nor their co-director, John Burrell, made a success of the Vic as an organization. They were responsible for establishing the Old Vic Centre, run jointly by Michel Saint-Denis, George Devine and Glen Byam Shaw, but this effort to run a theatre school, touring company and experimental theatre at the Vic never sat happily alongside the Old Vic company and inevitably lost the support of the governors before ending disastrously in 1951 amidst an embarrassing public airing of resentment and recrimination.[94] When the collapse of the Old Vic Centre threatened the company's future, it was to Guthrie that they again turned. He came back to the company for just a year, taking the characteristically pragmatic decision to engage the popular, if somewhat untameable, Donald Wolfit for a season in which he played Tamburlaine. Robert Shaughnessy observes of that production, of which Guthrie remained proud, that an 'unobtrusive stage direction ("One brings a map" [5.3.125]') cued the unfurling of a colossal map of the world across which Wolfit magnificently swayed and staggered, marking out the territory of his conquests'.[95] In Gielgud's 1940 portrayal of Lear, the line 'Give me the map there' was, as Terence Hawkes memorably argued, 'a dog that didn't bark': political resonances were sacrificed for heroic acting.[96] Here, by contrast, Guthrie was arguably attempting to harness his unruly star to a conception of the play that would reverberate strongly with contemporary geopolitics, as the British Empire likewise 'swayed and staggered'.

At about this time, however, Guthrie seems to have lost his taste for a high-profile career in British theatre. He handed the Old Vic company over to Michael Benthall in 1953, and in spite of having successfully laid the groundwork for a National Theatre based upon its model he chose not to pursue this ambition any further. Instead, he spent the greater part of his post-war career in North America, as far as possible from urban centres of power and artistic privilege. Before those pioneering excursions, he would spend a few years consolidating his international status as a director, through two mechanisms which, like his Draft Artistic Policy for the Old Vic, have become the stock-in-trade of Anglophone theatre directors in subsequent years: directing for the international festival circuit and re-staging key productions across the Atlantic.

Directing on the international stage: *Thrie Estates* and *Carmen*, 1948–52

The year 1947 saw the launch of the Edinburgh Festival, which was designed to present the highest quality work from major international artists working in a range of art forms. Scotland, however, provided only a backdrop to this spectacle, which did not feature Scottish artists. In its second year, Ivor Brown noted that '[t]he high standards achieved by Scottish actors, writers and producers in Scottish theatres, and principally the Citizens' Theatre of Glasgow, were held to justify a major contribution to the theatrical presentations'.[97] Nevertheless, the decision was taken not simply to include a production from the Citizens' Theatre in the festival but to commission 'a Scottish "classic"' for 'the Festival's first great experiment in purely Scottish drama'. Brown's account of the genesis of this project implies that the production needed not only to be Scottish, but overtly to perform Scottish identity in ways that bring to mind the Royal Edinburgh Military Tattoo, which began the following year under the title 'Something about a Soldier' and has been performed throughout the festival every year since. Brown describes Guthrie as 'the obvious choice as commander of these operations' because of his 'reputation as a producer of plays and spectacles', his previous association with 'the people with whom he would be working and his genius for production, particularly of the pageant-like, masquing kind'.[98]

Guthrie was offered a choice of three plays and rejected Alan Ramsay's pastoral *The Gentle Shepherd* and John Home's tragedy *Douglas*, choosing instead to stage Sir David Lindsay's sixteenth-century morality play, *Ane Satyre of the Thrie Estates* – a work that had not been performed in living memory – in the Kirk Assembly Hall in Edinburgh (now well known to Fringe-goers as the Assembly Hall venue).[99] Guthrie transformed the

Assembly Hall by constructing a platform stage 25 feet by 15, with a musicians' gallery opposite from where, according to Ivor Brown, 'Cedric Thorpe Davie could conduct his own admirable music with an eye looking down on the surge of movement that Guthrie was to organize'.[100] Guthrie used this structure to frame a quasi-Elizabethan *theatrum mundi* account of the play (see Figure 3.3), in which, in Brown's recollection, '[t]he three "estaits" which give the play its title were allotted their own quarters':

> The 'Spiritualitie' or Ecclesiastics were seated in pomp in the gallery over the stage, the 'Temporalitie' or Barons and the Burgesses or Merchants were quartered on the flanks of the 'Spiritualitie', while a fourth element, the common people, were strewn about the steps of the platform facing the exalted pews of the Lords Spiritual ... As a form of social landscape, this was not only proper to the theme of the play but notably decorative in itself.[101]

The propriety of Guthrie's staging was distinctly conservative. It both established a strong connection between aristocracy and divinity and occluded the absolute power of the ruling classes by seating the representatives of the church above them, implying that the tail of religious authority wagged the dog of property ownership.

FIGURE 3.3 *Tyrone Guthrie's production of* Ane Satyre of the Thrie Estaites *for the Edinburgh Festival, 1948 (Scottish Theatre Archive, University of Glasgow Library). Photo by Paul Shillabeer, by permission of University of Glasgow Library, Special Collections.*

The performance text of the *Thrie Estates* created for Guthrie by the Scottish writer Robert Kemp, which edited Lindsay's play from six or seven hours to two-and-a-half, was designed to render it palatable to both popular tastes and established authority. Kemp removed a long sermon and cut 'some light relief whose bawdy nature would not have been tolerated by the Censor or by the owners of the Assembly Hall [The Church of Scotland]'.[102] Guthrie's cast was drawn from the Glasgow Citizens' company, combined with amateur performers, and Brown notes that Guthrie managed to 'keep his crowds volatile and make his platform a sea of colourful movement' as everyone would have expected, but that it was also an 'agreeable surprise' to see 'each role […] become so realistic and each abstraction so charmingly concrete'.[103] As in his 1938 *Hamlet* with Guinness, so here Guthrie's customary pragmatism led him to renege somewhat upon his theoretical rejection of realism, and to use it as an aesthetic strategy to communicate to a popular audience. For example, the masque's allegorical figure of Sensuality was rendered as an entertaining, bouncy woman of relaxed morals, while the virtues appeared as 'dessicated maiden aunts'.[104] Such contemporary touches served to render a morality tale from another time, which might easily have been seen as lacking in both wit and drama, clear and intelligible to a broad audience: a strategy the production's huge success vindicated, and which Guthrie must have remembered when opening theatres in North America in the coming decades.

If masque form allowed Guthrie to make discoveries in this period, so too did opera. Looking back on his career, Guthrie reflected that his interest in opera was 'entirely accidental': he first grappled seriously with the art form as a result of his responsibilities to the combined companies of the Old Vic and Sadler's Wells after 1939. When he did, however, he found in opera an ideal site for his artistic signature, which combined virtuoso performances from star actors, skilled choreographic handling of large crowds, and a strong sense of the rhythmic composition of staging. With 'the right concatenation of conductor, work, cast, audience, décor and all the rest of it', he said, opera is 'an enormously soul-satisfying occasion'.[105] The somewhat distant tone of this praise reveals that Guthrie always felt himself to be a visitor in the opera house – a list published by Alfred Rossi acknowledges his direction of only eight operas in his entire career, plus two Gilbert and Sullivan operettas and the premiere of Leonard Bernstein's controversial musical picaresque, *Candide*[106] – but he was an influential visitor nonetheless. In 1952, for example, he directed a production of *Carmen* for the Metropolitan Opera in New York that made its star, the American mezzo-soprano Risë Stevens, the most famous Carmen of her generation (see Figure 3.4). Guthrie's conception of the opera – and indeed of its leading role – was created, however, not in New York, but in London, where he directed the opera at Sadler's Wells in 1949.

The Sadler's Wells production had rejected picturesque staging in favour of a seedier account of daily life in nineteenth-century Seville and starred Anna Pollak, whose Carmen also rejected sentimentality. She was, in

FIGURE 3.4 *Risë Stevens and Richard Tucker in Tyrone Guthrie's production of* Carmen *for the Metropolitan Opera, filmed for the 'Toast of the Town' show hosted by Ed Sullivan on 8 November 1953. Photo by Steve Ochs, courtesy of Michael Ochs Archives/Getty Images.*

Guthrie's words, 'not afraid to make Carmen the vulgar, violent slut the story demands'.[107] Guthrie's framing of misogynistic judgement as modern and realistic was not out of character; seeking to avoid a clichéd presentation of Ophelia as an ingénue in his 1963 Minneapolis *Hamlet*, he likewise swapped one side of misogyny's coin for the other, depicting her as a worldly and sexually available 'girl who knew a thing or two'.[108] However, audiences and critics seem to have been amenable to the gender politics of Guthrie's 1949 *Carmen*, which was widely admired, not least by Rudolf Bing, who would take over the directorship of the Metropolitan Opera the following year. It was therefore understood that the production of *Carmen* that he invited Guthrie to direct in New York in 1952 would be, substantially, a restaging of his London version. Guthrie continued to approach the story realistically, staging the opera's conclusion in the dressing-room of the bullfighter Escamillo rather than outside and thus confining Carmen, both literally and metaphorically, in a hidden corner of a world created for male display. Stevens was not new to the role, but her account of it seems to have been strongly influenced by Guthrie. *Time* magazine reported that the 'trace of well-bred sorority girl' that had featured in her previous performances was replaced by something 'just short of plain alley-cat'.[109] Although the recurring image of confinement in Guthrie's staging and *Time*'s description of Stevens's performance could be read as signalling a production that was proto-feminist in its intent to depict the structural violence inflicted on Bizet's heroine, that would ascribe an intent to Guthrie's staging that he never articulated himself. Likely, the very possibility of that reading emerged from a combination of the two instincts that defined so much of his work in this period: the desire to tweak established accounts of canonical texts and the willingness to deploy a combination of theatricality and realistic detail to that end.

Guthrie's Art and Importance, part 2: North America

A 'pioneer' across the pond

The fact that Guthrie's *Carmen* moved so confidently from London to New York underlines another characteristic aspect of his career. Among the great European directors of the twentieth century, Tyrone Guthrie is perhaps unique in his close relationship with North America: a relationship both institutional and ideological, which has entered into theatrical legend as few other transnational encounters between director and theatre have done. No other prominent director of his period can claim to have played such a pivotal role in the establishment of enduring theatrical organizations on a continent into which he was not born. As the founding artistic director of the Stratford Festival in Canada and the Guthrie Theater in the United States, he powerfully shaped both directorial practice and institutional policy in the emergent regional theatre infrastructure of North America. In the pages that follow, we will draw upon Knowles's materialist theatre semiotics to consider the close ties between the productions Guthrie created in this context, the critical controversies they produced, the legacies they left behind – and the spectre of colonialism that haunted the entire process.

By Guthrie's own account, his commitment to theatre-building in North America was the fruit not of commercial concerns but of fervent personal conviction: a conviction shaped by his experiences in both London and the provinces, and reflexive of the same dual instinct both to innovate and to preserve what he had developed during his years of work in the UK. In a

1964 interview recorded for the BBC, he declared, 'I think it's a great disaster of our times that the metropolitan cities gobble up all the plums and – and the rest just have to exist on the husks.'[110] When asked about decisions he had made on this principle, he immediately singled out his choice 'to go to Canada when they asked me, to start the Shakespeare Festival at Ontario'.[111] Describing the genesis of the Guthrie Theatre in Minneapolis, he similarly constructed this 'theatrical project aimed at those parts of the United States into which Broadway's influence did not penetrate' as an endeavour driven as much by 'missionary zeal' as by 'common sense'.[112]

Bound up with his commitment to theatre outside the metropolis was Guthrie's growing determination to find a home for the 'open' or thrust stage for which he believed Shakespeare's plays had been intended. When first asked by Dora Mavor Moore whether he would consider coming to small-town Stratford, Ontario, to help found a theatre, Guthrie wrote back that his interest in the project was inseparable from his eagerness 'to produce Shakespeare on a stage which might reproduce the actor-audience relationship for which he wrote'.[113] After working alongside designer Tanya Moiseiwitsch to create the famous thrust stage at the Stratford Festival Theatre, Guthrie returned to a similar plan for the Guthrie Theater, declaring that the 'open stage' would underline 'the experimental and pioneering character of the whole venture'.[114]

Guthrie's 'pioneering' rhetoric about these North American ventures is mirrored in the writing of many of his contemporaries, who viewed his new theatres as watersheds in their nations' cultural histories. The opening night of the Stratford Festival on 13 July 1953 has entered the annals of Canadian mythology as an event whose magnitude could be fully understood only by those privileged to be present. The Canadian critic Nathan Cohen, elsewhere a great opponent of Guthrie's work, remembered the audience's conviction that 'something absolutely original and world-important was going on' that night.[115] In a synoptic view of the first season at Minneapolis, Guthrie's friend and sometime collaborator Brooks Atkinson similarly constructed the director as a godlike progenitor of global theatres, 'roving the world like a Jovian Johnny Appleseed'.[116] In such encomia, Guthrie appears as innovator and benefactor, seeding new theatres with the courage and foresight of a trailblazer.

Over time, this frontiersman image of Guthrie has taken on a darker hew. As early as 1959, Nathan Cohen was describing the Stratford 'miracle' as a 'blight' on Canadian theatre, asserting that under the mask of innovation Guthrie had saddled the country with a classical stage whose standards, style and repertoire were all based upon those of Britain.[117] Such critiques have also been applied to the Guthrie Theater in Minneapolis; Joseph Ziegler remarks that its 'particular mission was very much based in colonialism',[118] while M.G. Aune has analysed its inaugural production of *Hamlet* as a prime example of 'British Cold War cultural colonization of the United States'.[119]

In this section, we will argue that these dual perspectives reflect Guthrie's own dual, conflicted identity and practice, to which he responded in North America by creating what might be called 'settler theatres' and working – both consciously and unconsciously – as a settler director. In *The Settler Colonial Present,* Lorenzo Veracini has defined settler colonists as those who distinguish themselves from 'colonial sojourners who would move on at the earliest opportunity and possibly return to a colonising metropole'.[120] Rather than longing to 'go home', settlers long to create permanent institutions and identities within their adopted land. Although Tyrone Guthrie did not arrive in either Canada or the United States with any plan to take up permanent residence there, he certainly strove to create theatres that would distinguish themselves from those of 'colonising metropoles' like London, and that would maintain permanent, localized identities within their communities. Like many settlers, moreover, Guthrie identified simultaneously with both 'old' and 'new' worlds, with both centre and margin. Even as he rebelled against established British artistic values, he sought to educate others in them. The result was a deeply contradictory institutional and artistic practice that evolved unique institutions for emergent markets while maintaining key tenets of dominant ones. The stages Guthrie built, the organizations he helped to found, the directorial tactics he used, and the controversial productions he created all reflected the viewpoint of a rebellious character deeply entrenched in – and, indeed, engaged in maintaining – the status quo.

Guthrie at Stratford: Fairy godfather or wicked uncle?

In *A Life in the Theatre*, Tyrone Guthrie describes his first visit to Canada in 1929 as a young director charged with managing a series of radio plays on Canadian history entitled *The Romance of Canada*. The project is a challenging one, for '[i]n those days there was no professional theatre in Canada'.[121] Guthrie has to winkle his casts out of the amateur theatres of Montreal, Ottawa and Toronto, and to cope with the limited store of 'obviously "radiogenic" episodes in Canada's rather brief history'.[122] Nevertheless, the director reports, 'I left Canada thrilled with what I had seen, eager to return and to be somehow, at some time and in some way a participant in the adventure of developing this land with its vast possibilities, so many of them still dormant, still undreamed – the romance of Canada'.[123] In this construction, Canada appears from the first as a Sleeping Beauty waiting to be rescued from its artistic slumber. Guthrie is determined to kiss her awake.

Guthrie's rhetoric here is perfectly fitted to his role in the founding of the Stratford Festival: one of the best-known fairy tales in twentieth-century theatre history. Guthrie himself participated enthusiastically in the making of this tale. In *A Life in the Theatre*, he tells how he received an initial phone call of invitation from Stratford businessman Tom Patterson, who asked, 'Will you come to Canada and give advice? We want to start a Shakespeare Festival in Stratford, Ontario.'[124] The enchantingly naïve enthusiasm of Patterson and his collaborators wins Guthrie round to its passion, and he agrees to help found the festival. He selects plays, auditions casts, finds a designer in his established friend and collaborator Tanya Moiseiwitsch, and survives multiple financial crises. Sometimes the venture appears as a comic lark, as when Guthrie describes rehearsing in a barn whose scenes of 'unbridled bird sexuality made the life of *Richard III* seem very anaemic and suburban'.[125] At others, the tone is more evangelical, as when he insists on a thrust stage configuration on the grounds that 'the best practical results would be gotten from a stage which closely conformed to what is known of the stage for which Shakespeare wrote, and by relating the audience to that stage in a manner which approximated to the Elizabethan manner'.[126] In the end, the fairy-tale denouement arrives: where the founders had hoped for a five-week run at houses 60 per cent filled, the 'first season played six weeks to 98-percent capacity [...] and a total audience of more than 68,000',[127] as well as to an enthusiastic critical reception both within and beyond Canada.

In the accounts of his collaborators and observers during that first triumphant season at Stratford, Guthrie as artistic director of Stratford is every inch the fairy godfather of Canadian theatre. William Hutt – one of the young actors who scored early success during those seasons and later went on to become a doyen of the Canadian stage – recalled that at a time when 'professional theatre in Canada was more or less in its infancy',[128] Guthrie was able to provide his inexperienced company with a sense of artistic purpose and highly concrete paths to achieving it. Hutt calls him 'one of the few directors in the world who could take absolutely rank amateurs and make them look all but totally professional. Because he had so many tricks, particularly with crowd scenes'.[129] Dawn Greenhalgh, who appeared in those crowd scenes during the first Stratford season, describes how this process worked:

> He'd pay such attention to detail. He loved it. So that even though I was just in the crowd scenes and understudying, he'd still say it was very important. And you'd be asked to do certain things right on the centre of the stage just as part of the crowd, which is what made it really exciting. You really had to be on your toes. He didn't miss a thing.[130]

In such accounts, Guthrie appears as a strategic, result-oriented shepherd figure, less interested in a particular concept or approach than in convincing his cast that they could achieve a goal and using his skills of *mise en scène* to ensure that they *did* achieve it. As Timothy Findlay, another young actor from that first season who went on to become a giant of the Canadian arts scene, puts it, 'He didn't shy away from saying "Look, come. Come up. Be better. Do more".'[131]

Recent scholarly interpreters of the Stratford Festival and its founding have cast a doubtful eye upon this inspiring tale. Robert Shaughnessy, for example, dismisses as 'disingenuous' Guthrie's yarn about the fortuitous call from Patterson, rightly noting that Guthrie had long been in conversation with Canadian interlocutors about his possible contributions to a Canadian National Theatre.[132] As for the nature of those contributions, Dennis Salter argues that they consisted in 'a set of reactionary ideas', fundamentally conservative and imperialist in bent.[133] In place of a truly organic tradition, Ric Knowles argues, Guthrie saddled his band of admiring young Canadian artists with 'a Shakespearean National Theatre in Canada after the British (imperialist) Model, in which Shakespeare was used to serve the interests of cultural colonization'.[134] Viewed from the standpoint of such critiques, all the qualities praised in Stratfordians' eulogies of Guthrie – his missionary zeal for the classics, his eye for talent, his 'tricks' and detailed instructions, his fatherly attitude towards his actors – appear as the deadening hand of established British tradition moulding an emergent theatre to its own, dominant form.

Pivotal to such critiques is the very aspect of the Stratford Festival that Guthrie viewed as most vital to its uniqueness and to his own legacy: the famed thrust stage designed by Tanya Moiseiwitsch, first for the tent in which the early Festival seasons took place, and later for the permanent Festival Theatre. Delighted by his fortuitous exploration of the open stage configuration during the 1937 tour of Olivier's *Hamlet* to Elsinore, Guthrie had come to the conclusion that progress in modern Shakespearean staging required the director 'first, to set the actors against a background with no concessions whatever to pictorial realism, the sort of background which the Elizabethan stage provided', and 'second, to arrange the actors in choreographic patterns, in the sort of relation to one another and to the audience which the Elizabethan stage demanded and the picture-frame stage forbids'.[135] Moiseiwitsch designed the Stratford stage with these specifications in mind; in a first-night review by Morley Safer, the result was vaunted as 'the first Elizabethan stage ever used in a large scale production, since the days of Queen Elizabeth herself'.[136] Canada, that colonial theatrical backwater, was suddenly at the forefront of innovation in theatre architecture. As J.L. Styan argued in *The Shakespeare Revolution*, 'the success of the thrust stage in Canada led to new thinking on both sides of the Atlantic'.[137] Guthrie's and Moiseiwitsch's vision was largely responsible for this coup.

From the first, however, dissident voices arose to underline the shortcomings of this theatre. Though he had shared the fervent enthusiasm engendered by the theatre's first night, Nathan Cohen came to see the thrust stage as a liability to the Stratford Festival, and the Festival itself as a liability to the Canadian theatre. The acoustics of the open stage, he argued, rendered Shakespeare's text inaudible to all but those lucky enough to be faced by the actor speaking at any given moment. To try to maximize the likelihood that spectators *would* be able to hear and see most of the actors on the stage at any given time, directors were forced to constantly to move them from one place to the next. The result, Cohen believed, was frantic 'squirming and rotating for the benefit of the audience on all three sides', which destroyed any chance of intimacy or stillness.[138] Cohen linked these disadvantages of the Festival stage directly to Guthrie's own strengths and weaknesses as a director; while admitting that Guthrie was a great manager of crowds and choreography, the critic believed that he tended to suppress 'those elements in the acting which fail directly to relate to zestfulness and drive'.[139] Under the influence of such directing and the stage upon which it took place, Cohen argued, Stratford had rapidly trained its audiences to look for spectacle instead of substance, 'persuad[ing] its public that they need not take Shakespeare seriously' and trapping them in a childish playground of movement and colour where they could find no contemporary relevance or insight.[140]

Cohen's inheritors have been harsher still in their judgements, viewing the Festival stage as a spatial inscription of colonialism that infantilized not only its spectators but also its actors and, indeed, the whole Canadian nation. Salter, for example, argues that Guthrie's platform stage knocked Canadian actors out of any sense of historical and geographical grounding as it placed them in a 'decontextualized, ahistorical, pseudo-universal, *un*naturally hybrid space' that laid claim to both past and present, both England and Canada, but actually inhabited neither.[141] What it does inhabit, Ric Knowles has argued, is a liberal space that views theatrical meaning – especially the meaning of classic plays like those of Shakespeare – as delocalized and universal.[142] In relation to such a space, performers are trapped in 'conventional actorly readings' as they struggle to replicate established and widely acceptable interpretations of Shakespearean characters.[143] By their very definition, such interpretations are likely to come from old, established theatrical centres and not from new and marginal ones such as Canadian small towns.

We are left with two possible images, not only of Guthrie as a director and founder at the Stratford Festival, but also of his legacy to Canada and its theatre: the fairy godfather on the one hand, and the wicked uncle on the other. Arguably, neither of these readings does full justice to the complexities inherent both in Guthrie's directorial practice at Stratford and in the durable institution he helped to create there. A striking corrective to both extremes is offered by Shaughnessy, whose analysis of Guthrie's 1953 Stratford *All's Well That Ends Well* underlines the optimism, tensions and complex implications of a production in which Guthrie imagined both Shakespeare's characters and the Canadian theatre as poised 'at the threshold of a new, and as yet unrealised, era of theatrical health, happiness and liberty'.[144] On what, in Guthrie's mind, might that dreamt-of era have depended, and how did he express this vision in directorial terms? To answer that question, we need, like Shaughnessy, to turn to one of Guthrie's own productions for Stratford.

'A strong thread of melodrama': *Richard III*, 1953

In his accounts of the Stratford Festival's founding, Guthrie focuses on the strategic choices he made in the moment, stressing not only their artistic value but also their ability to ensure the long-term survival of this fledgling institution. His approach mixed zeal for the future well-being of the Canadian stage with a bluntly commercial pragmatism. For example, after his initial meetings in Stratford, Guthrie returned to England on a 'star-shopping expedition' to find an actor who could headline the festival.[145] He fixed his sights on Alec Guinness, who was not only 'a great actor' and his own established collaborator but also 'well known to Canadians from his films': a box office draw, as well as an anchor for the cast.[146] Guinness, writes Guthrie, accepted the offer both out of a desire to play 'in the particular conditions our stage afforded, and also to take part in what he felt to be a pioneering venture of a gallant and unselfish kind'.[147] The Old World's star is cast as the New World's Prince Valiant, selflessly ready to offer himself for the good of the new stage – and, of course, to pull in the punters.

The key role in which Guthrie cast his leading man was that of Shakespeare's Richard III. Again, Guthrie's description of his motives in selecting the play is strategically focused:

> Guinness wanted to play it; I agreed that it was a suitable vehicle. We both felt that the complicated genealogy, the rather obscure historical background, were probably drawbacks for Canadian audiences but might be offset by the strong thread of melodrama.[148]

There is no sense, in such phrases, that Guthrie and Guinness are selecting this Shakespearean history in order to edify colonial spectators or to introduce them to the humanizing glories of the classical repertoire. The pros are its suitability for his star actor and its rip-roaring entertainment value, which Guthrie describes neither in Elizabethan nor in modernist terms but in nineteenth-century ones as 'melodrama'. The cons are its historical minutiae, which Guthrie assumes a Canadian audience will not understand. The Canadian spectator is constructed as star-loving, thrill-seeking, somewhat old-fashioned, and not particularly well educated; Guthrie is intent upon creating the opening night that will appeal to this demographic.

A glance at the *mise en scène* of Guthrie's Stratford *Richard III* shows this philosophy in action. From the first, the director's stated goals emerged clearly. The production began with a single spotlight on the figure of Richard; Guthrie's choice of lighting both celebrated his star player and offered a classic melodramatic focus on the fascinatingly malevolent anti-hero. Guinness's performance, too, was melodramatic in the sense described by Peter Brooks: an acting style 'predicated on the plastic figurability of emotion, its shaping as a visible and almost tactile entity'.[149] As his first speech began, he strolled onto the thrust stage's balcony as if to underline its Elizabethan qualities, then immediately disrupted the smooth integrity of its architecture by swinging a leg over its side. His performance was replete with grand guignol touches: he sloped down from the balcony to the main stage with a walk Hutt remembered as 'one of the most lascivious things he [had] ever seen',[150] and when Lady Anne spat in his face in the next scene, he dipped his finger in her spittle and sucked on it with lecherous pleasure.[151] Fifty years later, William Hutt still remembered 'things that Alec did that impressed me enormously', such as pressing his right foot against the ground 'as if he were squashing a bug' when he threatened Queen Elizabeth's brothers.[152] Such gestures were grandiose, but also recalled the detail of cinematic close-ups. Every idea, every emotion, was emphasized, externalized, made palpable.

The same melodramatic principles – gestural storytelling, spectacle, sensationalism, constant movement, a liberal dose of violence and an element of shock – dominated the entire production. The corpse of Henry VI, laid out between Lady Anne and Richard during their confrontation, oozed pus and blood; those who opposed Richard were 'kicked in the head and the crotch' before being flung through one of the new stage's quasi-Elizabeth trapdoors.[153] Guinness's crimson velvet coronation robe 'flowed across the stage like a river of blood'.[154] The climactic scene of the Battle of Bosworth Field, preserved on celluloid via the National Film Board of Canada documentary *The Stratford*

FIGURE 3.5 *Amelia Hall as Lady Anne and Alec Guinness as Richard in Tyrone Guthrie's production of* Richard III *at the Stratford Festival, Ontario, 1953. Photo by Peter Stackpole, courtesy of the LIFE Picture Collection and Getty Images.*

Adventure, began with a slow procession of soldiers onto the stage from all sides, accompanied by the steady beat of a single drum. Once they were all in place, Guthrie's direction ensured maximum suspense for the audience by holding the two armies in tense stand-off against one another, the drum suddenly silenced, before one soldier broke with a war cry and raised his sword against another. All hell then broke loose, with a bravura show of stage combat on the crowded stage. At the height of the battle, one soldier tried to scale the balcony and was flung off it into the arms of his comrades.[155] Seated up close to the rapidly flashing swords, the audience, reported William Hawkins in the *New York World-Telegram and Sun*, 'was dodging as none ever did at the most startling 3-D movie'.[156]

Though they can be read as squaring with Salter's view of Guthrie as a 'patriarch' who treated his colonial audiences with condescension,[157] the director's approach to *Richard III* had strategic value within the Canadian context of the 1950s, where the rise of talking pictures after the First World War had dealt a death blow to a well-established professional theatre network. Many theatre buildings, especially in smaller towns like Stratford, had been converted into cinemas; hence, cinema had become the representational lingua franca of most audience members, especially those outside the 'dominant elite' Knowles connects with Stratford.[158] With *Richard III*, Guthrie set out to speak to precisely these audience members. He used the language of melodrama: a theatrical vocabulary that would surely have appealed both to older audience members who associated it with the touring companies of their theatregoing youth and to younger spectators for whom it was the currency of many popular Hollywood movies. He offered them a film star they would recognize, and directed in a manner guaranteed to appeal to those habituated to the vocabulary of film: the constant swirl of movement onstage approximating a montage of cinematic shots, the lavish costumes and choreographed fight scenes presenting delights to equal those of Eastman Kodak's colour film processes and Hollywood 3-D cinema, both in vogue in the early 1950s.

At the same time, Guthrie's and Moiseiwitsch's thrust stage, with its 220-degree perspectives, its aisles through which actors brushed past audience members, and its multiple levels of action, offered its spectators an experience unavailable in any movie palace. Guthrie was showcasing classical theatre as an art form that could offer everything cinema and television could, but could also provide forms of excitement that were quite beyond their ken – all the while assuring the Canadian audience that it could see, on home soil, a spectacle to match the offerings of London, Broadway or Hollywood. In this, the evidence suggests, he succeeded. As Bruce Swerdfager, who as a young actor formed part of the *Richard III* cast, recalls: 'I don't think Canadians ever saw anything like this before. They had gone to Broadway, but this was still better than that. [...] [A]t the end, it was instant. They stood and they did not stop applauding.'[159]

Though they can certainly be seen as supporting Nathan Cohen's assertion that the Stratford Festival sought to 'persuade its public that they

need not take Shakespeare seriously', Guthrie's decisions in *Richard III*
seem to have been less successful when it came to his supposed aims of
ennobling the Canadian audience or imposing universalist, liberal humanist
values. Indeed, established reviewers complained that the production failed
abysmally at such goals. 'Mr. Guinness is fun to watch. Maybe too much
fun', sighed Walter Kerr; 'his performance is always interesting, but it still
falls short of this monster's full stature'.[160] 'Spectacular production; shallow
performance', concurred Brooks Atkinson:

> The acting does not get much beyond the surface of this most wild and
> horrifying play. The performance lacks the rude, elementary, concentrated
> power of an Elizabethan acting piece. Mr. Guthrie and Miss Moiseiwitsch
> [...] have concentrated on production. Infatuated with the mechanics of
> a very original stage and the ominous spectacle of a historical chronicle,
> they have left the drama loose and superficial.[161]

As spectacle, as melodrama, as entertainment, such critiques suggested,
Richard III succeeded. As Elizabethan drama, as Shakespeare, as *theatre* in
the elite sense, it failed.

If the Stratford *Richard III* and its reception teach us one thing about
Guthrie as a director, it may be that we need to mind the gap between his
theory and his practice – or rather, to consider the practical contradictions
that his theory, by its very nature, tended to create. As a theorist of the
performing arts and their cultural meanings, Guthrie espoused an image of
the classical repertoire as an improving, ennobling force. In a reflection on
the Stratford Festival written a year after its opening season, he applied this
insight to the Canadian context, opining that 'in Canada the audience [...]
needs to be trained for the Theatre. If you never get anything but margarine,
you lose the taste for butter'.[162] In practice, Guthrie's way of dealing with
the audience's taste for 'margarine' was by ensuring that butter tasted very
much like it. He worked strategically, not to edify his spectators, but to
entertain them. If the major New York critics objected that this approach
was disedifying, so be it; the key question for Guthrie was whether the
Canadian public would applaud, pay for seats and fund the future of this
new institution. When the first-night audience rose to its feet and gave
Richard III a seemingly endless standing ovation, he reportedly declared,
'All right, people, we just got away with it'.[163]

'Something they wanted and were willing to buy': Minneapolis, 1963

If the founding of the Stratford Festival and the staging of its first
production underline Guthrie's strategic melding of the roles of director
and artistic director, the founding of the Guthrie Theater in Minneapolis

and the story of its first production take us much further down the same path. Gone are the fairy-tale trappings of Stratford; as Shaughnessy writes, if the 'Stratford adventure' emerges from Guthrie's own writings as 'good-natured, idealistic and, on occasions, rather whimsical', the director's narrative of the Minneapolis project is 'pragmatic, jaundiced, and brutally honest'.[164] In both his 1964 book *A New Theatre* and his interview for the BBC recorded in the same year, Guthrie stresses the venture's basis in his disillusionment with America's established theatrical infrastructure, centred in New York City. His discussion of Broadway in *A New Theatre* is focused almost entirely on the economics of theatre as they shape its artistic possibilities: New York's lack of space, its exceedingly high rents and 'the tyranny of the unions',[165] Guthrie argues, all work together to ensure sky high ticket prices, which in turn 'discourage the habit of regular theatregoing' for all but the wealthy and those determined to see 'hits'.[166] Such a context leaves no room for experiment, honourable failure, or even 'moderate success' – a complaint that may be fuelled by Guthrie's own bitterness about the infamous box office disaster of his 1956 Broadway production of *Candide*.[167]

In response to this situation, Guthrie – along with the stage manager Peter Zeisler and the producer Oliver Rea – took the unusual step of advertising in the *New York Times* their interest in offering 'a classical programme' to 'any city which felt deprived of live theatre and would take us under its wing'.[168] They met with interest from a number of mid-sized American cities, including Cleveland, Milwaukee, Detroit and Minneapolis/St. Paul; in the end, their choice alighted upon the Twin Cities. In his 1964 interview for the BBC, Guthrie contrasts this home for a new theatre with the cities of the Old World in revealing terms:

> A great many, it seems to me, of our big cities are very complacent and satisfied with things as they are, and you would never get them to regard it as other than a reckless extravagance to spend money on a theatre, whereas in Minneapolis, they felt deprived without one, possibly not entirely for the right reasons but again possibly rightly, I think from our point of view, it was something they wanted to have and were willing to buy.[169]

The new theatrical organization appears here very explicitly as a commodity: one desired, according to Guthrie, by a group of businessmen and university professors due in large part to the benefits of revenue, community development and student enrolment they saw as likely to accrue from it. If these were not ideally 'right reasons' to build a theatre, Guthrie was nonetheless willing to seize upon them. Guthrie's rhetoric in describing these negotiations is unabashedly colonialist: he and his collaborators sallied forth, he writes, 'equipped with spears and blowpipes, with pretty beads, bright shells, and jews' harps to bribe the native chieftans'.[170] Like so many settlers before him, Guthrie sought to trade his skills for a foothold on the 'frontier' outside New York City.

As for what those skills might be, by this point in Guthrie's career he seems to have placed relatively little emphasis on his abilities as a director of specific plays. Instead, he underlined his role as an Artistic Director with an established facility for creating a lasting theatrical institution with a fully planned and coherent mandate or 'policy'. Early in *A New Theatre*, he emphasizes the notion that a theatre's policy, its audience, and its longevity are closely intertwined, arguing that '[p]olicy in the theatre demands continuity of aim and consistency of style. Without a policy, no theatre can possibly create its own public'.[171] The right spectators will be attracted to the right commodity, as long as they understand what it is. Guthrie lives up to his own requirements by defining the policy he imagines for the planned theatre in Minneapolis:

> Our programme would be classical; only those plays would be chosen which had seemed, to discriminating people for several generations, to have serious merit; which had, in fact, withstood the test of time. [...] We would each season offer not merely a series of classics, but of classics which in origin, style and content would contrast interestingly with one another, would pose the implicit question: what is a classic and what has made it so?[172]

This was more or less the same policy that had arisen at the Stratford Festival in Ontario in the years since Guthrie had left it: a programme designed to attract audiences already invested in the notion of 'classic' drama, as well as to educate those unfamiliar with the established repertoire.

In Stratford, such programming had given rise to vociferous criticism over the lack of new Canadian plays on the docket. At Minneapolis, Guthrie declared himself anxious to avoid 'appear[ing] as if once again Britain were trying to instruct the colonists'.[173] Although he was convinced America had not yet had time to develop an unimpeachably classic dramatist, he deemed it 'essential to include each season one American play of what we considered to be potential classical status; and to let it take its place in a programme of established classics'.[174] In other words, Guthrie understood this provincial theatre, not as a marginal institution, but as one that would perform a very central role within North American culture: that of establishing and sustaining a dramatic canon to which new American works might aspire. The new theatre would be a performative institution in all senses of the word; by playing the classics, it would sustain their shaping power for generations to come.

Guthrie knew that such aims were riven with potential pitfalls. He was sharply aware that many Americans were 'exasperated' by Europeans' tendency 'to give maddening little lectures intended of course for the betterment and instruction of a crude, young and, of course, totally materialistic society'.[175] If Minneapolis had 'bought' Guthrie's theatre because it was a commodity they wanted, it ill behoved him to impugn their taste.

He was faced, then, with a yet more difficult task than he had encountered as an invited guest at Stratford. If he were to start this new theatre off on the right foot, he had simultaneously to convince Minnesota audiences that they needed education in the classics *and* that this education was being offered to them in a spirit of equality rather than of condescension. The directorial convolutions required to achieve this objective proved challenging, even for the elder statesman of the transatlantic stage.

'You can stop depending on me': *Hamlet,* 1963

In creating the *Hamlet* that opened the Guthrie Theater on 7 May 1963, Guthrie was characteristically strategic, calling upon many of the tactics he had accrued over the course of his career to meet the needs of the audience and the moment. As he had with Guinness in 1938, he staged a 'modern dress' interpretation of the play – though in fact, as Shaughnessy notes of the earlier production, the costumes mixed Ruritanian military uniforms and evening gowns with more up-to-the-moment elements such as the umbrellas that appeared at both versions of Ophelia's funeral.[176] Such an approach had become habitual to Guthrie; it had also marked, for example, his well-received 1956 *Troilus and Cressida* at the Old Vic, which had transferred successfully to New York. Even in small-town Stratford, Guthrie and Moiseiwitsch had drawn upon similar design principles for their 1953 *All's Well That Ends Well* and met with very few objections. In writing about the Minneapolis *Hamlet*, however, Guthrie constructed his design decisions very explicitly as a concession to the American context. He opined that modern clothes would make the story clearer for spectators unfamiliar with *Hamlet*, since they render it 'possible at a glance to infer a number of things about the characters of the play, which are not apparent in period dress; the time of day, for instance, and the weather'.[177] He also suggested that modern dress would 'better suit an American cast, less at home with "period" plays than British actors who get more opportunities to appear in them'.[178] Such rationales imply that neither American audiences nor American actors are experienced enough to handle *Hamlet* without the designer's assistance.

At the same time, Guthrie devotes several pages of *A New Theatre* to arguing that modern dress helps to 'protect Shakespeare, [...] and all of us, from our passionate addiction to Romance and to Stereotype'.[179] 'Theatre audiences', he suggests, 'have an almost incurable tendency to romanticize': 'our natural inclination' is to see Hamlet as the sensitive, darkly poet Prince of Eugène Delacroix and Ophelia as the pure, pathetic heroine of the John Everett Millais.[180] Modern dress ruptures 'our' sentimental tendencies, encouraging us to see these well-known characters with fresh eyes. It helps 'us' to resist the dulling influence of culturally dominant notions of Shakespeare: notions that 'we' could scarcely espouse if we were bumbling colonials with little conception of the Bard's reputation or achievement.

As Aune argues, Guthrie's view of the Minneapolis audience is 'paradoxical': they are simultaneously 'intelligent, experienced theatregoers' and 'naïve auditors'.[181] In another example of this paradox, Aune mentions Guthrie's choice to play the text of *Hamlet* with very few cuts. This decision, Guthrie believed, would serve as an indication 'that the audience was being regarded as fully adult and willing to make a considerable effort of concentration, was not being condescended to'.[182] Here again, the effort to avoid any perception of patronizing colonial attitudes appears as a driving force behind Guthrie's directorial choices. A few pages later, however, the director is complaining that the show's first-night audience would have vastly preferred the excitement of 'a bullfight, or a belly dancer' to the uncut *Hamlet*'s demand for 'four hours of solid, concentrated attention'.[183]

Aune explains this contradiction by suggesting that Guthrie must have wanted to maintain a 'complete Shakespeare' even at the cost of a gruelling running time, because the bard's 'authority and [...] cultural capital lay in the words more than the costumes or sets'.[184] Yet Guthrie had never gone out of his way to present Shakespearean texts uncut at the Stratford Festival in Ontario, where he had stressed the Bard's authority and cultural capital for all they were worth. On Stratford's first night, he had cheerfully treated the Canadian spectators to a barnstorming melodrama; after all, they were self-admitted innocents who had asked for theatrical 'help' from their adopted Papa. The Minneapolis audience, by contrast, were customers who had paid good money for a theatre meant at once to supply their cultural deficits and to symbolize their cultural maturity. Guthrie directed accordingly, with choices that worked simultaneously to accommodate the audience's perceived shortcomings and to recognize its 'adult' competencies. Paradoxes were inevitable, for the production was designed around a construction of its audience as both 'them' and 'us': as the director's other, and as his other self.

Strikingly, the same tensions and contradictions informed Guthrie's work with his actors on the Minneapolis *Hamlet*, especially with his leading man. For the opening night at Stratford, Guthrie had gone to great lengths to cast Guinness, who carried with him both the cultural capital of the English stage and the instant iconicity of movie stardom. For the opening night at Minneapolis, he chose a 35-year-old American actor, George Grizzard (1928–2007), who had recently had a success in Edward Albee's *Who's Afraid of Virginia Woolf*, but had never before played Shakespeare professionally. In *A New Theatre*, Grizzard appears – like the Minneapolis audience to which he was to play – as a strange mixture of innate capability and utter ignorance. 'He was intelligent. He was witty. He was modest. He could suggest a prince,' writes Guthrie, but his 'voice was weak, harsh, and pitched too high. He had no idea of how, or when, or why to breathe'.[185] 'It seemed to us', concludes the director, 'that he had many of the assets needed for Hamlet, which are inborn and cannot be acquired; and that the assets which he lacked were of the kind which can be achieved by work'.[186] The very presence of Grizzard thus seemed to affirm that although the American theatre needed training from old hands like Guthrie, it nevertheless possessed within itself the qualities necessary for a thriving classical tradition. Grizzard was native here, but he was *also* to the manner born.

This complicated dialectic between condescension and respect seems to have shaped Guthrie's approach to his cast throughout the rehearsal period of the Minneapolis *Hamlet*. In his record of the production, Alfred Rossi reproduces a letter from Guthrie to Grizzard in which he rebukes his leading actor for suggesting that he would simply defer to his director's guidance when it came to his performance:

> You can stop right now depending on me for 98% of the performance. I know you don't mean it and only put it into your letter partly because you thought it was appropriate to neophyte Hamlet writing to elderly director. In fact the performance will be, *must* be almost entirely yours. [...] To put it another way: I shan't try (or anyway not consciously) to change YOU; only to help you to express what is already in you to express.[187]

Guthrie's description of his own directorial process here squares with those of actors like Guinness, who described him as 'enormously free and encouraging'.[188] Yet Rossi's account of the Minneapolis rehearsal process frequently highlights Guthrie's authoritarian directing style. Though Rossi, who served as Guthrie's Assistant on the production, clearly revered his boss, he observes with dismay that the director imposed line readings on his performers from the first rehearsal and that he 'seemed to be unwilling to let the actors discover things for themselves [... which] can't be very encouraging for them'.[189] 'Guthrie's directions to the actors ... were very specific', notes Rossi of a later scene, 'and there seems to be little freedom on the actors' parts – at least they don't seem to have the courage to ask for any'.[190] Despite Guthrie's strong claims for his performers' active role in the creative process, Rossi confessed to 'the feeling that the game is being played with marked cards, and Guthrie, as dealer, is the only one who knows how it will come out'.[191]

Rossi's notion of the play as a game recurs in the published reviews of the production; here, however, the game is one of chance or risk, and Guthrie features as an arch-gambler. In the *New York Herald Tribune*, Walter Kerr praised the production, declaring that the 'theater will never get anything done if it isn't willing to take a whack at it, and here are talented and determined people whacking in all directions. The score doesn't have to come out heavily in their favour. It is the game that counts just now'.[192] Brooks Atkinson agreed that 'Guthrie has cast the first stone with his familiar combination of recklessness, confidence and skill'.[193] Though these reviews were penned by the very critics who had attacked the Stratford *Richard III* for infantilizing the play and its audience, none of them accused Guthrie of the surface melodrama they had found in that earlier outing.

Some spectators, however, were less charitable, and their criticisms struck at some of Guthrie's most cherished aims. In the Chicago *Sunday Tribune*, Claudia Cassidy complained that Guthrie's was a 'singularly cheapened *Hamlet*', describing the show as 'amateurly acted and clumsily directed, with little indication of the freedom within disciplined form that is the basic classic style'.[194] Other reviewers, more circumspect in their criticisms, nevertheless echoed Cassidy's basic charge of a lack of actorly freedom, especially when it came to Grizzard's Hamlet. Henry Hewes found the actor 'disappointingly flat', and suggested that perhaps 'he and his director have concentrated too much on modulating the performance'.[195] Kerr agreed that Grizzard 'is never surprised; he knows the lines too well'.[196] Again and again, critics suggested that Grizzard was somehow constrained and over-cautious, perhaps even caught in Guthrie's shadow: a strong contrast to the free-wheeling English 'star' Hamlet of Olivier earlier in Guthrie's own career. 'A Hamlet who does not take off into space with the wild whirlings of his spirit can do serious damage to the heart's core of the play,' opined Herbert Whittaker: 'Still, there is a certain appropriateness to the fact that the first production at the Tyrone Guthrie Theater belongs plainly to Sir Tyrone.'[197]

There, arguably, was the rub. Though Guthrie had declared his intention to respect Minneapolis audiences and actors, granting them the liberty to play in Shakespeare's great drama, it was finally his own personality, rather than theirs, that shaped this *Hamlet*. Hewes could not 'help admiring the way Guthrie has staged Claudius's death with a spectacular backward fall against an overturning couch that seems to break his neck'.[198] Whittaker remembered its 'parade of fine theatrical tricks', among which he counted not only the umbrellas at the funeral and the pistol Laertes carried, but also the fact that Ellen Greer's Ophelia was clearly pregnant and that Graham Brown's Horatio was 'dark-skinned'.[199] Not only character choices, but even actors' ethnic identities were read as markers of the director's signature thrill-laden style. Perhaps it was with such points in mind that Hewes described Guthrie's 'inventive, sure-handed staging and audacity' as 'cumulatively self-defeating'.[200] Guthrie had encouraged his actors to 'stop depending on me', and had constructed his theatre as a marker of the burgeoning maturity with which they – and their spectators – might embrace and assimilate the classical tradition. In the end, however, his *Hamlet* spoke to these critics not of the grown-up freedom of American actors and audiences, but of the overpowering personality of Tyrone Guthrie himself.

Conclusion: Guthrie's shadow

After the opening of the Guthrie Theater, Tyrone Guthrie still had almost a decade left to live. In Minneapolis, he would go onto direct a number of projects that were arguably more successful than the much-debated

Hamlet. His Chekhov productions for the company were greatly applauded, beginning with a gently realist *Three Sisters* (1963) that somewhat gave the lie to the director's avowed disdain for illusionism on the open stage. Also notable was a masked, all-male version of Aeschylus's *Oresteia, The House of Atreus* (1967), which Guthrie revived the following year not only in Minneapolis but at the Billy Rose Theatre in New York and at the Mark Taper Forum in Los Angeles. In the *Chicago Tribune*, Clive Barnes complained of the 'wilful and tawdry gimmickry' of the New York outing of *The House of Atreus*, pointedly remarking that 'Sir Tyrone is one of the old school of British directors who have always worked hard for their effects'.[201] In Los Angeles, however, Cecil Smith declared that though Guthrie's *Atreus* initially seemed 'high camp – Aeschylus salted with touches of Disneyland', by the end the spectator was 'caught in the bloody maelstrom, sucked in, touched, moved, anguished, even exalted by the mighty drama'.[202] At the end of his career, Guthrie still occasioned controversy: to some, the embodiment of old-fashioned, middlebrow conservatism; to others, the master of ever-new and astonishing theatrical effects.

In the immediate aftermath of Guthrie's sudden death at the age of seventy-one, it was to the master that his collaborators paid tribute. The reminiscences recorded by Alfred Rossi return again and again to Guthrie's invention, energy and generosity of spirit. 'I always believe in the man who can make you argue, go back to the text, flip over the pages, read speeches aloud,' declared J.C. Trewin; 'Even when he maddened me, I did feel: "Thank heaven I've been here tonight".'[203] George Grizzard remembered that Guthrie's 'rehearsals were joyous. [...] Whenever he would correct or stop someone from doing something, he did it with great love and wit, so that you never felt put down by him'.[204] In the midst of the tributes, however, the voice of John Gielgud sounded a somewhat chilling note, comparing Guthrie to the younger and irresistibly ascendant Peter Brook: 'I would say that Brook is a genius (a pocket genius, perhaps) and Tony Guthrie was only a brilliant man, both remarkable talents and with a certain amount in common. But, to me, Peter has a kind of integrity, a sort of solid quality, that I think Tony lacked.'[205] This, arguably, is the judgement that has stuck: to this day, Guthrie is often perceived as a flashy but somewhat insubstantial director, memorable chiefly for his scenic innovations rather than as a 'genius' to rank with the greatest names of the twentieth-century stage.

When we consider the mainstream Anglo-North American theatre today, however, Guthrie's influence is everywhere visible – and not only in the many stages inspired by his and Moiseiwitsch's work at Stratford and Minneapolis. His approach to 'modern dress' Shakespeare, with its combination of Ruritanian military uniforms, elegant ball gowns and snappy two-piece suits, is still to be seen on the stages of the RSC, the Royal National Theatre and the Metropolitan Opera, as well as in Stratford and at regional theatres across England and North America. His practical willingness – even in the face of his avowed anti-illusionism – to mix the conventions of realism, melodrama, historical pageant and comedy in order to move and delight audiences has proved an indelible influence on later directors of both classical and musical theatre, such as Trevor Nunn, Nicholas Hytner, Adrian Noble, Gregory Doran and Marianne Elliott. His understanding of theatre 'policy' and approach to season programming still dominates subsidized urban and regional stages in Britain and North America. Perhaps his longest shadow, however, falls in the area of theatrical organization and infrastructure. If, as we have argued, he was the first great artistic director of the twentieth-century stage, his approach to that role has shaped many of the regimes that followed.

During his tenure at the Old Vic, as we have seen, Guthrie devoted a great deal of time and energy to forming a solid and lasting alliance between the theatre and its funders, CEMA foremost among them. This partnership launched the first collaboration between the subsidised and commercial sectors in the UK theatre: the model of production that would subsequently underpin the work of almost all successful directors and producers in Britain. The organizational labour of Peter Hall (1930–2017), who established the pattern of transferring work from the NT to the West End and Broadway, and Cameron Mackintosh, who developed the musical *Les Misérables* with Trevor Nunn and John Caird at the subsidised RSC, follows in Guthrie's footsteps at the Old Vic. This model of production finance continues today and underpins arguably the most significant development in theatre production in the twenty-first century to date: the live theatre broadcast.

The practice of broadcasting performances live to cinemas, although by no means new, has become an established part of the theatre landscape in the period since 2006.[206] Like the Old Vic/CEMA tours, extracts of which were also broadcast on the radio, live theatre broadcast was designed to broaden audiences for theatre, opera and ballet beyond the metropolitan centres where they have consistently catered to the elite. Principal among the producers of such broadcasts is NT Live, a commercial subsidiary of the NT, which has been shown significantly to extend the geographical reach of NT productions and to have had more modest but significant success in broadening the socio-economic diversity of its audiences.[207] By locating the source of these patterns at the very start of the subsidised theatre movement in the UK, we can see how public funding for the arts has always been justified with paradoxical rhetoric that is simultaneously elitist and egalitarian. Moreover, such a reading corrects any temptation to assume that the subsidised theatre has become tainted by increased association with its commercial cousin over time. The two have, in fact, long been deeply imbricated with each other, if not existentially dependent upon each other's various resources.

Meanwhile, the two key subsidised theatres Guthrie helped to found in Canada and the United States remain among the most powerful, influential and financially successful theatrical organizations on the continent. In 2017, the Stratford Festival posted its fourth consecutive annual surplus after a 2016 season where attendance figures surpassed 50,000;[208] it also received a \$20 million pledge from the provincial government of Ontario to help renovate its third stage, the Tom Patterson Theatre.[209] A recent article in *Minnesota Business Magazine* boasted that the Guthrie was not only an 'architectural gem' whose 'theatrical influence' had an 'international reach' (see Figures 3.1 and 3.7), but also an 'anchor' for 'residential, commercial, and office development' in the city; in 2016, it played to 84 per cent capacity audiences and reported a budget surplus of \$47,408.[210] From the beginning of his career, Guthrie had longed to create institutions that would help to keep theatre alive in communities beyond the metropolis. In Stratford and Minneapolis, he achieved his goal; in that sense, these theatres were his crowning achievements.

At the same time, Guthrie's work in Stratford and Minneapolis underlines the contradictions and tensions built into his vision of the stage, of directing, and of the role of the artistic director that he helped to develop. Always uncomfortable within a dominant order, he was attracted to the 'romance' of the so-called New World: its openness, innocence, malleability and potential. He wished, not to replicate what existed in Britain and Europe, but to create something new. Nevertheless, his own assumptions about theatre, about the creative process, and about his North American audiences

FIGURE 3.6 *Tyrone Guthrie directing, 1950, from an article in* Picture Post: *'Where Does the Producer Come In?'. Photo by Karl Hutton, courtesy of* Picture Post *and Getty Images.*

FIGURE 3.7 *Portrait of Tyrone Guthrie passed by visitors to the Guthrie Theater, Minneapolis. Photo by Craig Lassig, courtesy of AFP/Getty Images.*

led him frequently to replicate in artistic terms precisely the same settler colonial attitudes he criticized in his peers: paternalism, authoritarianism, repetition of established styles and a condescending approach to spectators and performers. As John Gielgud remarked, 'he was a terrific pioneer' attracted to 'the idea of a new stage, a new world to conquer'.[211] Because he approached theatres as a conqueror, he risked constructing his collaborators and his audiences as the conquered.

Both in Britain and in North America, Tyrone Guthrie's work celebrated his own freedom as an iconoclastic and individualistic director, his actors' freedom to explore, and his audience's freedom to affirm both their cultural heritage and their contemporary enthusiasms. William Hutt described this love of 'freedom' as one of the quintessential attributes of his work: 'One felt when working with Tony that he would accept anything you did, however outrageous it might be if it was done with courage and conviction.'[212] Yet Michael Langham, Guthrie's successor at Stratford, argued that Guthrie gave the actor only 'the *illusion* of freedom',[213] adding that when someone 'thought he was making up his own mind [...], the truth often was that Tony had told him not only what to think, but what to do'.[214] Arguably, Guthrie was himself subject to this same cycle of influence. Even when he most believed that he was defying the standards of the West End and Broadway stages from which he longed to escape, he was deeply and irrevocably shaped by them: by their star systems, their commercial imperatives, their spectacle and their understanding of the dramatic canon. Perhaps, indeed, he was ruefully aware of his own imbrication within the assumptions of the metropolitan establishment he so often criticized. When he heard Langham's judgement that he gave actors only an illusion of freedom, Rossi tells us that 'Guthrie paused, a glint coming to his eyes, and said, "Freedom *is* an illusion"'.[215]

NOTES

Introduction to the Series

1 Simon Shepherd, *Direction* (Basingstoke: Palgrave Macmillan, 2012).

2 P.P. Howe, *The Repertory Theatre: A Record & a Criticism* (London: Martin Secker, 1910).

3 Alexander Dean, *Little Theatre Organization and Management: For Community, University and School* (New York: Appleton, 1926), 297–8.

4 Constance D'Arcy Mackay, *The Little Theatre in the United States* (New York: H. Holt, 1917).

5 William Lyon Phelps, *The Twentieth Century Theatre: Observations on the Contemporary English and American Stage* (New York: Macmillan, 1920); Hiram Kelly Moderwell, *Theatre of Today* (New York: Dodd, Mead & Co., 1914, 1923); Dean, *Little Theatre Organization and Management*.

Introduction to Volume 3

1 Tyrone Guthrie, *A Life in the Theatre* (London: Hamish Hamilton, 1961), 136.

2 Avra Sidiropolou, *Authoring Performance: The Director in Contemporary Theatre* (London: Palgrave Macmillan, 2011), 11.

3 Samuel L. Leiter, *From Belasco to Brook: Representative Directors of the English-Speaking Stage* (New York: Greenwood Press, 1991), 77.

4 For Simon Shepherd it was the period 'from the beginning of the century through to the mid-1930s that the figure of the director became more clearly defined' relating this more generally to the currency of Talyorism and ideas of organization, systematic analysis and training. *Direction: Readings in Theatre Practice* (London: Palgrave Macmillan, 2012), 86.

5 Guthrie, *A Life in the Theatre*, 135.

6 Leiter, *From Belasco to Brook*, 88.

7 Jacques Copeau, *Copeau: Texts on Theatre* (London: Routledge, 1990), 124.

8 Copeau, *Copeau: Texts on Theatre*, 125.

9 For more details see the chapter on Komisarjevsky in this volume.

10 Theodore Komisarjevsky, *Myself and the Theatre* (London: William Heinemann, 1929), 165, my emphasis.

11   Leiter, *From Belasco to Brook*, 89.

12   Mark Evans, *Jacques Copeau* (London and New York: Routledge, 2006), 88.

13   Leiter, *From Belasco to Brook*, 82.

14   Komisarjevsky, *Myself and the Theatre*, 82. For a full discussion of
     Komisarjevsky's ideas on ensemble see Jonathan Pitches, 'Star or Team?
     Theodore Komisarjevsky's Early Developments in Ensemble Playing in the
     UK', in *Encountering Ensemble* (London: Methuen, 2013), 94–110.

15   Mark Evans, 'The French Ensemble Tradition: Jacques Copeau, Michel St-
     Denis and Jacques Lecoq', in *Encountering Ensemble* (London: Methuen,
     2013), 113.

16   See Leiter, *From Belasco to Brook*, 84–6 (in the section 'Strengths in Staging').

17   Tyrone Guthrie, *In Various Directions: A View of the Theatre* (London:
     Michael Joseph, 1965), 176–7.

Chapter 1

1   **Suzanne Bing** was born in 1885 in Paris to a bourgeois French-Jewish
    family. In 1905 she trained for two years at the Paris Conservatory of Music
    and Declamation before living in Paris and Berlin with her husband, the
    avant-garde composer Edgard Varèse. In 1910 they had a daughter, Claude,
    but divorced shortly afterwards. She later had a son, Bernard, by Copeau.
    After her time working with the Compagnie des Quinze she did not return
    to teaching or devising. She did go on to act in various French films, teach
    elocution and give readings to students at the Sorbonne; she died in 1967.

2   **Michel Saint-Denis** (1897–1971) was Copeau's nephew and became his close
    assistant at the Théâtre du Vieux-Colombier and then with Les Copiaus.
    Saint-Denis established La Compagnie des Quinze after the disbanding of Les
    Copiaus and eventually settled in England where he had great success as a
    director and a teacher. His life, work and importance are covered in greater
    detail in a chapter on him within this series.

3   **Louis Jouvet** (1887–1951) was an important collaborator in the early years of
    the Vieux-Colombier project, developing some significant staging and lighting
    innovations. He left the company in 1922 and became a successful director in
    his own right.

4   **Charles Dullin** (1885–1949) was an early collaborator with Jacques Copeau,
    and in particular supported and encouraged Copeau's interest in rejuvenating
    the idea of an improvised comedy, similar to the Italian *commedia dell'arte*.
    He left Copeau's company in 1929 and had considerable success as an actor,
    director and teacher in his own right. At his Atelier in Paris he trained a range
    of significant figures of French theatre, including Antonin Artaud, Jean-Louis
    Barrault and Etienne Decroux.

5   **Jean Dasté** (1904–94) was a student at the Ecole Vieux-Colombier, who then
    followed Copeau to Burgundy and became a member of Les Copiaus and later
    the Compagnie des Quinze. He subsequently set up his own company after

the Second World War, the Comédie de St.-Etienne. He married Marie- Hélène Copeau, Copeau's daughter in 1928.

6   **Marie-Hélène Dasté** (1902–94). After the Compagnie des Quinze disbanded she worked as an actor and costume designer with Dullin and Jouvet, and also with George Baty. After the Second World War she worked in Jean Dasté's company, and following their separation she was one of the original members of the Renaud-Barrault Company working with Madeleine Renaud and Jean-Louis Barrault until she retired in 1982. With her cousin, Suzanne Maistre, she was responsible for the management of the Copeau archives and the publication of a number of his, and the company's, writings/notebooks.

7   **Jessmin Howarth** (1892–1984). Following her time with the Vieux-Colombier, Howarth worked as an assistant choreographer at the Paris Opera before encountering Gurdijeff's Movements and the Mensedniek System, which she was to subsequently to teach across America and Europe (1924–84).

8   See Cassandra Fleming, 'A Genealogy of the Embodied Theatre Practices of Suzanne Bing and Michael Chekhov: The Use of Play in Actor Training' (PhD diss., De Montfort University, 2013).

9   There are twenty arrondissement in Paris, marking the administrative structure of the city.

10   The sous was a small French coin of low domination.

11   Copeau, *Copeau: Texts on Theatre*, 211.

12   Ibid.

13   Ibid., 253.

14   Maurice Kurtz, *Jacques Copeau: Biography of a Theatre* (Carbondale and Edwardsville: Southern Illinois University, 1999), 15.

15   Kurtz, *Jacques Copeau: Biography of a Theatre*, 33.

16   Copeau in Kurtz, *Jacques Copeau: Biography of a Theatre*, 11. The reference to 'natural' talent implies an essentialist approach to the actor's self; Copeau was also arguing for an approach which removed some of the artifice of acting which he saw as prevalent in French theatre at this time. Such an approach drew on contemporary notions of the natural which are contextualized and discussed in more detail in Mark Evans, *Movement Training for the Modern Actor* (London and New York: Routledge, 2009).

17   Charles Dullin in Kurtz, *Jacques Copeau: Biography of a Theatre*, 12.

18   Ibid.

19   Jacques Copeau, 'An Essay of Dramatic Renovation: The Théâtre of the Vieux-Colombier', *Educational Theatre Journal* Part Four (1967): 452.

20   At this point in time, although Stanislavksi was known internationally by reputation, there was little or no access to his writings, so knowledge of his practice and pedagogy was very limited outside of Russia.

21   Poster for the opening of the Vieux-Colombier Theatre, 15 October 1913, author's translation.

22   Various authors have previously acknowledged Bing's significant contribution (e.g. Baldwin, Donahue, Evans, Fleming, Kurtz, Kusler, Rudlin) and her work

is also discussed in the chapter on Michel Saint-Denis in this series. Bing's wider profile is however limited; although her work continued through the activities of Saint-Denis and Jean and Marie-Hélène Dasté, she herself did not achieve the public recognition for it that this chapter argues she deserved.

23 Copeau's various affairs arguably exploited the loyalty of both his wife, Agnès, and his lover, Suzanne. Agnès knew of the affair with Bing and of Copeau's child, Bernard, through this relationship – at times they were all living in the same house. She chose to remain with Copeau, but was sometimes painfully aware of this (and many of his other) infidelities (see Thomas Donahue, *Jacques Copeau's Friends and Disciples: The Théâtre du Vieux-Colombier in New York City, 1917–1919* (New York: Peter Lang, 2008) for more detail).

24 Bernard Bing, 'Le Souvenir de Suzanne Bing', *Revue d'histoire du théâtre*. Revue Trimestrielle, Janvier-Mars Trente-Cinquième Année (1). Paris, Ministry of Culture (1983), 17.

25 Bernard Bing explained that his mother's feelings about Copeau were in fact very ambiguous and that she spoke of him 'with a sort of cracked excitation, a mixture of idolatry and resentment'. Bing, 'Le Souvenir de Suzanne Bing', 20.

26 **Margaret Naumburg** (1890–1983). In 1924 Naumburg ended her formal relationship with the school and went on to become a pioneer in art therapy in America. See Donahue, *Jacques Copeau's Friends and Disciples*; Fleming, 'A Genealogy of the Embodied Theatre Practices of Suzanne Bing and Michael Chekhov'. Naumburg had also been responsible for disseminating the ideas of Jaques-Dalcroze and Alexander in America see A. Frost and R. Yarrow, *Improvisation in Drama* (London: Palgrave Macmillan, 2007), 27.

27 See Barbara Leigh Kusler 'Jacques Copeau's School for Actors: Commemorating the Centennial of the Birth of Jacques', in *Copeau, Mime Journal: Numbers Nine and Ten* (Claremont, CA: Pomona College, 1979); Mira Felner, *Apostles of Silence: The Modern French Mimes* (Cranbury and London: Associated University Presses, 1985); Thomas Donahue, 'Improvisation and the Mask at the École du Vieux-Colombier: The Case of Suzanne Bing', *Maske und Kothurn* 44, no. 1–2 (1998): 61–72; Donahue, *Jacques Copeau's Friends and Disciples*; Fleming, 'A Genealogy of the Embodied Theatre Practices of Suzanne Bing and Michael Chekhov'.

28 Donahue, 'Improvisation and the Mask at the École du Vieux-Colombier', 69.

29 See Art section for more detail.

30 Donahue citing from Registres, IV 303, 'Improvisation and the Mask at the École du Vieux-Colombier', 69.

31 For further discussion of the historical development and cultural context of the Noble and Neutral masks and the training practices associated with them, see Evans, *Movement Training for the Modern Actor*.

32 Copeau uses the term 'New Comedy' (Copeau, *Copeau: Texts on Theatre*, 156), but we have inserted the word 'Improvised' as it gives a clearer sense of the form of theatre and the connection with Commedia del'Arte, its historical antecedent, is clearer. This is explained in more detail in the section on Les Copiaus later in this chapter.

33 Copeau, *Copeau: Texts on Theatre*, 34–5.

34 Donahue, *Jacques Copeau's Friends and Disciples*, 118.

35 Copeau and Bing translated and adapted this play. They were later to translate other Shakespearean tragedies and comedies into French.

36 'Naked stage' is the literal translation, but the word *tréteau* also implies something closer to the raised rostra of the touring commedia companies of the early European Renaissance. There are interesting echoes of this concept in Peter Brook's use of the phrase 'the empty space' (Peter Brook, *The Empty Space* (Harmondsworth: Penguin Books, 1968)). Further details of Copeau's notion of the *tréteau nu* are given later in this chapter.

37 Regardless of the fact that Bing was the central pedagogue (Kusler, 'Jacques Copeau's School for Actors', 33; Etienne Decroux, 'Words on Mime', trans. Mark Piper, *Mime Journal* (Claremont, CA: Pamona College, 1985); Fleming, 'A Genealogy of the Embodied Theatre Practices of Suzanne Bing and Michael Chekhov'), Copeau appointed Jules Romains, a successful writer who shared their idea for a school based on a clear set of principles and a strong group ethos, as 'Director' when the school expanded in 1921. However, records indicate that Romains did not contribute in a significant way to the school and that '[he] had little understanding or interest in acting' (Kusler, 'Jacques Copeau's School for Actors', 26).

38 Kusler 'Jacques Copeau's School for Actors', 37. Dorcy identifies Copeau and Bing as joint directors of the School (Dorcy, *The Mime* (New York: Robert Speller, 1975), 11).

39 **Georges Hébert** (1875–1957) began his career as a naval officer, but his fascination with natural fitness led him to devise a training system that rejected the formal gymnastics of the time. He was also an early advocate of physical exercise for women. His regime was based on the natural activities of walking, running, jumping, climbing, throwing, etc. His work influenced the later development of obstacle courses, parkour and some of Jacques Lecoq's training exercises.

40 John Rudlin, *Jacques Copeau* (Cambridge: Cambridge University Press, 1986), 48.

41 Kurtz, *Jacques Copeau: Biography of a Theatre*, 103.

42 Copeau in Kurtz, *Jacques Copeau: Biography of a Theatre*, 105.

43 Ibid., 105.

44 Ibid., 118.

45 Ibid., 41.

46 Key members of Footsbarn trained with Lecoq who in turn drew on Copeau and Bing's earlier practice. Evans references communication with Footsbarn which confirms an awareness of Copeau's influence on their work and ethos (Evans, *Jacques Copeau*, 158).

47 Rudlin, *Jacques Copeau,* 84.

48 Baldwin notes that the rules introduced by Copeau were particularly restrictive for the younger women, who had to comply to additional limitations:

'cafes were off-limits without special authorization, smoking and drinking prohibited' (Jane Baldwin, *Michel Saint-Denis and the Shaping of the Modern Actor* (Westport, CT: Praeger, 2003), 28).

49 Rudlin, *Jacques Copeau*, 85. This idea of the value of poverty has interesting echoes with the work of Jerzy Grotowski in the 1960s and 1970s. The notion of poverty clearly relates to Copeau's personal asceticism and his deep spiritual convictions. He sees theatre as a form of monastic commitment, and sought to take his actors away from what he saw as the superficial distractions of conventional success. In the cases of Copeau's group and Grotowski's Laboratory Theatre, it ultimately meant that the actors stayed because they believed deeply in the value of the work beyond their own professional and commercial careers.

50 Kusler, 'Jacques Copeau's School for Actors', 51.

51 Rudlin, *Jacques Copeau*, 86.

52 Ibid., 86.

53 Rudlin (*Jacques Copeau*) argues that Saint-Denis exaggerates his involvement in the Paris school in his publications; he was only an interested observer.

54 One of these shows was rehearsed but never performed.

55 Kusler, 'Jacques Copeau's School for Actors', 92.

56 Copeau, *Copeau: Texts on Theatre*, 170.

57 Rudlin, *Jacques Copeau*, 110.

58 Baldwin, *Michel Saint-Denis and the Shaping of the Modern Actor*, 36.

59 Villard in Rudlin, *Jacques Copeau*, 110.

60 Ibid., 111.

61 Ibid., 93.

62 Baldwin, *Michel Saint-Denis and the Shaping of the Modern Actor*.

63 There is confusion on the exact dates for the company, the first production was in January 1931 and last performance was autumn 1934 (Baldwin, *Michel Saint-Denis and the Shaping of the Modern Actor*, 57).

64 Saint-Denis's accounts of this early work do not acknowledge this application of Bing's pedagogy and theatre-making techniques in the work of the Compagnie des Quinze. Michel Saint-Denis, *The Rediscovery of Style* (New York: Theatre Arts Books, 1969) and *Training for the Theatre: Premises and Promises* (London: Heinemann, 1982).

65 Kurtz, *Jacques Copeau: Biography of a Theatre*, 145.

66 Evans, *Jacques Copeau*, 38.

67 Kurtz, *Jacques Copeau: Biography of a Theatre*, 85.

68 Jacques Copeau in Kurtz, *Jacques Copeau*, 13.

69 Jacques Copeau, *Registres IV: Les Registres du Vieux Colombier deuxième partie America* (Paris: Gallimard, 1984), 175.

70 There are interesting connections here with Stanislavsky's development of the Method of Physical Action, which he started work on in the 1930s. There is no

clear evidence of any influence from Copeau's work, although the two met in Paris and corresponded frequently.

71 Bettina Knapp, *The Reign of the Theatrical Director: French Theatre 1887–1924* (Albany, NY: Whitston, 1988), 211.

72 *Boston Eagle*, 28 November 1917.

73 Copeau in Rudlin, *Jacques Copeau*, 72.

74 Martin du Gard in ibid., 72.

75 Ibid., 68.

76 Kurtz, *Jacques Copeau: Biography of a Theatre*, 83. See also Evans, *Jacques Copeau*, 14–16.

77 Rudlin, *Jacques Copeau*, 71.

78 Sincerity may now seem a problematic and unusual term. For Copeau, it captured some of the moral integrity, reliability and the searching for truth, that he saw as central to the work of the actor. This particular quality should be understood in the context of what Copeau saw as the superficiality of the *belle epoque* and the danger of the falseness inherent in *cabotinage*.

79 See chapter on Stanislavsky elsewhere in this series.

80 Kusler, citing Copeau's notes 37 August 1919, 'Jacques Copeau's School for Actors', 19.

81 See Donahue, 'Improvisation and the Mask at the École du Vieux-Colombier: The Case of Suzanne Bing', in *Jacques Copeau's Friends and Disciples*; Fleming, 'A Genealogy of the Embodied Theatre Practices of Suzanne Bing and Michael Chekhov'.

82 Margaret Naumburg, *The Child and The World: Dialogues in Modern Education* (New York: Harcourt, Brace and Company, 1928), 310.

83 Copeau, *Copeau: Texts on Theatre*, 155.

84 Felner, *Apostles of Silence*, 42.

85 Bing, Suzanne. 'Bodily Technique', Jacques Copeau Archives, University of Kent at Canterbury, Archive No. 6 (JCA/KC/46), undated paper (probably 1920), 102.

86 Bing in Jacques Copeau, and Claude Sicard, *Registres VI: L'École du Vieux-Colombier* (Paris: Gallimard Edition, 2000), 114. (Trans. E. Levin, 2011.)

87 Evans, *Jacques Copeau*.

88 Fleming, 'A Genealogy of the Embodied Theatre Practices of Suzanne Bing and Michael Chekhov'.

89 Felner, *Apostles of Silence*, 41.

90 Jacques Lecoq, *The Moving Body: Teaching Creative Theatre* (London: Methuen, 2000), 71.

91 This represents a point of convergence between the practices of Bing and Copeau and those of Michael Chekhov. See Fleming, 'A Genealogy of the Embodied Theatre Practices of Suzanne Bing and Michael Chekhov'.

92 Copeau cited in John Rudlin, 'Jacques Copeau: The Quest for Sincerity' in *Actor Training*, ed. Alison Hodge (London and New York: Routledge, 2000), 60.

93   Bing's contribution is also acknowledged in the chapter on Saint-Denis in this series.

94   Kusler, 'Jacques Copeau's School for Actors', 36.

95   Saint-Denis, *Training for the Theatre*, 179.

96   Kusler, 'Jacques Copeau's School for Actors', 65.

97   Rudlin, *Jacques Copeau*, 108.

98   Villard in Kusler, 'Jacques Copeau's School for Actors', 65.

99   Phylis Akroyd in Rudlin, *Jacques Copeau*, 109.

100 Copeau in ibid., 112.

101 See Fleming, 'A Genealogy of the Embodied Theatre Practices of Suzanne Bing and Michael Chekhov'.

102 See Baldwin, *Michel Saint-Denis and the Shaping of the Modern Actor*.

103 Rudlin, *Jacques Copeau*, 116.

104 Kurtz, *Jacques Copeau: Biography of a Theatre*, 84.

105 Copeau in ibid., 14. Copeau did not of course mean a literally bare stage, without any use of structures, shapes and levels. Drawing on his exchanges with Craig and Appia, he saw the 'bare stage' as a stage unadorned with unnecessary objects and design, throwing attention to the elements of space, light and the rhythm and dynamics of design.

106 Copeau in D. Bablet, *The Theatre of Edward Gordon Craig* (London: Eyre Methuen. York: Routledge, 1981), 184.

107 Copeau, *Copeau: Texts on Theatre*, 97.

108 Jacques Copeau, *Copeau: Texts on Theatre*, edited and translated by John Rudlin and Norman Paul (London and New York: Routledge, 1990), 84.

109 Ibid., 87.

110 Copeau in Kurtz, *Jacques Copeau: Biography of a Theatre,* 84.

111 Appia in ibid., 84.

112 Copeau, *Copeau: Texts on Theatre*, 83.

113 Ibid., 84.

114 Ibid., 85.

115 Ibid., 87.

116 Ibid., 89 (written in 1941).

117 Villard had only undertaken some training in Division B of the School while an actor with the Vieux-Colombier company. Like Saint-Denis, he was never in the Apprentice Group and had not been a Student Monitor.

118 Dorcy, *The Mime*, 21.

119 Ibid., 20.

120 Jacques Lecoq, *Theatre of Movement and Gesture* (London and New York: Routledge, 2006), 98.

121 Felner, *Apostles of Silence*, 54.

122 Jean-Louis Barrault, *Reflections on the Theatre* (London: Thames and Hudson, 1951), 21–2.

123 Marjaana Kurkinen, 'The Spectre of the Orient: Modern French Mime and Traditional Japanese Theatre in the 1930s' (PhD diss., University of Helsinki, Finland, 2000), 169.

124 See Mark Evans, 'The Myth of Pierrot', in *Routledge Companion to Commedia dell'Arte* (London and New York: Routledge, 2013) for the significance of Deburau in the history of French mime.

125 See Vivian Appler, 'Mime, "Mimes" and Miming', in *Routledge Companion to Jacques Lecoq* (London and New York: Routledge, 2016) for a discussion of the importance of this film in the history of French mime.

126 Lecoq, *The Moving Body*, 4.

127 The Cartel des Quatres (1927–40) was an informal alliance between Dullin, Jouvet, Gaston Baty and Georges and Ludmilla Pitoëff, all of whom committed to a respect for the text, simple staging and a serious approach to theatre.

128 Thomas Donahue, Interview with authors (24 February 2017).

129 Georges Clemenceau (1841–1929) was a French politician and served as prime minister of France during the First World War.

130 Donahue, Interview with Authors.

131 Ibid.

132 Ibid.

133 'Copeau really thought that the word company meant those who break bread together' (ibid.).

134 Ibid.

135 Ibid.

136 Ibid.

137 Ibid.

138 Ibid.

139 Ibid.

140 The company's most notable productions have included *La Cuisine* (The Kitchen) (1967), *Les Clowns* (The Clowns) (1969), *1789* (1970), *L'Age D'Or* (The Golden Age) (1974), *Richard II* (1981) and *Les Atrides* (The House of Atreus) (1990).

141 Anne Neuschäfer, '1970–1975: Ecrire une *Comédie de notre temps* – La filiation avec Jacques Copeau', *Théâtre du Soleil website,* 2004. Available at: http://www.theatre-du-soleil.fr/thsol/a-propos-du-theatre-du-soleil/l-historique/1970-1975-ecrire-une-comedie-de?lang=fr

142 Judith Miller, Correspondence with authors (20 May 2017).

143 The Cartoucherie is a former armament factory in the Bois de Vincennes on the southeastern outskirts of Paris. The building was converted into a performance and rehearsal space by Mnouchkine and the Théâtre du Soleil in 1970.

144 Miller, Correspondence with authors.

145 See Evans, *Movement Training for the Modern Actor*.

146 Miller, Correspondence with authors.

147 Ibid.

148 It is interesting however that it appears that Catherine Dasté did publish a book in the 1970s which shows some of these links: Yvette Jenger, Josette Voluzan and Catherine Dasté, *L'enfant, le theatre, l'ecole* (Paris: Delachoaux et Nisetle, 1975).

149 Ariane Mnouchkine, *l'Art du Présent* (Paris: Actes Sud, 2016).

150 Miller, Correspondence with authors.

151 See Mark Evans, 'The French Ensemble Tradition: Jacques Copeau, Michel Saint-Denis and Jacques Lecoq', in *Encountering Ensembe*, ed. John Britton (London: Bloomsbury Methuen, 2013), 111–25.

152 See Lecoq, *The Moving Body*. and Jacques Lecoq, *The Moving Body*, trans. David Bradby (London: Methuen, 2000) and Jacques Lecoq, *Theatre of Movement and Gesture*, trans. David Bradby (London & New York: Routledge, 2007).

153 Suzy Willson, Interview with authors (3 April 2017).

154 Ibid.

155 Ibid.

156 For a full discussion of the *auto-cours* system, see Estevez in Mark Evans and Rick Kemp, eds, *The Routledge Companion to Jacques Lecoq* (London and New York: Routledge, 2016), 165–70.

157 Lecoq, *The Moving Body*, ix.

158 Willson, Interview with authors.

159 Ibid.

160 Evans, *Movement Training for the Modern Actor*.

161 Willson, Interview with authors.

162 Ibid.

163 Ibid.

Chapter 2

1 Komisarjevsky, *Myself and the Theatre*, 45.

2 Theodore Komisarjevsky, *The Theatre and a Changing Civilisation* (London: John Lane, 1935), 15.

3 Komisarjevsky, *The Theatre and a Changing Civilisation*, 19.

4 John Gielgud, 'Mr Komisarjevsky', *Times*, 21 April 1954, 19.

5 Shepherd, *Direction: Readings in Theatre Practice*, 5.

6 Victor Borovsky, *A Triptych from the Russian Theatre: An Artistic Biography of the Komissarzhevskys* (London: Hurst, 1988), 252.

7   Sheridan Morley, *John Gielgud: The Authorized Biography* (New York: Simon and Schuster, 2002), 63.

8   Qtd in Ralph Berry, 'Komisarjevsky in Britain', *Theatrephile* 2, no. 5 (Winter 1984/5): 17.

9   Headed notepaper, Harvard Collection.

10 Ctd in Jonathan Pitches, 'A Tradition in Transition: Komisarjevsky's Seduction of the British theatre', in *Russians in Britain*, ed. Jonathan Pitches (Abingdon: Routledge, 2012), 15.

11 In *Myself and the Theatre*, Komisarjevsky suggests that this humorous quip was said by a stage hand (109). However, it was almost certainly coined by Evans. At least it is generally attributed to her.

12 Borovsky, *A Triptych*, 51.

13 Ibid., xx.

14 Oliver M. Sayler, *The Russian Theatre* (New York: Brentano's, 1922), 182.

15 Komisarjevsky, *The Theatre and a Changing Civilisation*, 121.

16 Ibid., 147.

17 Pitches, 'A Tradition in Transition', 19.

18 Fëdor Komissarzhevsky to A.V. Lunacharsky, letter (June 1919) in *The Soviet Theater*, ed. Laurence Senelick and Sergei Ostrovsky (New Haven: Yale UP, 2014), 72–3.

19 Rebecca Beasley and Philip Ross Bullock, eds, *Russia in Britain 1880–1940* (Oxford: Oxford UP, 2013), 5.

20 Caroline Maclean, *The Vogue for Russia: Modernism and the Unseen in Britain* (Oxford: Oxford UP, 2015).

21 Rebecca Beasley, 'Modernism's Translations', in *The Oxford Handbook of Global Modernisms*, ed. Mark Wollaeger (Oxford: Oxford UP, 2012), 558.

22 Stuart Young, 'Formless, Pretentious, Hideous and Revolting: Non-Chekhov Russian and Soviet Drama on the British Stage', in *Russia in Britain 1880 – 1940*, ed. Rebecca Beasley and Philip Ross Bullock (Oxford: Oxford UP, 2013), 88–9.

23 http://www.phoenix-theatre.co.uk, accessed 23 September 2016.

24 Richard Gray, *One Hundred Years of Cinema Architecture* (London: Lund Humphries Publishers, 1996), 75.

25 Alexei Bartoshevich, 'Theodore Komisarjevsky, Chekhov and Shakespeare' in *Wandering Stars: Russian Émigré Theatre, 1905–1940*, ed. Laurence Senelick (Iowa City: Iowa UP, 1992), 103.

26 Dates and biographical information taken from Jacqueline Lyons, 'Theodore Komisarjevsky in the British Theatre' (unpublished MA by research thesis, University of Newcastle, New South Wales, 1991) and Norman Marshall, 'Komisarjevsky, Theodore (1882–1954)', in *Oxford Dictionary of National Biography* (Oxford: Oxford UP, 2004–16), http://www.oxforddnb.com/view/article/34361, accessed 22 September 2017.

27 Rebecca Walkowitz, *Cosmopolitan Style* (New York: Columbia UP, 2006), 20.

28 Komisarjevsky, *Myself and the Theatre*, 173.

29 Ibid., 175. For more information regarding this production see the J. Glyn Davies Papers at the National Library of Wales. Davies's version of *Yr Ymhonwyr* was published by R.H. Rees as part of the Educational Publishing Company's Welsh Drama Series in 1922. With thanks to the National Library of Wales for this information.

30 Pitches, 'A Tradition in Transition', 35 n7.

31 Young, 'Formless, Pretentious, Hideous and Revolting', 99.

32 Letter from Stephen Murray to Michael Mullin (30 September 1972), cited in Michael Mullin, 'Augures and Understood Relations: Theodore Komisarjevsky's *Macbeth*', *Educational Theatre Journal* 26, no. 1 (1974): 20.

33 Komisarjevsky, *Myself and the Theatre*, 161.

34 Komisarjevsky, *The Theatre and a Changing Civilisation*, 160.

35 Konstantin Rudnitsky, *Russian and Soviet Theatre: Tradition and the Avant-Garde* (London: Thames and Hudson, 2000), 224.

36 Rudnitsky, *Russian and Soviet Theatre*, 224.

37 *The Observer*, 2 May 1926, Cadbury Research Library, University of Birmingham, MS38/5226.

38 Ibid.

39 *The Sunday Times*, 29 May 1932, Cadbury Research Library, University of Birmingham, MS38/1123. 'Grock' here means 'clown-like'.

40 See Louise Peacock, *Serious Play: Modern Clown Performance* (Bristol: Intellect, 2009), 67–8.

41 *The Observer*, 29 May 1932, Cadbury Research Library, University of Birmingham, MS38/1123.

42 For more details about this play and Komisarjevsky's production see Steve Nicholson, 'Censoring Revolution: The Lord Chamberlain and the Soviet Union', *New Theatre Quarterly* 8 (November 1992): 32; Claire Warden, 'Moscow, St Petersburg, London: Hubert Griffith and the Search for Russian Truth', *Comparative Drama* 49, no. 1 (Spring 2015).

43 Hubert Griffith, 'Preface' in *Red Sunday* (London: Cayme Press, 1929).

44 Komisarjevsky, *Myself and the Theatre*, 156.

45 *The Stage*, 14 July 1929, Cadbury Research Library, University of Birmingham, MS38/236.

46 Komisarjevsky, *Myself and the Theatre*, 141.

47 Interview. *The Daily Telegraph*, 26 July 1932.

48 Borovsky, *A Triptych*, 400.

49 See Mullin, 'Augures and Understood Relations' for a more thorough description of this play.

50 Ibid., 25.

51 Komisarjevsky, *The Theatre and a Changing Civilisation*, 23.

52 Komisarjevsky, *Myself and the Theatre*, 45, 52, emphasis in original.

53 Ronald Mackenzie, *Musical Chairs* (London: Samuel French, 1940 [1932]), 7, 65.

54 Jonathan Croall, *John Gielgud: Matinee Idol to Movie Star* (London: Methuen, 2011), 145.

55 For a practical reading of Meyerholdian biomechanics see Jonathan Pitches, *Vsevolod Meyerhold* (London: Routledge, 2003), 67–73; for more on Tairov's *Shakuntala* see Rudnitsky, *Russian and Soviet Theatre*, 15–17.

56 David Allen, *Performing Chekhov* (London: Routledge, 2000), 163.

57 Komisarjevsky, *Myself and the Theatre*, 149.

58 Ctd in Borovsky, *A Triptych*, 294.

59 Komisarjevsky, *Myself and the Theatre*, 126–7.

60 Ibid., 171.

61 Alexander Tairov, *Notes of a Director* (Florida: Miami UP, 1983), 82.

62 Komisarjevsky, *Myself and the Theatre*, 149.

63 Incidentally Komisarjevsky's final production in the United States was also an opera: *Wozzeck* in 1952.

64 Borovsky, *A Triptych*, 308.

65 Cited in Bartoshevich, 'Theodore Komisarjevsky', 104.

66 See, for example, 'Prince Igor at Covent Garden', *Times*, 5 November 1919, 10.

67 Komisarjevsky, *The Theatre and a Changing Civilisation*, 25.

68 The string has been analysed as a pure symbol, as a sign of disconnect in the family, as comment on the tragedy of the historical moment or the passing of the old order. For further suggestions see A.G. Cross, 'The Breaking Strings of Chekhov and Turgenev', *The Slavonic and East European Review* 47, no. 109 (July 1969): 510–13; Maurice Valency, *The Breaking String: The Plays of Anton Chekhov* (Oxford: Oxford UP, 1966). For a more recent interpretation see Adrian Curtin, *Avant-Garde Theatre Sound: Staging Sonic Modernity* (Basingstoke: Palgrave, 2014), 44–51.

69 Desmond MacCarthy, *Theatre* (London: MacGibbon and Less, 1954), 101.

70 Laurence Senelick, *The Chekhov Theatre: A Century of Plays in Performance* (Cambridge: Cambridge UP, 1999), 140.

71 Robert Tracy, 'Komisarjevsky's 1926 *Three Sisters*', in *Chekhov on the British Stage*, ed. Patrick Miles (Cambridge: Cambridge UP, 1993), 65, 72.

72 N.C. Royde-Smith, 'Producers', *The Outlook*, 30 January 1926, 73 in Borovsky, *A Triptych*, 350.

73 Borovsky, *A Triptych*, 357.

74 Pitches, 'A Tradition in Transition', 31.

75 Norman Marshall, *The Other Theatre* (London: John Lehmann, 1947), 221.

76 Dan Dietz, *The Complete Book of 1940s Broadway Musicals* (Lanham: Rowman and Littlefield, 2015), 20.

77 Dietz, *The Complete Book of 1940s Broadway Musicals*, 21.

78   Ibid., 20.

79   Komisarjevsky, *Myself and the Theatre*, 142.

80   Ibid., 147.

81   Allen, *Performing Chekhov*, 167.

82   Komisarjevsky, *Myself and the Theatre*, 143.

83   Ibid., 145.

84   Ibid., 146.

85   Previously known as the Moscow Private Opera House. Komisarjevsky, *Myself and the Theatre*, 151.

86   Ibid., 171.

87   *The Manchester Guardian*, 27 August 1923.

88   Ibid.

89   *New York Times,* 25 February 1923.

90   Komisarjevsky, *Myself and the Theatre*, between 170 and 171 and 174 and 175.

91   *New York Times,* 25 February 1923.

92   Ibid., 11 February 1923.

93   Theodore Komisarjevsky and Lee Simonson, *Settings and Costumes of the Modern Stage* (London: Studio Publications, 1933), 97–8.

94   Simonson had seen Meyerhold's *Roar China* (which premiered on 23 January 1926 and then went on a foreign tour in 1929), praising it for its 'simplicity and unity of design', Komisarjevsky and Simonson, *Settings and Costumes of the Modern Stage*, 98.

95   In fact, as we have argued in the section on Komisarjevsky's **Art**, integrated theatrical thinking was by no means the norm in Britain either.

96   Komisarjevsky and Simonson, *Settings and Costumes of the Modern Stage*, 98.

97   Komisarjevsky, *Myself and the Theatre*, 172.

98   Borovsky, *A Triptych*, 357.

99   Norman Marshall cited in Allen, *Performing Chekhov,* 167.

100 See particularly Allen, *Performing Chekhov*; Tracy, 'Komisarjevsky's 1926 *Three Sisters*'; Senelick, *The Chekhov Theatre*; Victor Emeljanow, 'Komisarjevsky's Three Sisters: The Prompt Book', *Theatre Notebook* 41, no. 2 (1987): 56–66.

101 Komisarjevsky, *Myself and the Theatre*, 88.

102 Prompt book of *Three Sisters,* Houghton Archive. Robert Tracy has this line cut in his analysis (71) but the prompt copy is at best ambiguous as to whether this line was retained or not.

103 This march is sometimes attributed to John Sousa (for instance in Senelick's *The Chekhov Theatre*, 159) but it was originally composed by Austrian Joseph Wagner and became a favourite of the American Sousa's.

104 Prompt book of *Three Sisters,* Houghton Archive.

105 Ibid.

106 Allen, *Performing Chekhov*, 166.

107 John Gielgud, 'Tradition, Style and the Theatre Today', in *Shakespeare Survey Online* (Cambridge: Cambridge UP, 2007), 103.

108 Allen, *Performing Chekhov*, 167.

109 Play Direction, Synopsis of Lectures: Houghton Library, Harvard, HTC bMS Th 490, folder 68.

110 See Komisarjevsky, *Myself and the Theatre*, 149, for details of Bernardi.

111 Letter to Mr Bennett, 19 December 1927, Houghton Archive, emphasis in original. Compare this with his statement in Komisarjevsky, *The Theatre and a Changing Civilisation*: 'An artist-regisseur cannot help respecting the creative individualities of his actors and knows that no more can be achieved by the methods of the drill sergeant than by committee meetings' (18).

112 Shepherd, *Direction: Readings in Theatre Practice*, 5.

113 Komisarjevsky, *Myself and the Theatre*, 83.

114 Ibid.

115 Borovsky, *A Triptych*, 262.

116 In fact, Komisarjevsky's blend was comparable with other regimes of acting which were emerging at the time, including Meyerhold's. See Edward Braun, *Meyerhold on Theatre* (London: Methuen Drama, 1991), 153–6.

117 Oliver Sayler and Victor Borovsky are two of the exceptions to this with some details on Komisarjevsky's studio.

118 Komisarjevsky, *Changing Civilisation,* 22.

119 *Play Direction*, Houghton Archive.

120 Komisarjevsky, *Myself and the Theatre,* 82.

121 Pitches, 'A Tradition in Transition', 34.

122 There is a fuller consideration of Komis as a trainer of actors in Pitches, 'A Tradition in Transition', 13–37.

123 Young, 'Formless, Pretentious, Hideous and Revolting', 100.

124 *Times*, 29 November 1921, 8.

125 *New York Times*, 9 January 2008.

126 Lecture announcement, Houghton Archive.

127 Press Advert, 1939–40, Houghton Archive.

128 Group Courses in Drama: Curriculum, Houghton Archive.

129 See for instance Susie Eisner Eley, 'Trained to Teach: Five Dancers-Turned-Teachers Talk about How They Made the Transition from Performance to Education', *Dance Teacher* 22, no. 3 (March 2000): 50–2.

130 Marshall, 'Komisarjevsky, Theodore (1882–1954)'.

131 Ibid.

132 Gielgud, 'Mr Komisarjevsky'.

133 Marshall, 'Komisarjevsky, Theodore (1882–1954)'.

134   Dennis Kennedy, 'Confessions of an Encyclopedist', in *Theorizing Practice, Redefining Theatre History*, ed. W.B. Worthen and Peter Holland (Basingstoke: Palgrave, 2004), 46.

135   Thomas Postlewait, 'Writing History Today', *Theatre Survey* 41, no. 2 (2000): 95. See also Erica Fischer-Lichte's alternative definition of micro-histories in *The Routledge Introduction to Theatre and Performance Studies* (Abingdon: Routledge, 2014), 73.

136   Milly S. Barranger, *Margaret Webster: A Life in the Theater* (Michigan: University of Michigan Press, 2004), 53.

137   John Gielgud, *Early Stages* (London: Hodder and Stoughton, 1987), 65–6.

138   See Lewis Funke and John. E Booth, *Actors Talk about Acting: Nine Interviews with Stars of the Theatre* (London: Thames and Hudson, 1961), 6–7; Michael Billington, *Peggy Ashcroft* (London: John Murray, 1988), 53; Elsa Lanchester, *Charles Laughton and I* (London: Faber and Faber, 1938), 66.

139   These letters and Sewell's journal were first made available to me by the generosity of Richard Thompson. They are now housed in Brotherton Library's Special Collections at the University of Leeds.

140   In this sense viewed collectively the letters bear an uncanny resemblance to the fictional set of lessons conducted by Komis's countryman, Richard Boleslavsky, with his tutee, known only as the Creature in Boleslavsky, Richard, *Acting: the First Six Lessons* New York: Theatre Arts Books, 1933.

141   Letters, 17 June 1930.

142   Letters, 13 July 1930.

143   Letters, 14 September 1932.

144   Sewell's Journal, 10 August 1930. See Pitches's essay in *Russians in Britain* for an analysis focused on the training embedded in this statement.

145   Sewell was in Komisarjevsky's production of *Mesmer* at the Kings Theatre in Glasgow (1935).

146   Letters, 24 April 1950.

147   Letters, 12 May 1950.

148   Borovsky, *A Triptych*, 453.

149   David Bevington and David Scott Kastan, eds, *William Shakespeare: The Late Romances* (New York: Bantam Classics, 2008), 205.

150   Letters, 20 November 1949, emphasis in original.

151   Letters, 22 April 1939.

152   These dates are extrapolated from papers in the Houghton archive, Harvard: An advert of 1940 advertising the start of the School and a Komisarjevsky Drama Studio letter-head dated 1952.

153   Komisarjevsky and Simonson, *Settings and Costumes of the Modern Stage*, 14.

154   Komisarjevsky, *My Life*, 148.

155   Richard Mennen, 'Theodore Komisarjevsky's Production of the *Merchant of Venice*', *Theatre Journal* 31, no. 3 (1979): 389.

156 Mennen, 'Theodore Komisarjevsky's production of the *Merchant of Venice*', 398.

157 Ibid., 397.

158 Ibid.

159 Ibid.

160 Borovsky's section on Komisarjevsky (the younger) stretches to 246 pages. Blanch's name appears against one illustration (for *Giannina Bernadone*) but not in the main text, nor the index.

161 Sybil Rosenfeld, *A Short History of Scene Design in Great Britain* (Oxford: Basil Blackwell, 1973), 180.

162 Komisarjevsky and Simonson, *Settings and Costumes of the Modern Stage*, 29.

163 Cary DiPietro's *Shakespeare and Modernism* (Cambridge: Cambridge UP, 2006), for instance, cites both *Merchant* and *Macbeth* as pivotal in British Theatre history with no mention of Blanch (118–36).

164 In Dennis Kennedy, *Looking at Shakespeare* (Cambridge: Cambridge UP, 2001) Dennis Kennedy does acknowledge Blanch as a collaborator on *Merchant* (128) but not for the later production of *Macbeth*, on which Blanch also worked as a designer (129).

165 Lesley Blanch, *Journey into the Mind's Eye* (London: Eland Publishing, 2014, Kindle version, no pagination).

166 Lesley Blanch, *On the Wilder Shores of Love: A Bohemian Life* (London: Virago: 2015), 123.

167 Blanch, *On the Wilder Shores of Love*, 9.

168 Cf. *The Guardian*, Saturday 9 July 2005: 'There is something of a cult around Blanch. And cult members understand that her most famous title [*On the Wilder Shores of Love*] is only the starting point: *Under A Lilac-Bleeding Star* (1963), *Nine-Tiger Man* (1965), *Pavilions of the Heart* (1974), an extended introduction to Harriette Wilson's Memoirs: *The Memoirs of the Reigning Courtesan of Regency London* (1985), two hard-to-find but treasured cookbooks and the recently re-published *The Sabres of Paradise* (1960), *Journey into the Mind's Eye* (1968) and *Pierre Loti* (1983) all await the reader.' Blanch's executrix, Georgia de Chamberet identifies her as the author of twelve books, however. Lesley Blanch, *Far to Go and Many to Love* (London: Quartet Books, 2017).

169 See the MOMA press release from 13–14 January 1934: https://www.moma. org/momaorg/shared/pdfs/docs/press_archives/158/releases/MOMA_1933-34_0025_1934-01-13.pdf?2010

170 For an example of her costume design see Blanch, *Far to Go and Many to Love*, 9. For the original playbill see https://www.google. com/culturalinstitute/beta/asset/le-club-des-canards-mandarins/ MQF8aynNcZ213Q?hl=fr

171 MOMA press release, 2.

172 Kennedy, *Looking at Shakespeare*, 128.

173 Blanch, *On the Wilder Shores of Love*, 9.

174   Cf. Mel Gordon, *Stanislavsky in America* (Abingdon: Routledge, 2010),
      xiii–xiv. Of the twenty-five acting studios listed in *Theatre Arts Monthly*,
      eight were headed by Russians or East Europeans, which didn't include
      Komisarjevsky who is identified as 'anti-Stanislavsky' (xiv).

175   Letters, 24 October 1945, emphasis in original.

176   W. Gareth Jones, 'Far from the West End: Chekhov and the Welsh Language
      Stage 1924–1991' in *Chekhov on the British Stage*, ed. Patrick Miles
      (Cambridge: Cambridge UP, 1993), 102.

177   *Manchester Guardian*, 24 January 1927, 13.

178   Ibid., 30 July 1927, 6.

179   Ibid., 3 August 1927, 3.

180   Jones, 'Far from the West End', 103.

181   See the *Dictionary of Welsh Biography: Wales*, http://yba.llgc.org.uk/en/s2-
      JONE-EVA-1895.html

182   Jones, 'Far from the West End', 104.

183   Simon Shepherd, *The Cambridge Introduction to Modern British Theatre*
      (Cambridge: CUP, 2009), 104, square brackets in original.

184   Shepherd, *The Cambridge Introduction to Modern British Theatre*, 105.

185   Jim Davis et al., 'Researching Theatre History and Historiography', in
      Research Methods in Theatre and Performance, ed. Helen Nicholson and Baz
      Kershaw (Edinburgh: Edinburgh UP, 2011), 96.

186   Cf. Komisarjevsky, *Myself and the Theatre:* 'A perfect actor of the drama [...]
      must be able to combine all the forms of expression he has to use, create a
      synthesis of them subordinating all of them to his conception of the part and
      to the single rhythm of his emotions' (143–4).

187   DiPietro, *Shakespeare and Modernism,* 124.

188   Komisarjevsky, *Changing Civilisation,* 137–8.

189   Komisarjevsky, *Myself and the Theatre*, 86–7.

190   Catherine Schuler, *Women in Russian Theatre* (London: Routledge, 1996),
      183.

191   Cf., for instance, his letter to Philliada Swewell of 1945: 'The fact of my
      alienship was bluntly proved when I wanted to come to England to help my
      adoptive Country in its hectic war time, & nobody moved a finger to help in
      doing it, while rascals & jealous careerists, *a la* Barnes & Basil Dean, even
      refused to give me a job, & the Stratford Memorial Theatre, which made tons
      of money on my productions, let alone the artistic & idealistic significance
      of these, having changed its directors twice, didn't even think of offering that
      job to me!' Letters, 24 October 1945.

192   Berry, Ralph, 'Komisarjevsky in Britain', *Theatrephile* 2, no. 5 (Winter
      1984/5): 17–21.

193   Cf. Irving Wardle, *The Theatres of George Devine* (London: Jonathan Cape,
      1978), 27: Devine 'clung to Komisarjevsky for several years, absorbing
      two beliefs which shaped his career'. These were: (i) acting to innovate

surreptitiously within the establishment system and (ii) attaching acting schools to theatres.

194 Marshall, 'Komisarjevsky, Theodore (1882–1954)'.

195 See for instance Sheridan Morley: '*The Three Sisters* was not a success, but it had at least introduced Gielgud to the legendary Russian director and Stanislavsky disciple Komisarjevsky, who was soon to marry Peggy Ashcroft and was already widely known in rehearsal as "Come and seduce me" on account of his passion for young actresses' (*John Gielgud*, 62).

Chapter 3

1 Tyrone Guthrie, *A Life in the Theatre* (New York: McGraw-Hill, 1959), 2–5.

2 Harold Hobson, 'Guthrie, Sir (William) Tyrone (1900–1971)', in *Oxford Dictionary of National Biography* (Oxford: Oxford University Press, 2004; online edn, January 2011), http://www.oxforddnb.com.ezproxy.library.dal.ca/view/article/31182, accessed 4 September 2017.

3 Guthrie, *A Life in the Theatre*, 10.

4 Ibid., 10.

5 See, for instance, Jon Gielgud's comments in Sheridan Morley, *John Gielgud: The Authorized Biography* (New York: Simon and Schuster, 2002), 177.

6 Ric Knowles, *Reading the Material Theatre* (Cambridge: CUP, 2004), 9.

7 Knowles, *Reading*, 19.

8 Ibid., 204.

9 Guthrie, *A Life in the Theatre*, 16.

10 J.T. Grein, 'The World of the Theatre', *Illustrated London News*, 23 July 1932.

11 Alfred Rossi, *Astonish Us in the Morning: Tyrone Guthrie Remembered* (London: Hutchinson and Co., 1977), 291.

12 Rossi, *Astonish Us*, 27.

13 Robert Shaughnessy, *The Shakespeare Effect: A History of Twentieth-Century Performance* (Houndmills: Palgrave Macmillan, 2002), 89–91.

14 Shaughnessy, *Shakespeare Effect*, 83.

15 James Forsyth, *Tyrone Guthrie: A Biography* (London: Hamish Hamilton, 1976), 32.

16 Forsyth, *Tyrone Guthrie*, 94.

17 Paul Cornwell, *Only by Failure: The Many Faces of the Impossible Life of Terence Gray* (Cambridge: Salt Publishing, 2004), 178.

18 Guthrie tells this story directly in 'Conversations with Tyrone Guthrie': BBC Transcription of Conversations between Guthrie and an Unnamed Interviewer (London: BBC, 1964), Victoria and Albert Museum Theatre and Performance Archive, Reel 10, 1. He tells it more indirectly in *A Life in the Theatre*, 181, where Assistant Stage Manager George Chamberlain does the deed of standing up to 'Miss Tempest'. See also Rossi, *Astonish Us in the Morning*, 87.

19   Guthrie, *A Life in the Theatre*, 80.

20   Qtd in Forsyth, *Tyrone Guthrie*, 228.

21   Iain Mackintosh, *The Guthrie Thrust Stage: A Living Legacy* (London: Association of British Theatre Technicians and The Royal Shakespeare Company, 2011), 1.

22   Because this series is intended to focus on theatre, we do not address Guthrie's work in radio and other media in any detail. For a comprehensive account of his work across art forms, see Forsyth, *Tyrone Guthrie*.

23   Gay McAuley, *Space in Performance: Making Meaning in the Theatre* (Ann Arbor: University of Michigan Press, 1999), 9.

24   Shaughnessy, *The Shakespeare Effect*, 80.

25   Peter Rankin, *Joan Littlewood: Dreams and Realities* (London: Oberon, 2016), 14.

26   Peter Brook, *Threads of Time: A Memoir* (London: Methuen, 1998), 29; see also Robert Shaughnessy, 'Tyrone Guthrie,' in *Great Shakespeareans 15: Poel, Granville Barker, Guthrie, Wanamaker*, ed. Cary M. Mazer (London: Bloomsbury, 2013), 98.

27   Nicholas Wroe, 'Peter Brook: The Magus', *Guardian*, 12 May 2007.

28   'Conversations', Reels 7 and 8, 13.

29   'Conversations', Reel 6, 12.

30   'Conversations', Reels 7 and 8, 9.

31   Tyrone Guthrie, *Theatre Prospect* (London: Wishart and Co., 1932), 40.

32   'Conversations', Reel 9, 10.

33   'Conversations', Reels 10 and 11, 7.

34   'Conversations', Reels 10 and 11, 5.

35   Forsyth, *Tyrone Guthrie*, 77.

36   'Conversations', Reels 10 and 11, 5.

37   Dennis Kennedy, 'The Director, the Spectator and the Eiffel Tower', *Theatre Research International*, 30 (1 March 2005): 36–48, 44.

38   Simon Shepherd, *Direction* (Basingstoke: Palgrave Macmillan, 2012), 199, emphasis added.

39   Shaughnessy, 'Tyrone Guthrie', 104.

40   Guthrie, *Theatre Prospect*, 9, 10.

41   Ibid., 16.

42   Ibid., 17.

43   Ibid., 24.

44   'Conversations', Reel 3, 12.

45   Guthrie, *Theatre Prospect*, 49.

46   Ibid., 51.

47   Ibid., 52, 53, 54, 60.

48   Ibid., 61.

49 See Tom Cornford, 'Jacques Lecoq and the Studio Tradition', in *The Routledge Companion to Jacques Lecoq*, ed. Mark Evans and Rick Kemp (Abingdon: Routledge, 2016), 43–50.

50 Rankin, *Joan Littlewood*, 14.

51 Shaughnessy, 'Tyrone Guthrie', 101.

52 'Conversations', Reels 13 and 14, 1.

53 Knowles, *Reading the Material Theatre*, 19.

54 'Conversations', Reel 5, 11.

55 Guthrie, *Theatre Prospect*, 43.

56 Guthrie, *A Life in the Theatre*, 53–61. See also Cornwell, *Only by Failure*, 185–6.

57 Knowles, *Reading the Material Theatre*, 19.

58 Forsyth, *Tyrone Guthrie*, 111.

59 Ibid., 112.

60 Ibid., 113.

61 'Conversations', Reel 12, 12.

62 Qtd in Shepherd, *Direction*, 78.

63 Harcourt Williams, *Old Vic Saga* (London: Winchester Publications, 1949), 126.

64 Williams, *Old Vic Saga*, 133.

65 'Sweet Aloes', Internet Broadway Database Entry, https://www.ibdb.com/broadway-production/sweet-aloes-12102, accessed on 12 September 2017.

66 Michael Sidnell, *Dances of Death: The Group Theatre of London in the Thirties* (London: Faber and Faber, 1984), 52.

67 Sidnell, *Dances of Death*, 75.

68 Ibid., 75.

69 Shaughnessy, 'Tyrone Guthrie', 110.

70 *Old Vic and Sadler's Wells Magazine*, September–October 1936.

71 Croall, *John Gielgud*, 123, 126.

72 *The Sunday Times*, 20 October 1935.

73 *The Daily Telegraph*, 29 November 1935.

74 Ibid.

75 Laurence Olivier, *On Acting* (London: Weidenfeld and Nicholson, 1986), 71.

76 Olivier, *On Acting*, 70.

77 See, for example, Carol Rutter, *Enter the Body: Women and Representation on Shakespeare's Stage* (London: Routledge, 2001), 31.

78 Shaughnessy, 'Tyrone Guthrie', 113.

79 'Conversations', Reels 13 and 14, 13.

80 Rossi, *Astonish Us in the Morning*, 33.

81 Williams, *Old Vic Saga*, 144.

82   Alfred Rossi, *Minneapolis Rehearsals: Tyrone Guthrie Directs Hamlet* (Berkeley: University of California Press, 1970), 59.

83   Guthrie, *A Life in the Theatre*, 192.

84   'Conversations', Reels 13 and 14, 12.

85   'C.E.M.A and "Old Vic"', in the programme for the Old Vic tour of *The Merchant of Venice*, autumn 1941, V&A Theatre and Performance Collection, ACGB/34/76 (1 of 24).

86   'Report on the Recent Activities of the Old Vic and Sadler's Wells Companies', December 1941, V&A Theatre and Performance Collection, ACGB/34/76 (1 of 24).

87   'Conversations', Reels 13 and 14, 4.

88   'The Old Vic and Sadler's Wells, 1940–1941', in 'Report on the Recent Activities of the Old Vic and Sadler's Wells Companies', December 1941, V&A Theatre and Performance Collection, ACGB/34/76 (1 of 24).

89   Private Correspondence, 26 June 1941, in V&A Theatre and Performance Collection, ACGB/34/76 (3 of 24).

90   'Closer Co-operation with CEMA, Notes by T. Guthrie, 17 June 1942', V&A Theatre and Performance Collections, ACGB/34/76, 2 of 24.

91   Handwritten note, 4 July 1942, V&A Theatre and Performance Collections, ACGB/34/76, 2 of 24.

92   'Policy for Old Vic Drama' (dated 28 February 1944), submitted for consideration by a special meeting of the Old Vic Governors on 6 March 1944, V&A Theatre and Performance Collection, ACGB/34/76 (1 of 24).

93   'Conversations', Reels 13 and 14, 5.

94   See Tom Cornford, 'The English Theatre Studios of Michael Chekhov and Michel Saint-Denis 1935–1965' (PhD thesis, University of Warwick, 2012), 220–33 (http://webcat.warwick.ac.uk/record=b2684505~S1, accessed 12 September 2017).

95   Shaughnessy, 'Tyrone Guthrie', 131.

96   Terence Hawkes, *Meaning by Shakespeare* (London: Routledge, 1992), 130.

97   Ivor Brown, '*Ane Satyre of the Thrie Estaits* at the Edinburgh Festival', in *Ane Satyre of the Thrie Estaits*, ed. James Kingsley and Sir David Lindsay (London: Cassell and Company, 1954), 27.

98   Brown, '*Ane Satyre of the Thrie Estaits* at the Edinburgh Festival', 27.

99   Guthrie, *A Life in the Theatre*, 306.

100 Brown, '*Ane Satyre of the Thrie Estaits* at the Edinburgh Festival', 29.

101 Ibid., 29.

102 Ibid., 30.

103 Ibid., 31.

104 'Conversations', Reel 11, 21.

105 'Conversations', Reels 7 and 8, 11.

106 See Rossi, *Astonish Us in the Morning*, 297–302.

107 Guthrie, *A Life in the Theatre*, 250.

108 'Conversations', Reel 6, 8.

109 Qtd in Victoria Etnier Villamil, *'O Ma Carmen': Bizet's Fateful Gypsy in Potrayals from 1875 to the Present* (Jefferson: McFarland and Co., 2017), 118.

110 'Conversations', Reel 12, 10.

111 Ibid.

112 Guthrie, *A New Theatre*, 36.

113 Qtd in John Pettigrew and Jamie Portman, *Stratford: The First Thirty Years. Volume 1: 1953–1967* (Toronto: Macmillan, 1985), 29.

114 Guthrie, *A New Theatre*, 70.

115 Nathan Cohen, 'That Great First Night at Stratford', *Toronto Star*, 4 June 1966, B25.

116 Brooks Atkinson, 'Atkinson Assesses Minneapolis' First Repertory Season', *Chicago Tribune*, 21 September 1963, 1B:17.

117 Nathan Cohen, 'Theatre Today: English Canada', *Tamarack Review* 13 (Autumn 1959): 37.

118 Joseph Wesley Ziegler, *Regional Theatre: The Revolutionary Stage* (Minneapolis: University of Minnesota Press, 1973), 67.

119 M.G. Aune, 'Importing Shakespeare: Tyrone Guthrie and British Cold War Cultural Colonialism', *Shakespeare* 5, no. 4 (December 2009): 425.

120 Lorenzo Veracini, *The Settler Colonial Present* (Houndmills: Palgrave Macmillan, 2015), 2.

121 Guthrie, *A Life in the Theatre*, 74.

122 Ibid., 76.

123 Ibid., 77.

124 Ibid., 314.

125 Ibid., 329.

126 Ibid., 318.

127 Pettigrew and Portman, *Stratford*, 11.

128 Rossi, *Astonish Us in the Morning*, 184.

129 Ibid., 182.

130 Richard Ouzounian, *Stratford Gold: 50 Years, 50 Stars, 50 Conversations* (Toronto: McArthur and Co., 2002), 62.

131 Ouzounian, *Stratford Gold*, 50.

132 Shaughnessy, 'Tyrone Guthrie', 134.

133 Dennis Salter, 'Acting Shakespeare in Postcolonial Space', in *Shakespeare, Theory, and Performance*, ed. James C. Bulman (London: Routledge, 1996), 120.

134 Richard Paul Knowles, 'From Nationalist to Multinational: The Stratford Festival, Free Trade and the Discourses of Intercultural Tourism', *Theatre Journal* 47, no. 1 (March 1995): 26.

135 Guthrie, *A Life in the Theatre*, 207.

136 Qtd in Tom Patterson and Allan Gould, *First Stage: The Making of the Stratford Festival* (Toronto: McLelland and Stewart, 1987), 181.

137 J.L. Styan, *The Shakespeare Revolution: Criticism and Performance in the Twentieth Century* (Cambridge: CUP, 1977), 201.

138 Nathan Cohen, 'Stratford after Fifteen Years', *Queen's Quarterly* 75, no. 1 (Spring 1968): 35–61, 52.

139 Cohen, 'Stratford after Fifteen Years', 52.

140 Ibid., 56.

141 Salter, 'Acting Shakespeare in Postcolonial Space', 122.

142 Richard Paul Knowles, 'Shakespeare, 1993, and the Discourses of the Stratford Festival, Ontario', *Shakespeare Quarterly* 45 (1994): 219.

143 Salter, 'Acting Shakespeare in Postcolonial Space', 122.

144 Shaughnessy, *The Shakespeare Effect*, 146.

145 Pettigrew and Portman, *Stratford*, 37.

146 Guthrie, *A Life in the Theatre*, 319.

147 Ibid.

148 Ibid., 320.

149 Peter Brooks, *The Melodramatic Imagination: Balzac, Henry James, Melodrama, and the Mode of Excess* (New Haven: Yale UP, 1976), 47.

150 Pettigrew and Portman, *Stratford*, 5.

151 Martin Hunter, *Romancing the Bard: Stratford at Fifty* (Toronto: Dundurn Press, 2001), 15.

152 Ouzounian, *Stratford Gold*, 26.

153 Pettigrew and Portman, *Stratford*, 5.

154 Hunter, 16.

155 Details of this scene are featured in *The Stratford Adventure*, dir. Morton Parker (National Film Board of Canada, 1954).

156 William Hawkins, 'Canada's "Richard III" Brilliant', *New York World-Telegram and Sun*, 14 July 1953.

157 Salter, 'Acting Shakespeare in Postcolonial Space', 120.

158 Knowles, 'From Nationalist to Multinational', 26.

159 Ouzounian, *Stratford Gold*, 77.

160 Quoted in Patterson and Gould, *First Stage*, 182–3.

161 Brooks Atkinson, 'Stratford, Ont., Opens Its Bard Fete with Spectacular but Shallow "Richard III"', *New York Times*, 15 July 1953, 22.

162 Tyrone Guthrie, 'A Long View of the Stratford Festival', in *Twice Have the Trumpets Sounded: A Record of the Stratford Shakespearean Festival in Canada, 1954* (Toronto: Clarke, Irwin, and Co., 1954), 152–72, 156.

163 Pettigrew and Portman, *Stratford*, 7.

164 Shaughnessy, 'Tyrone Guthrie', 140.

165 Guthrie, *A New Theatre*, 23.

166 Ibid., 26.

167 Ibid.

168 Ibid., 45.

169 'Conversations', Reel 3, 3.

170 Guthrie, *A New Theatre*, 46. See Aune, 'Importing Shakespeare', 431, for a detailed analysis of the implications of Guthrie's rhetoric here.

171 Guthrie, *A New Theatre*, 26, emphasis Guthrie's.

172 Ibid., 41.

173 Ibid., 43.

174 Ibid.

175 Ibid., 42, emphasis Guthrie's.

176 Shaughnessy, 'Tyrone Guthrie', 113.

177 Guthrie, *A New Theatre*, 97.

178 Ibid., 103.

179 Ibid., 100.

180 Ibid., 100–1.

181 Aune, 'Importing Shakespeare', 434.

182 Guthrie, *A New Theatre*, 89.

183 Ibid., 109.

184 Aune, 'Importing Shakespeare', 434.

185 Ibid., 88.

186 Ibid.

187 Rossi, *Minneapolis Rehearsals*, 10.

188 Rossi, *Astonish Us in the Morning*, 58.

189 Rossi, *Minneapolis Rehearsals*, 6–7.

190 Ibid., 17.

191 Ibid., 55.

192 Walter Kerr, Rev. of *Hamlet* at the Guthrie Theatre, dir. Tyrone Guthrie, *New York Herald Tribune*, 9 May 1963.

193 Atkinson, 'Atkinson Assesses Minneapolis', B1:17.

194 Claudia Cassidy, Rev. of *Hamlet* and *The Miser* at the Guthrie Theatre, *Chicago Sunday Tribune*, 19 May 1963.

195 Henry Hewes, 'Broadway Postscript', *Saturday Review*, 25 May 1963, 24.

196 Kerr, Rev. of *Hamlet*.

197 Herbert Whittaker, 'Guthrie Gimmicks', in *Minneapolis Rehearsals: Tyrone Guthrie Directs Hamlet, Volume 1,* by Alfred Rossi (Berkeley, 1970), 11.

198 Hewes, 'Broadway Postscript', 24.

199 Whittaker, 'Guthrie Gimmicks', 11.

200 Hewes, 'Broadway Postscript', 24.

201 Clive Barnes, 'Aeschylus is No Match for Guthrie's Gimmicks', *Chicago Tribune*, 18 December 1968, Section 2, 7.

202 Cecil Smith, 'Tyrone Guthrie's "Atreus" Unveiled', *Los Angeles Times*, 24 July 1967, D1.

203 Rossi, *Astonish Us in the Morning*, 37.

204 Ibid., 216.

205 Ibid., 75.

206 See Martin Barker, *Live to Your Local Cinema, The Remarkable Rise of Livecasting* (Basingstoke, Palgrave Macmillan: 2013).

207 Hasan Bakshi and David Throsby, 'Culture of Innovation: An Economic Analysis of Innovation in Arts and Cultural Organisations', National Endowment for Science, Technology and the Arts, June 2010, 30, 32. https://www.nesta.org.uk/sites/default/files/culture_of_innovation.pdf, accessed 1 September 2017.

208 Debra Yeo, 'Stratford Festival Records Fourth Consecutive Surplus', *Toronto Star,* 25 March 2017. https://www.thestar.com/entertainment/stage/2017/03/25/stratford-festival-records-fourth-consecutive-surplus.html, accessed 21 August 2017.

209 Terry Bridge, 'Ontario Pledges $20 Million towards Stratford Festival's New Tom Patterson Theatre', *Stratford Beacon Herald,* 30 May 2017. http://www.stratfordbeaconherald.com/2017/05/30/ontario-pledges-20-million-towards-stratford-festivals-new-tom-patterson-theatre, accessed 21 August 2017.

210 Kevyn Burger, 'The Ecosystem of the Guthrie Theater', *Minnesota Business Magazine,* 30 March 2017. http://www.minnesotabusiness.com/ecosystem-guthrie-theater, accessed 21 August 2017.

211 Rossi, *Astonish Us in the Morning*, 65.

212 Ibid., 183.

213 Rossi, *Minneapolis Rehearsals*, 18.

214 Rossi, *Astonish Us in the Morning*, 277.

215 Rossi, *Minneapolis Rehearsals*, 18.

BIBLIOGRAPHY

General

Britton, John. *Encountering Ensemble*. London: Methuen, 2013.

Copeau, Jacques. *Copeau: Texts on Theatre*, edited and translated by John Rudlin and Norman Paul. London and New York: Routledge, 1990.

Evans, Mark. 'The French Ensemble Tradition: Jacques Copeau, Michel Saint-Denis and Jacques Lecoq'. In *Encountering Ensemble*, edited by John Britton, 111–25. London: Bloomsbury, 2013.

Evans, Mark. *Jacques Copeau*. London and New York: Routledge, 2006.

Guthrie, Tyrone. *A Life in the Theatre*. New York: McGraw-Hill, 1959.

Komisarjevsky, Theodore. *Myself and the Theatre*. London: William Heinemann, 1929.

Leiter, Samuel L. *From Belasco to Brook: Representative Directors of the English-Speaking Stage*. New York: Greenwood Press, 1991.

Pitches, Jonathan. 'Star or Team? Theodore Komisarjevsky's Early Developments in Ensemble Playing in the UK'. In *Encountering Ensemble*, edited by John Britton, 94–110. London: Methuen, 2013.

Sidiropolou, Avra. *Authoring Performance: The Director in Contemporary Theatre*. London: Palgrave Macmillan, 2011.

Shepherd, Simon. *Direction: Readings in Theatre Practice*. Basingstoke: Palgrave Macmillan, 2012.

Jacques Copeau

Appler, Vivian. 'Mime, 'Mimes' and Miming'. In *Routledge Companion to Jacques Lecoq*, edited by Mark Evans and Rick Kemp, 19–26. London and New York: Routledge, 2016.

Bablet, Denis. *The Theatre of Edward Gordon Craig*. London: Eyre Methuen, 1981.

Baldwin, Jane. *Michel Saint-Denis and the Shaping of the Modern Actor*. Westport, CT: Praeger, 2003.

Barrault, Jean-Louis. *Reflections on the Theatre*. London: Thames and Hudson, 1951.

Bing, Bernard. 'Le souvenir de Suzanne Bing'. *Revue d'histoire du théâtre*. Revue Trimestrielle, Janvier-Mars Trente-Cinquième Année (1). Paris, Ministry of Culture (1983): 17–21. (Unpublished translation by E. Levin 2011.)

Bing, Suzanne. 'Bodily Technique'. Jacques Copeau Archives, University of Kent at Canterbury, Archive No. 6, undated paper (probably 1920).

Brook, Peter. *The Empty Space*. Harmondsworth: Penguin, 1968.

Copeau, Jacques. 'An Essay of Dramatic Renovation: The Théâtre of the Vieux-Colombier'. *Educational Theatre Journal* (1967): 447–54.

Copeau, Jacques. *Copeau: Texts on Theatre*, edited and translated by John Rudlin and Norman Paul. London and New York: Routledge, 1990.

Copeau, Jacques and Claude Sicard. *Registres VI: L'École du Vieux-Colombier*. Paris: Gallimard Edition, 2000.

Dasté, Catherine. *L'enfant, le theatre, l'ecole*. Paris: Delachoaux et Nisetle, 1975.

Decroux, Etienne. *Words on Mime*, translated by M. Piper. Clarement, CA: Mime Journal, 1985.

Donahue, Thomas. 'Improvisation and the Mask at the École du Vieux-Colombier: The Case of Suzanne Bing'. *Maske und Kothurn* 44, no. 1–2 (1998): 61–72.

Donahue, Thomas. *Jacques Copeau's Friends and Disciples: The Théâtre du Vieux-Colombier in New York City, 1917–1919*. New York: Peter Lang, 2008.

Dorcy, Jean. *The Mime*. New York: Robert Speller, 1975.

Evans, Mark. 'The French Ensemble Tradition: Jacques Copeau, Michel Saint-Denis and Jacques Lecoq'. In *Encountering Ensemble*, edited by John Britton, 111–25. London: Bloomsbury, 2013.

Evans, Mark. *Jacques Copeau*. London and New York: Routledge, 2006.

Evans, Mark. *Movement Training for the Modern Actor*. London: Routledge, 2009.

Evans, Mark. 'The Myth of Pierrot'. In *The Routledge Companion to Commedia dell'Arte*, edited by Judith Chaffee and Olly Crick, 346–54. London and New York: Routledge, 2015.

Evans, Mark and Rick Kemp. *The Routledge Companion to Jacques Lecoq*. London and New York: Routledge, 2016.

Felner, Mira. *Apostles of Silence: The Modern French Mimes*. Cranbury and London: Associated University Presses, 1985.

Fleming, Cassandra. 'A Genealogy of the Embodied Theatre Practices of Suzanne Bing and Michael Chekhov: The use of Play in Actor Training'. PhD thesis, De Montfort University, 2013. Available at: https://www.dora.dmu.ac.uk/xmlui/bitstream/handle/2086/9608/Cassandra%20Fleming%20PhD%20Thesis.pdf;sequence=1

Frost, Anthony and Ralph Yarrow. *Improvisation in Drama*. London: Palgrave Macmillan, 2007.

Knapp, Bettina. *The Reign of the Theatrical Director: French Theatre 1887–1924*. Albany, NY: Whitston, 1988.

Kurkinen, Marjaana. 'The Spectre of the Orient: Modern French Mime and Traditional Japanese Theatre in the 1930s'. PhD thesis, University of Helsinki, Finland, 2000. Available at: http://ethesis.helsinki.fi/julkaisut/hum/taite/vk/kurkinen.

Kurtz, Maurice. *Jacques Copeau: Biography of a Theatre*. Carbondale & Edwardsville: Southern Illinois University, 1999.

Lecoq, Jacques. *The Moving Body: Teaching Creative Theatre*. London: Methuen, 2000.

Lecoq, Jacques. *Theatre of Movement and Gesture*. London and New York: Routledge, 2007.

Leigh, Barbara Kusler. 'Jacques Copeau's School for Actors: Commemorating the Centennial of the Birth of Jacques Copeau'. *Mime Journal: Numbers Nine and Ten*, 1979.

Mnouchkine, Ariane. *l'Art du Présent*. Paris: Actes Sud, 2016.

Naumburg, Margaret. *The Child and the World: Dialogues in Modern Education*. New York: Harcourt, Brace and Company, 1928.

Neuschäfer, Anne. '1970–1975: Ecrire une *Comédie de notre temps* - La filiation avec Jacques Copeau', *Théâtre du Soleil website* (2004). Available at: http://www.theatre-du-soleil.fr/thsol/a-propos-du-theatre-du-soleil/l-historique/1970-1975-ecrire-une-comedie-de?lang=fr

Rudlin, John. *Jacques Copeau*. Cambridge: Cambridge University Press, 1986.

Rudlin, John. 'Jacques Copeau: The quest for sincerity'. In *Actor Training*, edited by Alison Hodge, 43–62. London and New York: Routledge, 2000.

Saint-Denis, Michel. *The Rediscovery of Style*. New York: Theatre Arts Books, 1969.

Saint-Denis, Michel. *Training for the Theatre: Premises and Promises*. London: Heinemann, 1982.

Theodore Komisarjevsky

Allen, David. *Performing Chekhov*. London: Routledge, 2000.

Barranger, Milly S. *Margaret Webster: A Life in the Theater*. Michigan: University of Michigan Press, 2004.

Bartoshevich, Alexei. 'Theodore Komisarjevsky, Chekhov and Shakespeare'. In *Wandering Stars: Russian Émigré Theatre, 1905–1940*, edited by Laurence Senelick, 102–15. Iowa City: Iowa University Press, 1992.

Beasley, Rebecca. 'Modernism's Translations'. In *The Oxford Handbook of Global Modernisms*, edited by Mark A. Wollaeger and Matt Eatough, 551–70. Oxford: Oxford University Press, 2012.

Beasley, Rebecca and Philip Ross Bullock, eds. *Russia in Britain 1880–1940*. Oxford: Oxford University Press, 2013.

Berry, Ralph. 'Komisarjevsky in Britain'. *Theatrephile* 2, no. 5 (Winter 1984/5): 17–21.

Bevington, David and David Scott Kastan, eds. *William Shakespeare: The Late Romances*. New York: Bantam Classics, 2008.

Billington, Michael. *Peggy Ashcroft*. London: John Murray, 1988.

Blanch, Lesley. *Far to Go and Many to Love*. London: Quartet Books, 2017.

Blanch, Lesley. *Journey into the Mind's Eye*. London: Eland Publishing, 2014.

Blanch, Lesley. *On the Wilder Shores of Love: A Bohemian Life*. London: Virago: 2015.

Boleslavsky, Richard. *Acting: The First Six Lessons*. New York: Theatre Arts Books, 1933.

Borovsky, Victor. *A Triptych from the Russian Theatre: An Artistic Biography of the Komissarzhevskys*. London: Hurst, 1988.

Braun, Edward. *Meyerhold on Theatre*. London: Methuen Drama, 1991.

Croall, Jonathan. *John Gielgud: Matinee Idol to Movie Star*. London: Methuen, 2011.

Curtin, Adrian. *Avant-Garde Theatre Sound: Staging Sonic Modernity*. Basingstoke: Palgrave, 2014.

Davis, Jim, Katie Normington and Gilli Bush-Bailey, with Jacky Bratton. 'Researching Theatre History and Historiography'. In *Research Methods in*

Theatre and Performance, edited by Helen Nicholson and Baz Kershaw, 86–110. Edinburgh: Edinburgh University Press, 2011.

Dietz, Dan. *The Complete Book of 1940s Broadway Musicals*. Lanham: Rowman and Littlefield, 2015.

DiPietro, Cary. *Shakespeare and Modernism*. Cambridge: Cambridge University Press, 2006.

Eley, Eisner Susie. 'Trained to Teach: Five Dancers-Turned-Teachers Talk about How They Made the Transition from Performance to Education'. *Dance Teacher* 22, no. 3 (March 2000): 50–2.

Emeljanow, Victor. 'Komisarjevsky's *Three Sisters*: The Prompt Book'. *Theatre Notebook* 41, no. 2 (1987): 56–66.

Fischer-Lichte, Erica. *The Routledge Introduction to Theatre and Performance Studies*. Abingdon: Routledge, 2014.

Funke, Lewis and John E. Booth. *Actors Talk about Acting: Nine Interviews with Stars of the Theatre*. London: Thames and Hudson, 1961.

Gielgud, John. *Early Stages*. London: Hodder and Stoughton, 1987.

Gielgud, John. 'Tradition, Style and the Theatre Today'. In *Shakespeare Survey Online*. Cambridge: Cambridge University Press, 2007.

Gordon, Mel. *Stanislavsky in America*. Abingdon: Routledge, 2010.

Griffith, Hubert. *Red Sunday*. London: Cayme Press, 1929.

Gray, Richard. *One Hundred Years of Cinema Architecture*. London: Lund Humphries Publishers, 1996.

Jones, W. Gareth. 'Far from the West End: Chekhov and the Welsh Language Stage 1924–1991'. In *Chekhov on the British Stage*, edited by Patrick Miles, 101–12. Cambridge: Cambridge University Press, 1993.

Kennedy, Dennis. 'Confessions of an Encyclopedist'. In *Theorizing Practice, Redefining Theatre History*, edited by W.B. Worthen and Peter Holland, 30–46. Basingstoke: Palgrave, 2004.

Kennedy, Dennis. *Looking at Shakespeare*. Cambridge: Cambridge University Press, 2001.

Komisarjevsky, Theodore. *The Costume of the Theatre*. New York: Henry Holt and Co., 1932.

Komisarjevsky, Theodore. *Myself and the Theatre*. London: William Heinemann, 1929.

Komisarjevsky, Theodore. *The Theatre and a Changing Civilisation*. London: John Lane, 1935.

Komisarjevsky, Theodore and Lee Simonson. *Settings and Costumes of the Modern Age*. London: Studio Publications, 1933.

Komissarzhevsky, Fëdor to A.V. Lunacharsky, letter (June 1919). In *The Soviet Theater*, edited by Laurence Senelick and Sergei Ostrovsky, 72–3. New Haven: Yale University Press, 2014.

Lanchester, Elsa. *Charles Laughton and I*. London: Faber and Faber, 1938.

Lyons, Jacqueline. 'Theodore Komisarjevsky in the British Theatre'. MA diss., University of Newcastle, New South Wales, 1991.

MacCarthy, Desmond. *Theatre*. London: MacGibbon and Less, 1954.

Mackenzie, Ronald. *Musical Chairs*. London: Samuel French, 1940 [1932].

Maclean, Caroline. *The Vogue for Russia: Modernism and the Unseen in Britain*. Oxford: Oxford University Press, 2015.

Marshall, Norman. 'Komisarjevsky, Theodore (1882–1954)'. In *Oxford Dictionary of National Biography*. Oxford: Oxford University Press, 2004–16. http://www.oxforddnb.com/view/article/34361

Marshall, Norman. *The Other Theatre*. London: John Lehmann, 1947.

Mennen, Richard. 'Theodore Komisarjevsky's Production of the *Merchant of Venice*'. *Theatre Journal* 31, no. 3 (1979): 386–97.

Morley, Sheridan. *John Gielgud: The Authorized Biography*. New York: Simon and Schuster, 2002.

Michael Mullin. 'Augures and Understood Relations: Theodore Komisarjevsky's *Macbeth*'. *Educational Theatre Journal* 26, no. 1 (1974): 20–30.

Nicholson, Steve. 'Censoring Revolution: The Lord Chamberlain and the Soviet Union'. *New Theatre Quarterly* 8, no. 32 (November 1992): 307–9.

Peacock, Louise. *Serious Play: Modern Clown Performance*. Bristol: Intellect, 2009.

Pitches, Jonathan. 'A Tradition in Transition: Komisarjevsky's Seduction of the British Theatre'. In *Russians in Britain*, edited by Jonathan Pitches, 14–37. Abingdon: Routledge, 2012.

Pitches, Jonathan. 'Star or Team? Theodore Komisarjevsky's Early Developments in Ensemble Playing in the UK'. In *Encountering Ensemble*, edited by John Britton, 94–110. London: Methuen, 2013.

Pitches, Jonathan. *Vsevolod Meyerhold*. London: Routledge, 2003.

Postlewait, Thomas. 'Writing History Today'. *Theatre Survey* 41, no. 2 (2000): 83–106.

Rosenfeld, Sybil. *A Short History of Scene Design in Great Britain*. Oxford: Basil Blackwell, 1973.

Rudnitsky, Konstantin. *Russian and Soviet Theatre: Tradition and the Avant-Garde*. London: Thames and Hudson, 2000.

Sayler, Oliver M. *The Russian Theatre*. New York: Brentano's, 1922.

Schuler, Catherine. *Women in Russian Theatre*. London: Routledge, 1996.

Senelick, Laurence. *The Chekhov Theatre: A Century of Plays in Performance*. Cambridge: Cambridge University Press, 1999.

Shepherd, Simon. *The Cambridge Introduction to Modern British Theatre*. Cambridge: Cambridge University Press, 2009.

Shepherd, Simon. *Direction: Readings in Theatre Practice*. Basingstoke: Palgrave Macmillan, 2012.

Tairov, Alexander. *Notes of a Director*. Miami: Miami University Press, 1983.

Tracy, Robert. 'Komisarjevsky's 1926 *Three Sisters*'. In *Chekhov on the British Stage*, edited by Patrick Miles, 65–77. Cambridge: Cambridge University Press, 1993.

Valency, Maurice. *The Breaking String: The Plays of Anton Chekhov*. Oxford: Oxford University Press, 1966.

Walkowitz, Rebecca. *Cosmopolitan Style*. New York: Columbia University Press, 2006.

Warden, Claire. 'Moscow, St Petersburg, London: Hubert Griffith and the Search for Russian Truth'. *Comparative Drama* 49, no. 1 (Spring 2015): 1–21.

Wardle, Irving. *The Theatres of George Devine*. London: Jonathan Cape, 1978.

Tyrone Guthrie

Aune, Mark. 'Importing Shakespeare: Tyrone Guthrie and British Cold War Cultural Colonialism'. *Shakespeare* 5, no. 4 (December 2009): 423–40.

Bakshi, Hasan and David Throsby. 'Culture of Innovation: An Economic Analysis of Innovation in Arts and Cultural Organisations'. National Endowment for Science, Technology and the Arts, June 2010. Available at: https://www.nesta. org.uk/sites/default/files/culture_of_innovation.pdf

Barker, Martin. *Live to Your Local Cinema, The Remarkable Rise of Livecasting.* Basingstoke: Palgrave Macmillan, 2013.

Brooks, Peter. *The Melodramatic Imagination: Balzac, Henry James, Melodrama, and the Mode of Excess.* New Haven: Yale University Press, 1976.

Brook, Peter. *Threads of Time: A Memoir.* London: Methuen, 1998.

Brown, Ivor. 'Ane Satyre of the Thrie Estaits at the Edinburgh Festival'. In *Ane Satyre of the Thrie Estaits,* edited by James Kingsley and Sir David Lindsay, 27. London: Cassell and Company, 1954.

Burger, Kevyn. 'The Ecosystem of the Guthrie Theater', *Minnesota Business Magazine,* 30 March 2017. Available at: http://www.minnesotabusiness.com/ ecosystem-guthrie-theater

Cohen, Nathan. 'Stratford after Fifteen Years'. *Queen's Quarterly* 75, no. 1 (Spring 1968): 35–61.

Cornford, Tom. 'The English Theatre Studios of Michael Chekhov and Michel Saint-Denis 1935–1965'. PhD thesis, University of Warwick, 2012. Available at: http://webcat.warwick.ac.uk/record=b2684505~S1

Cornford, Tom. 'Jacques Lecoq and the Studio Tradition'. In *The Routledge Companion to Jacques Lecoq,* edited by Mark Evans and Rick Kemp, 43–50. Abingdon: Routledge, 2016.

Cornford, Tom. 'Reconstructing Theatre: The Globe under Dominic Dromgoole'. *New Theatre Quarterly* 26, no. 4 (November 2010): 319–28.

Cornwell, Paul. *Only by Failure: The Many Faces of the Impossible Life of Terence Gray.* Cambridge: Salt Publishing, 2004.

Croall, Jonathan. *John Gielgud: Matinee Idol to Movie Star.* London: Methuen, 2011.

Forsyth, James. *Tyrone Guthrie: A Biography.* London: Hamish Hamilton, 1976.

Guthrie, Tyrone. *A Life in the Theatre.* New York: McGraw-Hill, 1959.

Guthrie, Tyrone. 'A Long View of the Stratford Festival'. In *Twice Have the Trumpets Sounded: A Record of the Stratford Shakespearean Festival in Canada, 1954,* 152–72. Toronto: Clarke, Irwin, and Co., 1954.

Guthrie, Tyrone. *A New Theatre.* New York: McGraw-Hill, 1964.

Guthrie, Tyrone. *In Various Directions: A View of the Theatre.* London: Michael Joseph, 1965.

Guthrie, Tyrone. *Theatre Prospect.* London: Wishart and Co., 1932.

Hawkes, Terence. *Meaning by Shakespeare.* London: Routledge, 1992.

Hobson, Harold. 'Guthrie, Sir (William) Tyrone (1900–1971)'. In *Oxford Dictionary of National Biography.* Oxford: Oxford University Press, 2004; online edn, January 2011. http://www.oxforddnb.com.ezproxy.library.dal.ca/ view/article/31182, accessed 4 September 2017.

Hunter, Martin. *Romancing the Bard: Stratford at Fifty.* Toronto: Dundurn Press, 2001.

Kennedy, Dennis. 'The Director, the Spectator and the Eiffel Tower'. *Theatre Research International* 30, no. 1 (March 2005): 36–48.

Knowles, Richard Paul. 'From Nationalist to Multinational: The Stratford Festival, Free Trade and the Discourses of Intercultural Tourism'. *Theatre Journal* 47, no. 1 (March 1995): 19–41.

Knowles, Richard Paul. *Reading the Material Theatre*. Cambridge: Cambridge University Press, 2004.

Knowles, Richard Paul. 'Shakespeare, 1993, and the Discourses of the Stratford Festival, Ontario'. *Shakespeare Quarterly* 45 (1994): 211–25.

Mackintosh, Iain. *The Guthrie Thrust Stage: A Living Legacy*. London: Association of British Theatre Technicians and The Royal Shakespeare Company, 2011.

McAuley, Gay. *Space in Performance: Making Meaning in the Theatre*. Ann Arbor: University of Michigan Press, 1999.

Morley, Sheridan. *John Gielgud: The Authorized Biography*. New York: Simon and Schuster, 2002.

Olivier, Laurence. *On Acting*. London: Weidenfeld and Nicholson, 1986.

Ouzounian, Richard. *Stratford Gold: 50 Years, 50 Stars, 50 Conversations*. Toronto: McArthur and Co., 2002.

Patterson, Tom and Allan Gould. *First Stage: The Making of the Stratford Festival*. Toronto: McLelland and Stewart, 1987.

Pettigrew, John and Jamie Portman. *Stratford: The First Thirty Years. Volume 1: 1953–1967*. Toronto: Macmillan, 1985.

Rankin, Peter. *Joan Littlewood: Dreams and Realities*. London: Oberon, 2016.

Rossi, Alfred. *Astonish Us in the Morning: Tyrone Guthrie Remembered*. London: Hutchinson and Co., 1977.

Rossi, Alfred. *Minneapolis Rehearsals: Tyrone Guthrie Directs Hamlet*. Berkeley: University of California Press, 1970.

Rutter, Carol. *Enter the Body: Women and Representation on Shakespeare's Stage*. London: Routledge, 2001.

Salter, Dennis. 'Acting Shakespeare in Postcolonial Space'. In *Shakespeare, Theory, and Performance*, edited by James C. Bulman, 113–32. London: Routledge, 1996.

Shaughnessy, Robert. *The Shakespeare Effect: A History of Twentieth-Century Performance*. Houndmills: Palgrave Macmillan, 2002.

Shaughnessy, Robert. 'Tyrone Guthrie'. In *Great Shakespeareans, Vol. 15: Poel, Granville Barker, Guthrie, Wanamaker*, edited by Cary M. Mazer, 98–150. London: Bloomsbury, 2013.

Shepherd, Simon. *Direction: Readings in Theatre Practice*. Basingstoke: Palgrave Macmillan, 2012.

Sidnell, Michael. *Dances of Death: The Group Theatre of London in the Thirties*. London: Faber and Faber, 1984.

Styan, J.L. *The Shakespeare Revolution: Criticism and Performance in the Twentieth Century*. Cambridge: Cambridge University Press, 1977.

Veracini, Lorenzo. *The Settler Colonial Present*. Houndmills: Palgrave Macmillan, 2015.

Villamil, Etnier Victoria. *'O Ma Carmen': Bizet's Fateful Gypsy in Potrayals from 1875 to the Present*. Jefferson: McFarland and Co., 2017.

Williams, Harcourt. *Old Vic Saga*. London: Winchester Publications, 1949.

Ziegler, Joseph Wesley. *Regional Theatre: The Revolutionary Stage*. Minneapolis: University of Minnesota Press, 1973.

INDEX